International
Finance
Regulation

Founded in 1807, John Wiley & Sons is the oldest independent publishing company in the United States. With offices in North America, Europe, Australia, and Asia, Wiley is globally committed to developing and marketing print and electronic products and services for our customers' professional and personal knowledge and understanding.

The Wiley Finance series contains books written specifically for finance and investment professionals as well as sophisticated individual investors and their financial advisors. Book topics range from portfolio management to e-commerce, risk management, financial engineering, valuation, and financial instrument analysis, as well as much more.

For a list of available titles, visit our web site at www.WileyFinance.com.

International Finance Regulation

The Quest for Financial Stability

GEORGES UGEUX

WILEY

Published by John Wiley & Sons, Inc., Hoboken, New Jersey.
Published simultaneously in Canada.

For general information on our other products and services or for technical support, please contact our Customer Care Department within the United States at (800) 762-2974, outside the United States at (317) 572-3993 or fax (317) 572-4002.

Wiley publishes in a variety of print and electronic formats and by print-on-demand. Some material included with standard print versions of this book may not be included in e-books or in print-on-demand. If this book refers to media such as a CD or DVD that is not included in the version you purchased, you may download this material at http://booksupport.wiley.com. For more information about Wiley products, visit www.wiley.com.

Library of Congress Cataloging-in-Publication Data:
Ugeux, Georges.
 International finance regulation : the quest for financial stability / Georges Ugeux.
  pages cm. — (Wiley finance)
 Includes bibliographical references and index.
  ISBN 978-1-118-82959-2 (Hardcover) — ISBN 978-1-118-82962-2 (ePDF) — ISBN 978-1-118-82961-5 (ePub)   1. International finance.   2. International finance—Law and legislation.   3. Banks and banking.   I. Title.
  HG3881.U34 2014
  332′.042—dc23

                                                                2014003248

Printed in the United States of America
10 9 8 7 6 5 4 3 2 1

To Moritz Erhardt—who died of a seizure after 72 hours without sleep in investment banking—as well as those whose personal, professional, and financial well-being has been destroyed by the selfishness of the leadership of the financial services industry.

With the hope that this book will contribute to make finance a better world.

Contents

Preface

et's face it: finance betrayed itself, its customers, and the public at large.[1]
This time, finance has become itself a source of instability. This situation
creates a completely different approach to regulation. Financiers hate it but
provoked this new wave by their own irresponsibility.

Can it be regulated in a way that will no longer make it destabilize the
economy? Can it solve its own crises without requesting interventions that
use taxpayers' money? Can it regain a lost trust and reputation?

Antony Jenkins, chief executive officer of Barclays Plc, said it may take a
decade to rebuild trust in the bank after a series of scandals from interest-rate
manipulation to selling customers insurance they didn't need. "It is about
what you do, not what you say," Jenkins said on the BBC's *Today* radio
program. "Until people start to perceive the change, Barclays will not begin
rebuilding that trust."[2]

The various financial crises[3] that have populated the past 50 years have
demonstrated the huge challenges facing any attempt to regulate global finance. While domestic regulation is in itself an unsatisfactory way to prevent such crises, regulating global finance presents huge challenges.

One cannot expect finance to be stable in an unstable world. What needs
to be addressed is the ways and means to ensure that finance itself does not
become an additional factor of global instability to the real economy.

Since the beginning of the twenty-first century, at least 20 financial institutions have had to be rescued one way or another. Will Slovenian banks
be rescued without European intervention? The last failing bank, Monte dei
Paschi di Siena, in Italy, dates back to the beginning of 2013. It has 3,000
branches and 33,000 employees.

*When the Monte dei Paschi di Siena bank was founded in 1472,
Michelangelo was not born, Columbus had still to discover America
and Henry VIII of England had yet to split from the church of Rome.*

*More than half a millennium later, the world's oldest bank is
facing nearly $1 billion of trading losses in a scandal that has forced
Italian authorities to issue reassurances about the stability of the
Siena institution.*[4]

The swift bailout by the Italian authorities made this crisis discreet, since the *Partito Democratico* was directly involved, in the middle of the Italian political crisis.

> *Even as the rest of the euro zone emerges from the economic crypt, Italy alone continues to dig its grave, tragically unaware of Warren Buffett's maxim: "The most important thing to do if you find yourself in a hole is to stop digging.*[5]

When Lehman Brothers, on the fateful weekend of September 15, 2008, was dropped by the U.S. and U.K. authorities and filed for bankruptcy, AIG was about to go under. The U.S. Treasury, the Federal Reserve, and a massive support from the U.S. banking industry eventually rescued AIG, but Lehman collapsed. What looked like domestic crises immediately turned into a global crisis (see Figure P.1).

Fifteen months later, in December 2009, after those dramatic Wall Street events, the revelation of the amplitude of the Greek indebtedness plunged Europe, and particularly those countries using the euro as their common currency (eurozone[6] countries), into a sovereign debt crisis whose consequences quickly affected global markets.[7]

As this book comes to press, it would be naïve to believe that this sovereign debt crisis is fully resolved—somber clouds are still casting their shadow on economic recovery and global financial stability. The level of indebtedness of Japan, the United States, and western Europe is unsustainable and presents a systemic risk at least as important as the banking risk.

IS FINANCE IN A STAGE OF PERMANENT CRISIS?

One of the reasons why the world constantly seems unprepared for a new financial crisis is probably that we tend to look at the history of finance as a stable one agitated by external periodic disruptions. Furthermore, economists look at historical numbers and project them without integrating the current signals of what could go wrong, often when it is too late to take preventive measures.

Each crisis leads to a new set of institutional and regulatory initiatives that are not always productive. Is it the right approach? I would argue that finance does not need, by nature, to be unstable. It is a gigantic sounding board where all kinds of economic, social, and financial shocks resonate. As a result of complex and global evolutions, financial markets are never in a stable situation because the environment in which they operate is not stable.

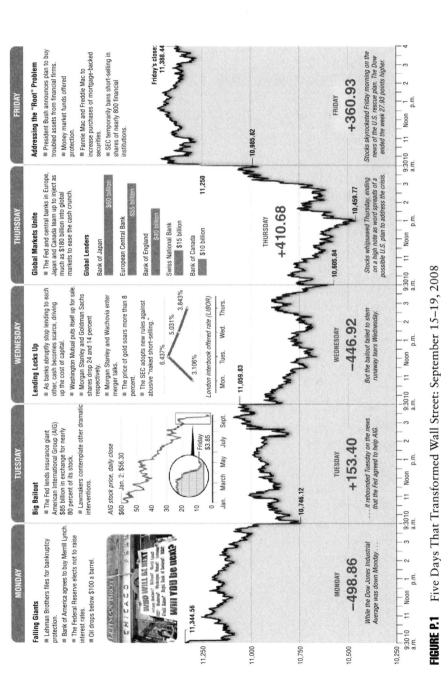

FIGURE P.1 Five Days That Transformed Wall Street: September 15–19, 2008

Source: www.washingtonpost.com/wp-dyn/content/graphic/2008/09/20/GR2008092000318.html.

Beyond the world disturbances that affect markets, investors and traders represent a variety of opinions about the meaning of those events, and more important, the anticipation of their impact on the economy.

GLOBAL MARKETS ARE INTERCONNECTED

The International Monetary Fund (IMF) summarizes this state of inter-dependence.

> *Countries are financially interconnected through the asset and liability management strategies of their sovereigns, financial institutions, and corporations. This financial globalization has brought benefits as well as vulnerabilities. In particular, the speed with which illiquidity and losses in some markets can translate into global asset re-composition.*[8]

Interconnectedness has become the natural framework of finance. It makes it subject to systemic risks. This implies that the monitoring of global finance must be a permanent exercise.

The IMF chart in Figure P.2 illustrates the interconnectedness of large complex financial institutions (LCFIs).

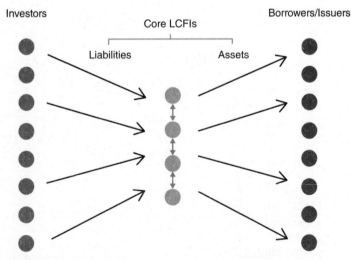

FIGURE P.2   LCFIs at the Center of the Global Financial System
Source: www.imf.org/external/np/pp/eng/2010/100410.pdf.

Rather than jumping from one crisis to another, regulation should be, first and foremost, in charge of providing the framework for global financial stability.

Regulators must consider what can be done to make the U.S. financial system itself more stable, without compromising the dynamism and innovation that has been its hallmark, stated Ben Bernanke, the Chairman of the Federal Reserve Board—two months before the Lehman bankruptcy.[9]

His conference was explaining how excruciating and surprising the Bear Stearns collapse had been and how the Federal Reserve played a crucial role in making its takeover by JPMorgan Chase possible.

Our analyses persuaded us and our colleagues at the Securities and Exchange Commission (SEC) and the Treasury that allowing Bear Stearns to fail so abruptly at a time when the financial markets were already under considerable stress would likely have had extremely adverse implications for the financial system and for the broader economy. In particular, Bear Stearns' failure under those circumstances would have seriously disrupted certain key secured funding markets and derivatives markets and possibly would have led to runs on other financial firms. To protect the financial system and the economy, the Federal Reserve facilitated the acquisition of Bear Stearns by the commercial bank JPMorgan Chase.[10]

This, in turn requires from the authorities an ability to gather relevant data, and, more importantly, anticipate financial trends that could potentially create a systemic risk. The former boss of Northern Rock, Adam Applegarth, pinpointed the start of the first credit crunch as August 9, 2007.[11]

The first massive intervention of the Federal Reserve and the European Central Bank took place on August 10, 2007, as a result of the U.S. subprime crisis that immediately reverberated in Europe. The European Central Bank scrambled to head off a potential financial crisis by making an emergency injection of €94.8 billion ($131 billion) worth. The Fed added a total of $31.25 billion into temporary reserves, more than market participants had expected. They intervened the same day because two major financial institutions, IndustrieKredit Bank (IKB) from Germany and BNP Paribas in France, had been immediately affected.

BNP Paribas decided to suspend the redemptions of investment funds.

An alternative name is the "Panic of 2007," which is dated as beginning with the announcement by BNP Paribus on August 9, 2007, of its suspension of redemptions for three of its investment funds. This name stresses the financial crisis as the precipitating event leading up to the severe decline in real economic activity slightly more than a year later.[12]

The rescue of IKB was fairly dramatic. Probably unbeknownst to its own board, IKB management had started developing in Ireland speculative activities outside of its core business—long-term financing to German companies. That activity was heavily dependent on outside financing (like all consumer institutions that were not collecting deposits).

It literally exploded that same week and had to be rescued by the German government, which was its largest shareholder through Kreditbank fur Wiederaufbau (KfW). In 2008 it needed a new injection of 2 billion euros.[13] It was Lone Star, a hedge fund specializing in purchasing distressed assets globally, that eventually bought IKB.[14]

REGULATING FINANCE IN A WORLD IN CRISIS

Finance is probably one of the most regulated industries in the world. The structure of regulation itself is nothing else than the accumulation of the various rules and institutions created to solve the problem of the previous crises since 1929.

The world is similar to a volcano. It is a huge magma of tectonic forces that constantly collide more or less strongly. The energy spent in focusing on new rules that aim at avoiding a repetition of the previous crisis would be better applied at monitoring and understanding the global forces that can affect the financial system today. It is nothing else than what volcanologists do for a living: monitor the forces that could provoke eruptions and take preventive actions to limit the consequences of this eruption.

This structural instability is a sobering message. We cannot expect, and neither should we forecast, that finance can be more stable or provide stability to the rest of the world. After all, the Financial Stability Forum, assembling the smartest and the brightest central bankers and experts, did not see the crisis coming.[15]

Despite the damage of the previous financial crises, the International Monetary Fund (IMF) and the Financial Stability Board (FSB) have not been turned into the seismic monitor of world finance. I picture such a monitoring as a huge interconnected information technology (IT) system that would have the ability to catch all the signals of eruption, as tiny as they are, and detect what could be the convergence or interconnectedness of those signals.

To a large extent, global financial stability is still managed in a fragmented and incoherent way. However, both the Federal Reserve and the

European Central Bank set up bodies to look at the systemic risks associated with finance in their own constituencies.

In this context, one must understand that regulators primarily protect themselves from criticism or liabilities. They look first and foremost at auditable criteria that will minimize the use of judgment and protect them from having to act accordingly. Better to be compliant than right. They aim to do the right thing, but the political environment that puts pressure on regulators as if they were able to rule finance makes it too dangerous, and even lethal for their future.

A WEB OF INSTITUTIONAL COMPLEXITY

This incoherent approach does not fare well for the future of finance. But what threatens it even more is the complexity of the institutions and the rules they publish and implement.

After the U.S. financial crisis, it became patently clear that too many cooks had parts of the meal and produced a disaster. Furthermore, they were keeping their own data, making it impossible to integrate the warning signals.

While the Financial Stability Oversight Council,[16] created as part of the Dodd-Frank Act (DFA) of 2012, puts the 22 U.S. regulators around a common table run by the U.S. Treasury, no attempts has been made to rationalize this inextricable web.

> *The DFA establishes a regulatory framework of which the FSOC is a consultative council. The new regulatory regime incorporates several policy tools to address systemic risk. The FSOC facilitates communication among financial regulators, collects and evaluates financial data to monitor systemic risk, and designates which financial institutions and financial market utilities will be subject to prudential regulation by the Federal Reserve Board (the Fed). Upon a determination of a threat to financial stability, a covered non-bank financial institution in danger of failing may under certain conditions be resolved by the Federal Deposit Insurance Corporation (FDIC), rather than through the bankruptcy process. The FSOC may under certain circumstances set aside some financial regulations for consumers if the rules create systemic risk.[17]*

One of the unintended consequences of institutional complexity is to diffuse the responsibilities and fragment regulation and information. It is the reign of unaccountability.

It also is an unnecessary burden for financial institutions, even though they derive unintended advantages in regulatory arbitrage. It allows them to present their requests at the point of least resistance. The recent tug-of-war between JPMorgan Chase's (JPM) CEO, Jamie Dimon, and former Federal Reserve Board (FRB) Chairman Paul Volcker is a perfect example of the way the banking sector tries to take advantage of complexity.

> *Just a couple weeks before Jamie Dimon announced publicly that his banking firm JPMorgan had lost a stunning $2 billion betting with depositor funds, he took to Fox News to criticize the Volcker Rule, meant to ban federally backstopped banks from engaging in proprietary trading.*[18]

It ended up as a $6 billion loss for JPM. To that amount lawyer costs and $920 million fines were added. Jamie Dimon had described it when it first emerged as a *tempest in a teacup.*[19]

WILL GLOBAL FINANCIAL REGULATION BECOME LEX AMERICA?

The complexity of global regulation, the difficulty of Europe to come up with a coherent and executable banking regulation, as well as the Asian absence from the global regulatory debates create a situation that might provide the United States with an opportunity to impose its regulatory model on the rest of the world.

Washington is certainly not shy to impose its rules on foreign institutions and foreign countries. This extraterritorial outreach is in contradiction with the basic rules of international private law. It applies to everything the United States cares about.

Recently, the National Security Agency's (ab)use of its powers is still denied by the White House but seriously damaged the reputation of the United States as applying the rule of law.

> *Before President Obama left for his 17-day vacation in Hawaii, White House officials made it clear that his holiday reading would consist of a lot more than beach novels to escape the stresses of Washington. He'd also be studying a 300-page report on how to rein in the government's controversial surveillance programs that had just been delivered to him by a high-level panel of experts.*[20]

The global regulatory process is dominated by the United States, even though it is not certain that it will feel bound to apply common rules. The United States refuses multilateral oversight, whether it is the criminal court of the Hague or other sanctions.

The most recent spreading was on the tax side. Taxes stop at a country's borders. The United States is the only country in the world that applies the principle of universal taxation. The U.S. Supreme Court is unambiguous about it:

> *In other words, the principle was declared that the government, by its very nature, benefits the citizen and his property wherever found, and therefore has the power to make the benefit complete. Or, to express it another way, the basis of the power to tax was not and cannot be made dependent upon the situs of the property in all cases, it being in or out of the United States, nor was not and cannot be made dependent upon the domicile of the citizen, that being in or out of the United States, but upon his relation as citizen to the United States and the relation of the latter to him as citizen.*[21]

The recent use of foreign banks as tax informants under Foreign Account Tax Compliance Act (FATCA) rules does not seem to bother anybody, and in the absence of any legal arguments, the United States is threatening an additional tax and uses blackmail with governments around the world.[22]

As far as regulation is concerned, there are serious concerns about the spreading of Lex America. The application of Basel III will be an interesting case. However, the most immediate impact will be on large banks that operate in the United States. For Deutsche Bank, UBS, and other large banks, the application of derivative regulation as well as the capital adequacy and the Volcker Rule will make Lex America the law of the land as they are systemically important financial institutions (SIFIs) wherever they operate as long as it includes the United States of America.

While criticism of that position has been loud, one must recognize that the United States has taken initiatives and applied rules and regulations after the financial crisis much faster and more decisively than Europe or Asia. Whether it is influence or power, it puts the United States in the driving seat. As Columbia Law School Professor John C. Coffee puts it:

> *Bilateral negotiations among them (particularly between the U.S. and the E.U.) and the assertion of extraterritorial jurisdiction by them is necessary to create a governance structure under which highly mobile financial institutions cannot flee to less regulated venues. Ultimately, this assertion of extraterritorial authority (which both the U.S. and the E.U. have now done) may be an interim stage*

in the longer term development of adequate international "soft law"
standards. But, absent the assertion of such authority, the commons
will predictably collapse again into tragedy.[23]

On February 18, 2014, the Federal Reserve published the rules that will
apply to foreign banks operating in the United States.[24]

The days later, the Financial Times announced that Deutsche Bank announced it was reducing the balance sheet of its US unit by 25 percent. This
amounts to $100 billion, and raises the question of the impact on the U.S.
markets and their liquidity of the reduction of the foreign banks.

APPLYING GLOBAL REGULATORY CONVERGENCE

In a system of institutional complexity, one should not be surprised by possible regulatory incoherence. Whether it is in Europe or in the United States,
regulations are built in vertical silos, with a system of consultation that affects some segments of the financial industry more than others.

Such a process can only land a forest of regulation where each tree is
trying to do the best for itself, and nobody is in charge of coherence. One
would believe that there might be a level of the regulatory process that looks
at the consistency of regulation in a horizontal way.

What exists in many countries for legislation does not exist for international regulation. Many legislative systems provide for the arbitrage of a
form of administrative instance that looks at the constitutionality and the
consistency of the laws of the country. There is an urgent need, at European
and U.S. levels, to have an administrative court that will look at the consistency and coherence of the various financial regulatory initiatives.

Navigating the web of regulation has become one of the main sources
of law firms' assignments. Regulators themselves are generally lawyers, and
will—after a stay in a regulatory agency—end up in a law firm or the legal
department of one of the regulated entities. Bloomberg estimates the total
fees related to the financial crisis in the United States at $100 billion.[25]

There is little chance that regulation will protect us from financial instability and regulatory incoherence. It is the reason why, often enough, the reaction to an unexpected and new crisis gives this impression of improvisation.
Even worse, as the European crisis showed, political action operates sometimes in perfect illegality.[26] Who cares about being legal when the ship sinks?

However, the precedents created in Greece or Cyprus will haunt for
a long time the European authorities that perpetrated legally questionable
actions using their political muscle rather than assuming their own responsibilities. Breaking the law is also breaking the trust.

REGULATOR AND REGULATED: THE INFERNAL COUPLE

When their masters blame regulators, whether they are governments, parliaments, or public opinion and media, regulators become angrier and defensive vis-à-vis financial institutions. Needless to say, the indispensable dialogue between regulators and financial institutions has become extremely difficult.

Regulators, sometimes legitimately, suspect financial institutions of creating, behind what looks like acceptable suggestions, the next trap in which they will fall at the next crisis. When investment banks asked the Securities and Exchange Commission (SEC) to allow a larger leverage to enable them to compete with large global banks, they obtained what they wanted. The price to pay was a specific reporting to the SEC, which was never properly staffed. It was the single most important regulatory failure that explains the Lehman Brothers collapse.

There is also a subtler divide: money. Regulators are paid like civil servants, and deal with the best-paid financial executives and partners of law firms. This monetary divide has a perverse effect: one should not expect regulators to be as equipped, and even sometimes competent, as those they need to regulate who have at their service armies of specialists in every single discipline and law. This unbalance is rarely openly discussed. It does, however, explain some serious misunderstandings.

I would argue that it is up to the regulated institutions to present their proposals in a way that allows regulators to monitor and understand the products or the activities they are responsible for. It is not good enough to disagree with the initiatives of regulators if one is not capable of coming forward with concrete proposals that will allow the regulators to understand them and monitor them.

Can a level playing field be created that would give regulators the means to deal evenly in the legislative and regulatory processes? As long as lobbying continues to channel hundreds of millions of dollars for financial services alone, it seems doubtful.

FINANCE CANNOT BE LEFT UNREGULATED

The financial crisis was the kiss of death to self-regulation.

Whether they like it or not, financial institutions played self-regulation at the Russian roulette, took a huge bet that everything would be well at the end, and they lost. Regulators and politicians became painfully aware that banks did not have fiduciary or prudential attitudes that would have led them to manage their risks properly.

The top management of financial institutions did not include their own regulators or risk managers. They were hardly listened to. It was true across the border, but especially in innovative finance. Even worse, the riskier the bets become, the higher their bonuses are. Whether it is the demise of Kidder Peabody and Salomon Brothers, or the collapse of Bear Stearns, Merrill Lynch, and Lehman Brothers, it is always the same combination of *Greed and Glory on Wall Street*[27] playing *Liars' Poker*.[28]

Finance needs strong regulation and strong regulators. It requires statutory, financial, and human power and leadership. Financiers are no longer trusted, and even, in some substantial part of public opinion and the media, hated for the perpetration of "crimes" against households.

The usury interest rates on credit cards, the manipulation of the London interbank offered rate (LIBOR), and the London Whale are there to remind us that even the most iconic and reputable financial institutions have continued to behave beyond the boundaries of legality, hoping not to be caught. They suffer from a gigantic deficit of trust and credibility. Those were, when I became a banker, the two ingredients that allowed banks to intermediate and play their role for the good of their clients and society at large. Those days are gone, and restoring credibility is a complex undertaking that few of them seem to be in a hurry to even start.

FIVE YEARS AFTER LEHMAN, REGULATION COULD NOT CHANGE THE CULTURE

The movie *The Wolf of Wall Street* is there to remind us of behaviors, sometimes criminal, that dominate a substantial part of the financial services industry. With some exaggeration, it does paint a picture of what the financial industry has had a hard time eradicating.

I wish a more optimistic diagnostic could be made after five years of efforts, rules, political debates, and bank lobbying. The reality is that nothing has changed in the financial culture. It is as arrogant, irresponsible, bullying, and selfish as it has ever been. In its September 23, 2013, issue, *TIME* magazine's front page contained an unambiguous statement: *How Wall Street Won: Five Years after the Crash, It Could Happen All Over Again . . . The Myth of Financial Reform*.[29]

We will look at the reasons why, after Lehman, several financial scandals continued to affect global finance, and especially the mother of all: the LIBOR crisis.[30]

It goes back to the basis of moral philosophy and natural law: it is the individuals who are ethically responsible. Short of criminal actions in the case of fraud, the global regulatory landscape does not look at enforcing its rules by making individuals, management committees, or boards of directors personally responsible for acting wrongly.

After the Lehman crisis, further frauds appeared: the LIBOR crisis, the collapse of Monte dei Paschi, and the London Whale, and the accounts on the malpractice of mortgage loan marketing are still being settled five years after that.

A CULTURE OF OUTLAWS

"There is a need for a cultural shift," Thomas Baxter, the New York Fed's general counsel, told bankers at an industry conference yesterday. "You need to focus on making examples of people, and nothing focuses the attention like a hanging. How are people promoted, how did those people get into those senior seats? This is another powerful way to send a message."[31]

As to the culture of some parts of finance, in particular trading rooms, they are purely and simply despicable.

A survey, by law firm Labaton Sucharow, also found that more than a third of younger respondents (those with 10 years or less experience) believe financial professionals need to behave unethically or illegally in order to be successful.

Interestingly enough, the women surveyed felt that things are even worse. More women than men believe that colleagues as well as competitors are engaged in misconduct, and more believe their own firm's top management would ignore wrongdoing from a top performer. Strikingly, women are almost twice as likely as men to fear retribution if they report wrongdoing.[32]

Bullying, sexual harassment, machismo, and other primary instincts continue to dominate the world of finance. In the words of a management consultant to a lady involved in this business, "For women, there is one choice: being easy or being difficult."

Those who have personality and integrity are automatically considered to be "difficult." Alcohol and drugs continue to dominate the life of traders and sales executives. Trading rooms remain the equivalent of school playgrounds, except that nobody oversees behaviors.

Goodness was not taken into account on the trading floor. It just was. Or it wasn't," wrote Michael Lewis in Liar's Poker *of Salomon Brothers, the pioneering bond trading firm of the 1980s. "The place was governed by the simple understanding that the unbridled pursuit of self-interest was healthy."*[33]

General management continues to have complacent standards provided that money flows. They do not dare to impose ethical standards to big money makers. They are effectively accomplices of a deterioration of the integrity of finance, away from client services. It is the responsibility of the top management to turn a blind eye on such behaviors they "purchase" with top dollars that needs to be questioned.

> *In the longer-term, the question is how to reform high street banks that now employ financial traders who exclaim: "Dude, I owe you big time! Come over one day after work and I'm opening a bottle of Bollinger," to a colleague who distorts a quasi-official index for profit.*[34]

Boards of directors refuse to care about such behaviors, and no audit on human decency has ever been requested by a board of a major financial institution. Unless the remuneration system and the governance of the capital market activities evolve, little will change, despite all the efforts of regulation.

The most dramatic case happened in London in 2012, when an intern died of a seizure after 72 hours without sleep.

> *Bank of America–Merrill Lynch intern Moritz Erhardt worked day and night in the weeks before his death, sending e-mails to his parents and colleagues in the early hours of the morning.*
>
> *The 21-year-old died of an epileptic seizure while taking a shower on Aug. 15, a London coroner said after an inquest yesterday. He never once complained about his workload, Erhardt's parents and co-workers said, even when staying up until 5 A.M.*[35]

Will it take a CEOs being jailed or severely fined for management to create a culture of responsibility and respect? One thing is certain: banking management and boards are accomplices to a culture that violates ethical and even legal human relations standards.

I WILL NEVER GIVE UP

Barbara Streisand's inspiring song "I Will Never Give Up"[36] comes to mind when approaching the challenges of this book.

In front of that situation, the temptation to give up is huge. By and large, public opinion has given up the hope that regulation will make bankers and financiers honest. They lost ethical standards, so why bother writing a book on global financial regulation?

The reality is simple: millions of financiers and bankers are honest and want to live in an industry they can be proud of, not only because of its performance and success, but because of its values. Millions of them are involved in regulation around the world. Whether they are practitioners or lawyers, they are subject to the complex web of regulators and regulations.

This book, inspired by my experience in the public, semipublic, and private financial sectors, as well as teaching European Banking and Finance at the Columbia University School of Law,[37] is an attempt to assist those professionals as well as the public who try to better understand and reform the world of finance.

In front of the size of the challenge, it does not even pretend to be comprehensive: rather, it will try to focus on the core of what inspires regulation, in a number of critical fields. It will also confront these objectives, with a sense of practical reality, and sometimes argue that some rules and regulations would not or will not reach such objectives.

The buzzword is unintended consequences. Regulations are made in silos, with very little coherence, let alone awareness that many of those rules will have unintended consequences. Using a French expression, it *tries to kill a bee with a cannonball*.

This huge undertaking has only one objective: assisting the reader in his or her exploration of financial regulation, opening windows to texts that will allow further investigation and look at the possible legal and practical dilemmas facing those who, in their day-to-day life, are confronted with the daunting task of making some sense of it. I hope that some policymakers, bankers, academics, students, corporate executives, and investors will find here a few thoughts that might improve the situation locally, if not globally.

It is also a tribute to the millions of financiers and regulators who, in the worst of circumstances, remained honest, refused corruption, and accepted to dedicate the whole or part of their life to try to keep finance at the service of its customers, rather than as a money machine for its executives.

It would be helpful if individual and institutional clients of banks were to take into consideration the ethical reputation and practices of some banks before mandating them to assist them financially.

NOTES

1. Georges Ugeux, *The Betrayal of Finance: Twelve Ways to Restore Confidence*. New York, Galileo Global Institute, September 2011, 295 pp.

(Available at www.amazon.com/The-Betrayal-Finance-Georges-Ugeux/dp/125776943X.)

2. www.bloomberg.com/news/2013-12-31/barclays-s-ceo-say-rebuilding-trust-may-take-10-years.html.

3. http://en.wikipedia.org/wiki/List_of_banking_crises.

4. www.reuters.com/article/2013/01/25/us-montepaschi-derivatives-profile-idUSBRE90O0R820130125.

5. Eric Reguly, "Italy's Economic Woes Pose Existential Threat to Euro Zone," *Globe and Mail*, Toronto, Canada. November 1, 2013. www.theglobeandmail.com/report-on-business/international-business/european-business/italys-economic-woes-pose-existential-threat-to-euro-zone/article15224210/.

6. The eurozone has 17 members, all countries who abandoned their national currencies for the euro. www.eurozone.europa.eu/.

7. Georges Ugeux, "Greece Evidences the Weakness of the Euro," *Huffington Post*, December 21, 2009. www.huffingtonpost.com/georges-ugeux/greece-evidences-the-weak_b_393972.html.

8. International Monetary Fund, "Understanding Financial Interconnectedness," Washington, DC. www.imf.org/external/np/pp/eng/2010/100410.pdf.

9. Ben Bernanke, at the Federal Deposit Insurance Corporation's Forum on Mortgage Lending for Low and Moderate Income Households, Arlington, Virginia, July 8, 2008. www.federalreserve.gov/newsevents/speech/bernanke20080708a.htm.

10. Ibid.

11. Jill Treanor, "Credit Crunch Pinpointed to 9 August 2007—The Day the World Changed," *The Guardian*, December 1, 2011. www.theguardian.com/business/2011/dec/01/credit-crunch-pinpointed-august-2007.

12. Joseph S. Tracy, executive vice president, Federal Reserve Bank of New York, "What the Fed Did and Why." Remarks at the Westchester County Bankers Association, Tarrytown, New York, June 25, 2010.

13. John O'Donnell and Patricia Nann, "Subprime Stricken IKB Attempts Third Rescue," Reuters, Frankfurt, February 8, 2008. www.reuters.com/article/2008/02/08/us-ikb-rescue-idUSWEB456520080208.

14. Carter Dougherty, "Lone Star Buys German Bank IKB at a Major Discount," *New York Times*, August 21, 2008. www.nytimes.com/2008/08/21/business/worldbusiness/21iht-bank.4.15525666.html?_r=0.

15. Enrique R. Carrasco, "The Global Financial Crisis and the Financial Stability Forum: The Awakening and Transformation of an International Body." University of Iowa. www.uiowa.edu/~tlcp/TLCP%20Articles/19-1/carrasco.finalfinal.mlb.022510.pdf.

16. It is interesting to note that the Council is chaired by the U.S. Treasury, and not by the Federal Reserve. It is on the Treasury's web site that the information is available. www.treasury.gov/initiatives/fsoc/Pages/home.aspx.

17. www.bbc.co.uk/news/business-24159801.

18. http://talkingpointsmemo.com/dc/volcker-to-dimon-just-give-up-your-banking-license-and-we-re-cool-video.

19. www.marketwatch.com/story/dimon-london-whale-issues-tempest-in-a-teapot-2012-04-13-937450.

20. www.thedailybeast.com/articles/2013/12/31/obama-s-defining-fight-how-he-will-take-on-the-nsa-s-surveillance-state-in-2014.html.

21. www.irsmedic.com/2010/12/04/the-history-of-universal-tax-jurisdiction/.

22. http://clsbluesky.law.columbia.edu/2013/06/19/should-lex-americana-be-universal-fatca-turns-foreign-banks-into-tax-informants/.

23. John C. Coffee, "Extraterritorial Financial Regulation: Why E.T. Can't Come Home," Columbia Law and Economics Working Paper No. 459, October 2013. http://papers.ssrn.com/sol3/papers.cfm?abstract_id=2347556##.

24. www.federalreserve.gov.newevents/press/bcreg/20140218a.htm.

25. www.bloomberg.com/news/2013-08-28/u-s-bank-legal-bills-exceed-100-billion.html.

26. Georges Ugeux, "Cyprus: What Happened to the Sanctity of Insured Deposits?" Columbia Law School's *Blue Sky* blog, March 21, 2013. http://clsbluesky.law.columbia.edu/2013/03/21/cyprus-what-happened-to-the-sanctity-of-insured-deposits/.

27. Ken Auletta, *Greed and Glory on Wall Street: The Fall of the House of Lehman.* New York: Random House, 1986, is a riveting account by a *New York Times* journalist of the first collapse of Lehman Brothers.

28. Michael Lewis, *Liar's Poker: Rising through the Wreckage on Wall Street.* Markham, Ontario: Penguin Books Canada. This book described the way Salomon Brothers worked and was influential in the demise of its CEO, John Gutfreund. Citibank would ultimately buy Salomon Brothers, a fixed-income-dominated firm.

29. Rana Foroohar, "The Myth of Financial Reform," *TIME,* September 23, 2013, pp. 29–39. http://content.time.com/time/covers/0,16641,20130923,00.html.

30. The BBC managed to explain in very simple terms what this crisis is all about. www.bbc.co.uk/news/business-19199683.

31. www.bloomberg.com/news/2013-11-22/n-y-fed-s-baxter-says-bankers-need-punishment-to-shift-culture.html.

32. "'The Wolf of Wall Street': Women and Sexual Harassment in the 1980s," TIME.com. http://entertainment.time.com/2013/12/30/what-the-wolf-of-wall-street-is-missing-the-women/#ixzz2pAEgn2kU.

33. www.ft.com/intl/cms/s/0/da40a9d8-c4fb-11e1-b6fd-00144feabdc0
.html#axzz2oX3RhPnK.

34. Ibid.

35. Ben Woshinsky, in Bloomberg.com, November 22, 2013, http://bloom
.bg/18UeJyr.

36. Barbara Streisand, "I Will Never Give Up." www.vagalume.com.br/barbra-
streisand/never-give-up.html provides the text. This is the sung version:
www.youtube.com/watch?v=CWx0lSVWaKs.

37. http://web.law.columbia.edu/courses/L8138#.UrtrLPZRZdc.

CHAPTER 1

The Multiple Objectives of Financial Regulation[1]

"Globalization requires us to act in consistent ways. If we don't do that, we have fragmentation, we have regulatory arbitrage and in the worst cases a race to the bottom. We have just agreed . . . to look much more deeply at how we can coordinate our regulatory efforts on a global level."

— IOSCO Director General David Wright

The scope of this book is those regulatory issues that threaten the mere existence of financial institutions, and even more crucial, the areas where finance threatens the stability of the world economy. It does not look at all the aspects of regulation of financial institutions.

The number of legal disciplines and regulations that affect financial institutions creates a unique level of complexity. One can understand that, being at the center of the circulation, and even the creation, of money, their impact needs to be tempered and their activities have to be legitimate.

Laws and regulations that apply to financial institutions are structured to achieve many purposes, and that explains why they are sometimes perceived to be overreaching. The recent evolution has focused on the consequences of the financial crisis that developed in several parts of the world since 2008. In Europe, it additionally included the complex regulation issues raised by the sovereign crisis, making it even more complex.

However, in order to understand the dynamics of those regulations, it is important to look at some of the key objectives of regulation. At this stage, let's look at the key elements of the financial regulation by focusing on the diversity of objectives pursued by the authorities.

In an article published by Professor Alan Binder of Princeton University, he summarized the key objectives of financial regulation:

> *I suggest the following four main reasons for (different kinds of) financial regulations, all of which play major roles in this paper:*
>
> 1. *Consumer protection:* To protect customers from anti-competitive behavior (and hence from excessively high prices), from fraud, from deceptive practices, and perhaps even—though this is far more controversial—from their own foolishness and gullibility.
> 2. *Taxpayer protection:* To limit the costs to taxpayers of the government's safety net for financial institutions. The huge bailout costs that taxpayers in many countries are now bearing are spectacular examples. Ex ante taxpayer protection often involves guarding against or limiting moral hazard. Ex post taxpayer protection involves, inter alia, such things as least-cost resolution.
> 3. *Financial stability:* To protect the financial system against various sorts of systemic risks that might be triggered by contagious runs, breakdowns of the "financial plumbing," or failures of large institutions that are either too big or too interconnected with others to fail—or, rather, to fail messily.
> 4. *Macroeconomic stability:* To limit the adverse spillover effects of financial shocks on the real economy and/or to limit the financial propagation and magnification of shocks that originate outside the financial sector—in short, to mitigate booms and busts.[2]

STOP (AB)USING TAXPAYER MONEY

The main objective of the new banking regulation is to provide a resolution mechanism that provides for a recovery of financial institutions without using taxpayer money. The outrage created by the interventions of U.S. and European governments to rescue their banks during the subprime crisis led most of them to adopt policies that aim at resolving banking problems within the system (bail-in rather than bailout).

As President Obama put it in his State of the Union address in 2009:

> *I intend to hold these banks fully accountable for the assistance they receive, and this time they will have to clearly demonstrate how*

taxpayer dollars result in more lending for the American taxpayer. This time, CEOs won't be able to use taxpayer money to pad their paychecks, or buy fancy drapes, or disappear on a private jet. Those days are over. . . . Our job is to govern with a sense of responsibility. I will not spend a single penny for the purpose of rewarding a single Wall Street executive, but I will do whatever it takes to help the small business that can't pay its workers or the family that has saved and still can't get a mortgage.[3]

As noble as this objective is, regulation will not be sufficient to reach it. It will create the framework within which financiers will operate, and how to rescue financial institutions when they fail. Governments and central banks will have to take emergency measures if they have not been able to anticipate the imbalances that led to the collapse of the institution(s).

The Global Stability Report, published twice a year by the International Monetary Fund (IMF)[4] looks at the developments in this field and, among others, the stability of the financial markets. Its preface states that:

If these policy challenges are properly managed, and if reforms are implemented as promised, the transition toward greater financial stability should prove smooth and provide a more robust platform for financial sector activity and economic growth. But a failure to implement the reforms necessary to address the many policy challenges highlighted above could trigger profound spillovers across regions and potentially derail the smooth transition to greater stability.[5]

The Congressional Budget Office (CBO) released a report with what seemed like good news: the bailout of 2008, which fronted $700 billion in taxpayer funds to prop up the financial institutions that brought the economy to the brink, ended up with a profit. The estimated cost of the General Motors bailout to American taxpayers was $10 to $12 billion cheaper than expected. The price tag of the $700 billion TARP was revised down to $21 billion from $42 billion.[6]

PROTECT RETAIL AND SMALL INVESTORS AND DEPOSITORS

History tells us that unscrupulous financiers have always been trying to defraud retail and small investors. The objective of investor protection goes beyond shareholders who are inevitably the first victims of problems in financial institution bankruptcy. It first and foremost provides depositor protection through the creation of some form of insurance for retail deposits. This objective, despite its own legislation, was clearly broken recently in Europe. In the case of the Cyprus rescue, the European Council publicly broke the sanctity of insured deposits and its own regulation by proposing a haircut on deposits below the 100,000 euros guarantee. They had to backtrack immediately in front of the uproar that such a precedent was raising.[7]

In the United States, regulation is aiming at protecting retail investors. Accredited investors are allowed to access other financial instruments. They include:

- A natural person who has individual net worth, or joint net worth with the person's spouse, that exceeds $1 million at the time of the purchase, excluding the value of the primary residence of such person.
- A natural person with income exceeding $200,000 in each of the two most recent years or joint income with a spouse exceeding $300,000 for those years and a reasonable expectation of the same income level in the current year.[8]

The absence of an equivalent definition in Europe is the main reason why, for instance, the Lehman Brothers bankruptcy and the Madoff Ponzi scheme hit retail investors in Europe, while they did not in the United States.

There is no European equivalent to the U.S. rule on suitability of investments known as "know your customer":

> FINRA's [Financial Industry Regulatory Authority] suitability rule states that firms and their associated persons "must have a reasonable basis to believe" that a transaction or investment strategy involving securities that they recommend is suitable for the customer. This reasonable belief must be based on the information obtained through the reasonable diligence of the firm or associated person to ascertain the customer's investment profile.[9]

Not all assets can be sold legitimately to all investors. The need for a global suitability ruling, to be then defined at national or regional levels, would certainly make the unscrupulous sellers accountable for their abuse.

The Cyprus crisis has taught the European Union that it needs to respect the sanctity of insured deposits defined as up to 100,000 euros. However, everything else is pretty much up for grabs.

Deposits above this amount will be asked to accept a haircut to contribute to the bail-in of the bank under European rules. Europe has decided to sacrifice deposits and will create a handicap for the funding of

European banks. Large depositors will hesitate to deposit their money with European banks.

This in turn might make European banks more fragile and increase their market dependency. One of the many unintended consequences of its new resolution and recovery system might be to create a competitive disadvantage for European banks.

ENSURE TRANSPARENCY OF MARKETS AND INSTITUTIONS

The amplitude of the crises took the world by storm. It raises the question of the transparency and the availability of critical information that would allow markets and investors to act in time. Its objective should be to prevent some of the explosions that did transform into a systemic risk. The chair of the European Securities and Markets Authority (ESMA) articulates this argument:

> *Having said that transparency brings overall benefits to the market, improving its efficiency and good functioning and ultimately contributing to financial stability, we may argue that the market should have sufficient incentives to develop, adopt and implement measures to foster market transparency. However, opacity favours and benefits the individual positions of market players, allowing exploitation of information asymmetries. Therefore, this is a typical situation where decisions adopted in the general interest benefit all players, but, individually, there are not sufficient incentives to move ahead alone.*
>
> *Given the lack of sufficient and credible steps made by market led initiatives of a self-regulatory nature, transparency is an area where regulators had and have to intervene in the general public interest to restore conditions of adequate levels of transparency to reduce the information gaps and ensure good conditions of market functioning.*[10]

This objective is critical to market efficiency and investors' confidence. Capital market regulators or securities regulators have been fighting a constant battle to ensure proper information of the markets and its transparency. However, this is not unanimously shared around the world.[11]

Trust requires disclosure. An institution or a market cannot rely on investors' confidence if they hide substantial risks from them. Two of the tests will be both on securitization and on sovereign debt.

IMPLEMENT A TRULY RISK-ADJUSTED REMUNERATION SYSTEM

Remunerations had no limits or regulation before the financial crisis. The structure of remuneration in finance is a blend of several components that could affect the way risks are being taken. No incentive to increase the risk profile of the assets and trading positions can be tolerated. The Group of 20 (G20) launched this global initiative, and the Financial Stability Board (FSB) published its "Principles for Sound Compensation Practices" in April 2009, a few months after the Lehman crisis.

> *The Principles are intended to reduce incentives towards excessive risk taking that may arise from the structure of compensation schemes. They are not intended to prescribe particular designs or levels of individual compensation.*[12]

Europe chose another way. The new rules are:

> *Upfront cash bonuses will be capped at 30 percent of the total bonus and to 20 percent for particularly large bonuses. In place of upfront cash between 40 and 60 percent of any bonus must be deferred and can be recovered if investments do not perform as expected. Moreover at least 50 percent of the total bonus would be paid as "contingent capital" (funds to be called upon first in case of bank difficulties).*
>
> *Bonuses will also have to be capped to salary. Each bank will have to establish limits on bonuses related to salaries, on the basis of E.U. wide guidelines, to help bring down the overall, disproportionate, role played by bonuses in the financial sector.*
>
> *Finally, bonus-like pensions will also be covered. Exceptional pension payments must be held back in instruments such as contingent capital that link their final value to the underlying strength of the bank. This will avoid situations, similar to those experienced recently, in which some bankers retired with substantial pensions unaffected by the crisis.*[13]

With the best intentions, those rules are unfortunately misguided. First, they focus on bonuses only: the reason is that the European authorities do not have the power to address salaries and, as a consequence, global compensation. As a result of these rules, if a firm believes it needs to pay a trader $1 million, it will be forced to pay this individual a higher salary, making its fixed costs higher.

While lawmakers hailed the vote as a major victory, many in Europe's finance sector questioned whether the new laws would lead to overall reductions in bankers' pay. Analysts warned that many firms would look to skirt the new restrictions by offering higher base salaries for their top earners, which would allow them to continue to receive multi-million dollar salaries despite the cap on bonuses.[14]

Second, there is no attempt to correlate the remuneration packages with risks. A mergers-and-acquisitions (M&A) banker who uses no equity is treated the same way as an equity derivative trader who relies heavily on the bank's equity.

Unfortunately, the European Commission disregarded this approach. Unable to structure an adequate remuneration system and under the pressure of the Parliament, it chose a shortcut that disconnects its remuneration system from the risk considerations.

The web of regulation will certainly provide loopholes for bankers, as Edmond T. FitzGerald, partner and head of the Executive Compensation Group at Davis Polk & Wardwell, analyzes in the Harvard Law School blog.[15]

PROTECT DEPOSITS FROM TRADING

In order to avoid the contamination of risks that would in effect threaten the deposit base and consumer confidence, the European Commission tried to set up a European scale deposit guarantee system. While this objectively is unanimously shared, its definition is complex. Michel Barnier, the EU commissioner for the single market, asked a high group of experts to make extensive suggestions on this subject.

This report, known as the Liikanen Report, concluded that:

The central objectives of the separation are to make banking groups, especially their socially most vital parts (mainly deposit-making and providing financial services to the non-financial sectors in the economy) safer and less connected to high risk trading activities and to limit the implicit or explicit stake of taxpayer in the trading parts of banking groups. The Group's recommendations regarding separation concern businesses, which are considered to represent the riskiest parts of trading activities and where risk positions, can change most rapidly.

It is at the core of the debate on separation of banking activities and the question whether some banks should not be allowed to conduct joint activities since they have become too big to fail, manage, or regulate. We will further analyze this in Chapter 8, which is dedicated to the degrees of separation in financial institutions.

Eventually, the European deposit guarantee scheme was recast and capped at 55 billion euros. It was adopted on March 20, 2014.

NOTES

1. Financial regulation: laws and rules that govern what financial institutions such as banks, brokers, and investment companies can do. These rules are generally promulgated by government regulators or international groups to protect investors, maintain orderly markets, and promote financial stability. The range of regulatory activities can include setting minimum standards for capital and conduct, making regular inspections, and investigating and prosecuting misconduct. *Financial Times* lexicon, http://lexicon.ft.com/Term?term=financial-regulation.
2. Alan Binder, "It's Broke, Let's Fix It: Rethinking Financial Regulation," *International Journal of Central Banking,* December 2010. www.ijcb .org/journal/ijcb10q4a13.htm.
3. www.whitehouse.gov/the_press_office/Remarks-of-President-Barack-Obama-Address-to-Joint-Session-of-Congress.
4. International Monetary Fund, Global Stability Report, October 2013, Washington DC, 166 pages. www.imf.org/External/Pubs/FT/GFSR/ 2013/02/index.htm.
5. Ibid., p. xiii.
6. www.commondreams.org/view/2013/05/28-5.
7. This post I published on the website of Columbia Law School (the CLS *Blue Sky* blog) on March 21, 2013, when the news erupted, was denouncing the breach of the sanctity of insured deposits. The European Union was forced to amend its decision and agreed not to apply haircuts to insured deposits. http://clsbluesky.law.columbia.edu/2013/03/21/ cyprus-what-happened-to-the-sanctity-of-insured-deposits/.
8. The SEC definition of accredited investors. www.sec.gov/answers/ accred.htm.
9. The FINRA rule on suitability. www.finra.org/investors/protectyourself/ beforeyouinvest/p197434.
10. Steven Maijoor, "Market Transparency: Does It Prevent Crisis?" FMA Supervision Conference, Vienna, September 29, 2011. www.esma.europa .eu/system/files/2011_322.pdf.

11. Robert J. Bloomfield and Maureen O'Hara, "Market Transparency: Who Wins and Who Loses?" *Review of Financial Studies* 12(1). Available at SSRN: http://ssrn.com/abstract=122708.
12. Financial Stability Forum, "Principles for Sound Compensation Practices," April 2009. www.financialstabilityboard.org/publications/r_0904b.pdf.
13. www.europarl.europa.eu/sides/getDoc.do?language=en&type=IM-PRE SS&reference=20100630IPR77285.
14. Mark Scott and James Kanter, "Europe Votes to Curb Banker Bonuses," *New York Times*, Deal Book, April 16, 2013. http://dealbook.nytimes .com/2013/04/16/europe-votes-to-curb-banker-bonuses/.
15. Edmond T. FitzGerald, "Remuneration Regulation in the European Financial Services Industry," Harvard Law School blog, August 18, 2013. http://blogs.law.harvard.edu/corpgov/2013/08/18/remuneration-regulation-in-the-european-financial-services-industry/.

CHAPTER 2

A Quarter Century of Banking Crises and the Evolution of Financial Institutions

"The crisis has resulted from a confusion about the appropriate roles of the government and the market. We need to find the right balance again, and I am hopeful we will."

—Reserve Bank of India Governor Raghuram Rajan

In May 2007, on both sides of the Atlantic Ocean, two crises erupted, in Europe and in the United States, and central banks stepped in to avoid a systemic crisis. It was the first evidence that markets were so interconnected that the impact of problems in a major country immediately affects the global markets.

Within a week, information hit the market in the United States and in Europe, and both the Federal Reserve ($30 billion)[1] and the European Central Bank[2] (€95 billion [$ 135 billion]) had to intervene on Friday, August 10, 2007.

One of the most spectacular and dramatic market indicators is the three-month Eurodollar (TED) rate that measures the spread between U.S. Treasuries and the Eurodollar market for the same 90 days' maturities (see Figure 2.1). U.S. Treasuries benefit from the interest rate management of the Federal Reserve, while the Eurodollar rate was "free" to fluctuate purely on supply and demand.

The London interbank offered rate (LIBOR) was therefore the key indicator of the confidence of the banks in each other since it is an interbank deposit rate.

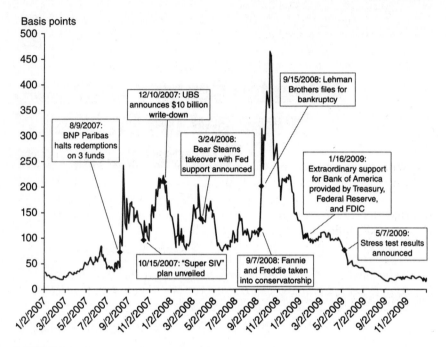

FIGURE 2.1 Three-Month TED Spread
Source: Federal Reserve Bank of St. Louis FRED database.[3]

One is constantly surprised to see how little is remembered of the previous crisis and how little is learned in the solutions proposed to avoid the next one. The similarities between the Société Générale in 2009[4] and the Baring Brothers[5] case in 1985 is striking: same lack of disclosure, insufficient scrutiny of positions by the management, and inadequacy of reporting.

BANKING CRISES ARE NOT EXACTLY A RECENT PHENOMENON

In a speech at *The Economist*'s Buttonwood Conference in 2009, in New York, Larry Summers,[6] in his capacity of adviser to President Obama, made the comment that:

Roughly every three years for the last generation, a financial system that is supposed to manage, distribute and control risk has, in fact, been a source of risk, with devastating consequences for workers, consumers and taxpayers. He added that while there is no disagreement about the importance of ethics and of better market infrastructure. Commissions are formed. Recommendations are made. And the world moves on. All this is constructive, to a point but only to a rather limited point, because it relies on the basically implausible premise that you can improve outcomes by improving human nature.

Without going into the whole history of banking, I might add that, at least since the creation of modern banking under the Medici's Venetian Court, who also came to the verge of collapse, during the Quattrocento (fourteenth century), banking or financial crises have accompanied all types of wars and conflicts throughout the world.

Some specific crises are, however, worth more specific attention.

THE TWO MAIN EMERGING-MARKET CRISES

To Larry Summers' point, the two main emerging-market crises were a repetition of the same types of causes and remedies. The Latin American[7] and Asian[8] crises had some of the same ingredients. In both cases, governments started over borrowing by borrowing short term to reduce the budgetary impact of long-term financing. As the situation worsened, the short-term debt exploded and could not be refinanced.

Countries could no longer borrow on capital markets and had to be rescued by the International Monetary Fund (IMF) with constraints that they often resented. It was, however, the only condition for them to go back to creditworthiness.

Even today, countries such as Argentina have not yet acted responsibly to their obligations and are cut off from market funding. The Yacimientos Petrolíferos Fiscales (YPF) "Marxist" nationalization made the situation even worse. The IMF, for the first time, censored the country for providing false economic data, particularly on inflation.[9] A new tax was levied: 35 percent on the foreign currency credit card hits one of Argentina's resources—tourism.

During those two critical crises, a new framework started to develop about the best way to handle sovereign crises. They would have been helpful to cure some of the European sovereign crises. However, these crises have led financiers to reflect on this common wisdom statement: countries don't get bankrupt, or the banks who lend to them.

This has been proved right and, today, concerns about a possible emerging-market crisis are being expressed. The chief economist of the IMF, Simon Johnson, expresses a cautious optimism, but remains vigilant:

> *Do the world's middle-income countries—known in the investment business as "emerging markets"—face a serious risk of crisis? If such a crisis unfolds in one country, could there be contagion, with panic spreading around the world?*
>
> *My answer is a cautious "no" on both questions. But it would be a mistake to dismiss or ignore these questions, in part because they are being asked by smart people in financial markets and in part because sometime in the not-too-distant future the answer could be a decisive "yes"—with disastrous consequences.*[10]

SUBPRIME CRISIS

While the previous crises were driven by macroeconomic trends, the subprime crisis emerged from the lack of discipline of the financial system that, with the active participation of the rating agencies, securitized assets that they did not properly underwrite.

The U.S. Treasury, in its initial report, describes how consumers were insufficiently protected against possible frauds:

> *Prior to the current financial crisis, a number of federal and state regulations were in place to protect consumers against fraud and to promote understanding of financial products like credit cards and mortgages. But as abusive practices spread, particularly in the market for subprime and nontraditional mortgages, our regulatory framework proved inadequate in important ways. Multiple agencies have authority over consumer protection in financial products, but for historical reasons, the supervisory framework for enforcing those regulations had significant gaps and weaknesses. Banking regulators at the state and federal level had a potentially conflicting mission to promote safe and sound banking practices, while other agencies had a clear mission but limited tools and jurisdiction. Most critically in the run-up to the financial crisis, mortgage companies and other firms outside of the purview of bank regulation exploited that lack of clear accountability by selling mortgages and other products that were overly complicated and unsuited to borrowers' financial situation. Banks and thrifts followed suit, with disastrous results for consumers and the financial system.*[11]

The combination of a change in the way banks started as well as the securitization of their assets deteriorated the quality of underwriting practices and credit analyses. Rating agencies began to water down their rating standards, providing an incentive to further securitization. The explosion was unavoidable and hit first and foremost specialized mortgage providers such as Countrywide.[12]

Jeffrey Shafer provides a description of the combination of factors that explain the explosion of the subprime crisis:

> *The buildup to the crisis took place amid easy monetary conditions and a rising external imbalance in the U.S. economy, which drained the supply of safe financial assets and pushed economic activity into sectors that did not compete with foreign production, such as housing. Complacency infected the markets and regulators, allowing growing risks to be overlooked. A number of factors in the mortgage market contributed to excesses:*
>
> - *Long-standing policy support for housing got new impetus from the Clinton and Bush Administrations, both of which sought to extend homeownership to those who would not have qualified for mortgages earlier.*
> - *Looser credit standards extended to the mainstream mortgage market.*
> - *Structured retail mortgage-backed securities (RMBS) grew explosively in response to the shortage of safe assets.*
> - *Packaging and distribution of RMBS was often accompanied by credit ratings, many of which, in retrospect, appear to have been based on assumptions that failed to capture what eventually happened. The role of ratings was exaggerated by their use in setting bank capital requirements.*
> - *Fannie Mae and Freddie Mac responded aggressively to the loss of market share, using their implied U.S. government guarantee and "AAA" ratings to push into alt-A and subprime mortgages.*
> - *Standards of documentation of mortgages collapsed, masking a collapse of underwriting standards by originators.*[13]

At the core of the subprime crisis is a deterioration of bank lending standards. Where are we today on this? Banks have become notaries: they created a set of complex internal rules that will have a long-term effect on the mortgage market. They are making this business the worst administrative nightmare.[14] However, mortgage marketing remains as aggressive and misleading as it used to be. The main difference is that they are scarcer.

LEHMAN CRISIS

Lehman Brothers, Bear Stearns, and Merrill Lynch were crises of overleverage. The intense lobbying of investment banks led to a reduction of regulatory and capital adequacy standards in 2004,[15] following the repeal of the Glass-Steagall Act. Jeffrey Shafer continues:

> *Over the period of the Great Moderation, four trends in financial markets led to the creation of an extraordinarily fragile system:*
>
> 1. *Rising leverage, which left the system much more sensitive to changes in the value of outside assets, such as housing.*
> 2. *Increasing maturity transformation—the financing of long-term assets with short-term liabilities—in securities portfolios.*
> 3. *More opaque financial instruments and markets generated by financial innovation, which resulted in an increase in information asymmetries—one side of the market with knowledge that the other side lacks.*
> 4. *Increasing intensity of incentive-based compensation in financial institutions. Here as well, the causes are not linked to the previous crisis. However, the European leadership pretended and managed to convince its people that there was one financial crisis, meaning that the U.S. financial crisis financial crisis spilled over to Europe.*

The spreading of the U.S. financial crisis to European banks was a result of their investments in subprime assets through asset-based securities (ABSs) and collateral loan obligations (CLOs). Banks needed to be supported, nationalized, or bailed out. Several European governments had to step in to support their banks. However, by the time the European sovereign crisis started heating up, most of the borrowings had been repaid and the equity had been placed on the market. This does not stop the political leaders, media, and public opinion from continuing to see the financial crisis as a single event.

Lehman's collapse did not in itself seriously affect the European banking industry.

As to the sanctions on the chairman and CEO of Lehman, the latest reports do not seem to point to any form of serious punishment.

> *Take Richard Fuld. Five years after Lehman Brothers Holdings Inc., the 158-year-old company he ran, collapsed under the weight of bad investments and sent a tidal wave of panic through the global financial system, Richard Fuld is living comfortably.*

> *He has a mansion in Greenwich, Conn., a 40-plus-acre ranch in Sun Valley, Idaho, as well as a five-bedroom home in Jupiter Island, Fla. He no longer has a place in Manhattan, since he sold his Park Avenue apartment in 2009 for $25.87 million.*[16]

EUROPEAN SOVEREIGN DEBT CRISIS

The Greek government debt was underestimated[17] to allow the country's joining the euro. Europe had not applied its own Pact for Stability and Growth.

> *The one post-Maastricht element, finalized at the June 1997 meeting of the European Council in Amsterdam, is the Pact for Stability and Growth. The pact clarifies the provisions of the Excessive Deficit Procedure. It calls for fiscal positions to be balanced or in surplus in normal times so that automatic stabilizers can operate.*[18]

Behind those statements lies a complex political reality. The ambitious goals of the European Union can be implemented only through a unanimous consent. The rule of unanimity[19] was essential in a small group of six Member States. However, as the European Union grew to its current size of 27 members, the rule became gradually an obstacle to quick decisions.

When a sovereign debt crisis erupts, all Member States become hostages to the failing member, but the defaulting country has no alternative but to accept the strict conditions associated with the bailout organized by the European Union. In the case of Greece, the IMF recognized that the troika (European Commission, European Central Bank, and the IMF) had underestimated the consequences of those austerity rules on Greece.[20]

The mismanagement of this crisis is now widely recognized. What was a €100 billion crisis evolved in three years into a €300 billion crisis.[21] This is one of the reasons why questions are asked about the ability of the European Commission to resolve future crises in Europe and its role in banking resolution.

EUROPEAN BANKING CRISIS

Often confused with the sovereign crisis, the European banking crisis takes its roots from the massive mismanagement of risk and liquidity by some banks in Europe.

Governments as well as the European Union had to step in to rescue the banks and, in turn, saw their indebtedness increase and their cost of financing increase. Distinguishing banking crises from sovereign crises is essential, since the remedy is substantially different.

The case of Ireland is exemplary. The country was not overly indebted, but its banks had extended mortgage loans that created a near-collapse of the Irish banking system. The bailout of Allied Irish Banks and Bank of Ireland put pressure on Irish public finance,[22] and the country had to be bailed out by the Eurozone. However, the measures taken gradually restored the health of the Irish banking system, and the country is now well on its way to recovery.[23] Declaring the imminent end of an "economic emergency," Prime Minister Enda Kenny predicted in October 2013 that Ireland would emerge from an international bailout program in December.[24]

For different reasons, banks in the United Kingdom, Ireland, Germany, Spain, and Portugal had become overleveraged, mostly through their exposure to the mortgage market. Governments had to step in to rescue the banks and, in turn, saw their indebtedness increase and their cost of financing increase. Here were the sources of those problems:

1. United Kingdom:
   a. The United Kingdom had to nationalize and sell Northern Rock, which they rescued at the beginning of the crisis. It cost the taxpayers GBP 2 billion.[25]
   b. The emergency nationalization of Royal Bank of Scotland (RBS) is soon going to be terminated : Fed up with the lack of lending, "senior government figures" are discussing whether to spend £5 billion buying up the 18 percent of RBS the state doesn't own. Alistair Darling, the chancellor of the Exchequer, has just announced the world's biggest bailout for a single bank in a bid to rescue the RBS.[26]
   c. The nationalization of Lloyds Bank: £17 billion is to be injected into the merged HBOS–Lloyds TSB, meaning 41 percent of the new "super bank" will effectively be owned by the public.[27]
2. Ireland created a fund to rescue its banks and injected $34 billion to rescue its banking system. It needed to be supported in doing so by the European Union rescue mechanism. However, the European Union and Ireland are at odds. While the bondholders will have to contribute to the bail-in of banks, the president of the European Commission accused Ireland of being the cause of the crisis (!) as if Greece did not exist.

In his comments, President Barroso has completely ignored the role played by European authorities in the full cost of bailing out Irish banks being shouldered by the Irish state. He should be reminded that the ECB flatly rejected efforts by the previous and current governments to impose losses on unguaranteed senior bondholders.[28]

3. Spain had to bail out its savings banks and, in particular, merged five of them into a new entity, Bankia, surrounding the Caja de Madrid.

The European Commission approved a payment of 37 billion euros, or $48 billion, from the euro zone bailout fund to four Spanish banks on the condition that they lay off thousands of employees and close offices.[29] Spain renounced to ask for more money from the European Union and Bankia is now profitable.

4. Germany had to rescue its banks, without EU funds. The situation of the Landesbanken was particularly fragile.

West LB was closed, with some of its assets going to Helaba. Sachsen LB was folded into Landesbank Baden-Wurttemberg (LBBW) and Landesbank Berlin is being dismantled into a savings bank and real estate business, with its capital markets arm moving to Deka. State control at both Bayern and LBBW has been eased, after the European Commission insisted on less state representation on their supervisory boards.[30]

The cost of the bailout is estimated between $44 and $64 billion.

5. Portugal had to rescue its banks.

Three leading Portuguese banks will draw on funds provided under the country's 78 billion euro ($96 billion) international bailout to meet tough new capital requirements as they struggle with the country's debt crisis.[31]

LIBOR MANIPULATION

The most memorable incidents in earth-changing events are sometimes the most banal. In the rapidly spreading scandal of LIBOR (the London inter-bank offered rate) it is the very everydayness with which bank traders set about manipulating the most important figure in finance. They joked, or offered small favours. "Coffees will be coming your way," promised one trader in exchange for a fiddled number. "Dude. I owe you big time! . . . I'm opening a bottle of Bollinger," wrote another. One trader posted diary notes to himself so that he wouldn't forget to fiddle the numbers the next week. "Ask for High 6M Fix," he entered in his calendar, as he might have put "Buy milk."[32]

LIBOR[33] is the interbank rate fixed on several currencies in London at 11 A.M. based on the data obtained from a select group of leading global banks. It became the reference of most floating-rate loans and bonds amounting to $350 trillion and regulated by the British Bankers Association (BBA).[34]

The largest scandal in recent years was undoubtedly the LIBOR crisis. It exposed the unregulated small group of banks that dominated their market and manipulated rates that influenced the cost of borrowing of $360 trillion of loans, bonds, derivatives and other debt instruments. The "regulator" was the BBA, the United Kingdom's leading association for the banking and financial services sector, representing the interests of more than 240 member organizations with a worldwide presence in 180 countries.[35]

The Wheatley Review to the U.K. Treasury, named after the CEO of the Financial Services Authority of the United Kingdom,[36] was the result of an unprecedented joint effort of 10 national regulators around the world. The LIBOR concept was indeed a model that applied to a number of currencies.

> *The Review has concluded that submission of false or misleading information in connection with a benchmark such as LIBOR is a form of wider market manipulation and should therefore be brought within the scope of market abuse.*
>
> *Benchmarks should be brought within scope in their own right, due to their importance to market functioning, rather than requiring competent authorities to establish a consequent effect on a particular financial instrument.*[37]

Following several inquiries, European banks had to pay fines amounting to around $1 billion per bank. Several leaders had to leave their post. The regulatory system was overhauled.[38]

Ultimately, the New York Stock Exchange was granted the privilege to act as the LIBOR platform.

> *On 9 July 2013, the Hogg Tendering Advisory Committee for LIBOR announced that, following a rigorous selection process, NYSE Euronext Rate Administration Limited had been appointed as the new administrator for LIBOR. As the new administrator, we plan to return credibility, trust and integrity to LIBOR, by bringing the essential combination of strong regulatory framework and market-leading validation techniques, administered by a pre-eminent market infrastructure provider.*[39]

Recently, Fannie Mae announced its intention to sue nine banks in connection with the LIBOR fraud. Fannie says it suffered $800 million in damages from the manipulation of the LIBOR and other financial benchmarks that are used to set interest rates on mortgages, credit cards, and other financial products around the world.[40]

Following an in-depth probe into suspected manipulation of benchmark eurozone interest rates, the EU competition regulators have announced their intention to fine Deutsche Bank, JPMorgan, HSBC, Royal Bank of Scotland, Crédit Agricole, and Société Générale.[41]

How will the LIBOR markets be supervised? There are calls for some form of public oversight. Germany's banking watchdog has called for government involvement in the setting of benchmark interest rates, such as LIBOR.

"Reference prices that are just based on more or less random estimates are not sound," Raimund Röseler, the head of banking supervision at BaFin, said in a Sunday newspaper interview. "The most relevant numbers must also be checked by a government body. It should not be left only to the private sector."[42]

WILL THE FOREIGN EXCHANGE MARKET BE NEXT?

For years, the chatroom cacophony in the clubby world of foreign exchange traders was peppered with allusions to drinks, drugs and women. But in the spring of 2012, debate in the private Bloomberg chats suddenly turned serious.

The conversations centred on a committee meeting of an elite group of the City of London's most senior currency traders and their counterparts at the Bank of England. Traders were agitated about rumours that BoE representatives may have raised concerns in an April meeting over possible manipulation of daily currency fixings, said people familiar with the interbank chatroom conversations.

While the traders' chatter does not chime with the meeting's minutes, it would not have been the first time that regulators had discreetly raised the issue in the past two years. One member of the BoE committee said regulators had asked senior traders on various occasions whether the daily "fix" could be manipulated but those traders had repeatedly allayed their apprehensions.

Several authorities are now scrutinizing the largest market in the world with $5 trillion worth of daily transactions. Names such as UBS, Deutsche Bank, Goldman Sachs, Lloyds and BNP Paribas *are putting aside money for legal bills as the regulatory machine is focusing on the international currency market.*[43]

It is likely that we will need more time before the amplitude of the collusion between traders as well as the huge concentration of the foreign exchange market becomes more transparent. Citibank and JPMorgan Chase are putting foreign exchange traders on leave:

Rohan Ramchandani, Citigroup's head of European spot trading, was told yesterday he will be placed on leave, said one of the people who asked not to be identified because he wasn't authorized to talk publicly. Richard Usher, JPMorgan's chief dealer in London, went on leave two weeks ago, said another person. Both are taking leave by mutual agreement with their employers and neither has been suspended.[44]

The foreign exchange market is characterized by "fixes" that are short time "auctions":

The fixes are snapshots of traded currencies rates gathered at set times of day that are used by companies and investors as benchmark reference points. The most popular is at 4 P.M. in London. Around 1 percent to 2 percent of global currencies flows are executed at this fix, which is computed by examining trades in a one-minute window.[45]

With the combination of the concentration of forex dealers and those fixes, the risk of manipulation is fairly similar to the structure of the LIBOR. The authorities are starting to investigate measures that could improve the situation. Here again, the world central banks are cooperating in trying to resolve the crisis before it erupts into a world scandal.

The European Commission has already opened an inquiry.

The European Commission is studying information about possible manipulation of foreign exchange markets, but no decision has been made about whether to open a formal investigation, the European Competition Commissioner said on Thursday.

"We have internal information regarding possible manipulation of forex benchmarks, but we are still looking at the information, I cannot anticipate anything will happen. We are in the preliminary steps," Joaquin Almunia told journalists in Dublin.[46]

The situation is taken sufficiently seriously to explain the recent statement by the Governor of the Bank of England, Mark Carney, on March 10, 2014:

> *The alleged manipulation of foreign exchange markets is "as serious as" the Libor rate rigging scandal that rocked the financial sector, Bank of England governor Mark Carney said Tuesday.*
>
> *"This is extremely serious . . . this is as serious as Libor, if not more so, because this goes to the heart of the integrity of markets and we have to establish the integrity of markets," Carney told a panel of British lawmakers.*[47]

NOTES

1. Stephen G. Cecchetti, "Crisis and Responses: The Federal Reserve in the Early Stages of the Financial Crisis," *Journal of Economic Perspectives,* Winter 2009, pp 51–75. http://econ.ucsd.edu/~grondina/pdfs/week5_cecchetti_earlyfedresponse.pdf.
2. "ECB Injects €95bn to Help Markets." www.ft.com/intl/cms/s/0/a8c5829a-466e-11dc-a3be- 0000779fd2ac.html#axzz2fdRjX9Zv.
3. www.mhfigi.com/wp-content/uploads/2013/09/Five-Years-Later-Paper-by-Jeff-Shafer1.pdf.
4. George Gilligan, "Jérôme Kerviel the 'Rogue Trader' of Société Générale: Bad Luck, Bad Apple, Bad Tree or Bad Orchard? *The Company Lawyer* 32(12), September 20, 2011, pp. 355–362. Available at http://papers.ssrn.com/sol3/papers.cfm?abstract_id=2014487.
5. Nick Leeson, *Rogue Trader: How I Brought Down Barings Bank and Shook the Financial World.* New York: Little Brown & Company.
6. Larry Summers, "The 2007–2009 Financial Crisis and the Future of Finance." Remarks at *The Economist*'s Buttonwood Conference, October 16, 2009, National Economic Council. www.whitehouse.gov/administration/eop/nec/speeches/the-2007-2009-financial-crisis-and-the-future-of-finance.
7. In the 1990s, several Latin American countries had overindebted themselves and, in order to reduce their costs of borrowing, borrowed for short maturities. When the markets became doubtful about Latin American stability, the level of short-term borrowings created an explosion. See Robert Devlin and Ricardo French Davis, The Great American Debt Crisis: A Decade of Asymmetric Adjustment. *Revista de Economia Politica,* July–September 1995, Brazil. www.rep.org.br/pdf/59-8.pdf.

8. In 1997, the crisis started in Thailand with the realization of the weakness of the banking system. It touched Malaysia, Indonesia, and eventually affected all emerging markets, including Europe and Latin America. An IMF Staff Paper, published in 1998, summarizes the Asian crisis and its causes and cures. www.imf.org/external/pubs/ft/fandd/1998/06/imfstaff.htm.

9. www.economist.com/news/americas/21591882-official-figures-paint-rosy-picture-so-why-are-argentines-rioting-still-lying-after-all.

10. http://economix.blogs.nytimes.com/2013/09/05/the-next-emerging-market-crisis/?_r=0.

11. U.S. Treasury, "A New Foundation: Rebuilding Financial Supervision and Regulation." Washington, DC, 2009.

12. Benathy Maclean and Jo Niocera, "How the Roof Fell on Countrywide." *Fortune*, December 23, 2010. http://finance.fortune.cnn.com/2010/12/23/how-the-roof-fell-in-on-countrywide/.

13. www.mhfigi.com/wp-content/uploads/2013/09/Five-Years-Later-Paper-by-Jeff-Shafer1.pdf.

14. Arthur Delaney, "Wells Fargo 'Nightmare' for Homeowner Applying for Help under Administration's Anti-foreclosure Program." *Huffington Post*, November 12, /2010. www.huffingtonpost.com/2010/11/12/wells fargo-makes-it-near_n_782634.html.

15. The new legislation provided extended leverage against closer scrutiny by the SEC that never adequately staffed the relevant unit. Stephen Labaton summarizes the impact of this rule on the financial crisis in "Agency's '04 Rule Let Banks Pile Up New Debt," *New York Times*, October 2, 2008. www.nytimes.com/2008/10/03/business/03sec.html?pagewanted=all&_r=0.

16. http://finance.yahoo.com/blogs/daily-ticker/ceo-behind-lehman-collapse-isn-t-sorry-dick-131017662.html.

17. It took years for the Greek government to admit that its accounts were fraught. http://www.europolitics.info/greece-on-defensive-after-underestimating-deficit-art251882-38.html.

18. Barry Eichengreen and Charles Wyplosz, "Stability Pact, More than a Minor Nuisance," IMF, University of California, Berkeley, CEPR and NBER; Graduate Institute of International Studies, Geneva, and CEPR, Economic Policy, April 1998, pp. 67–113. www.aueb.gr/users/kalyvitis/Wyplosz.pdf.

19. From the beginning the European Union could only be construed on a unanimous decision by its six Member States: Belgium, France, Germany, Italy, Luxembourg, and the Netherlands.

20. www.economist.com/blogs/charlemagne/2013/08/greeces-bailout.

21. www.bbc.co.uk/news/business-13856580.

22. www.independent.ie/irish-news/taxpayer-is-picking-up-ailing-anglo-irish-bank-26506105.html.
23. Ireland obtained a reduction of the interest rate it had to pay to the EFSF.
24. www.nytimes.com/2013/10/14/world/europe/setting-pace-ireland-predicts-december-exit-from-bailout.html?_r=0reland.
25. http://news.bbc.co.uk/2/hi/6994099.stm.
26. www.wsws.org/en/articles/2009/11/scot-n09.html.
27. www.theguardian.com/business/blog/2011/oct/13/taxpayer-losses-rbs-lloyds-shares.
28. "EU Betrayed Ireland over Debt." www.independent.ie/irish-news/eu-betrayed-ireland-over-debt-29855752.html.
29. www.nytimes.com/2012/11/29/business/global/european-commission-approves-bailout-of-four-spanish-banks.html.
30. www.reuters.com/article/2013/09/17/banking-germany-landesbanken-idUSL5N0H820520130917.
31. www.reuters.com/article/2012/06/04/portugal-millennium-idUSL5E-8H43EA20120604.
32. "The Rotten Heart of Finance," *The Economist,* July 7, 2012. www.economist.com/node/21558281.
33. LIBOR stands for London interbank offered rate. LIBOR is a key benchmark rate that reflects how much it costs banks to borrow from each other. It is the reference rate for about $350 trillion of financial products, ranging from interest rate swaps and corporate loans to credit cards, mortgages and savings accounts. http://lexicon.ft.com/Term?term=LIBOR.
34. Evan Weinberger, "British Bankers Group Agrees to Give Up Libor-Setting Duties," February 25, 2013. www.law360.com/articles/418285/british-bankers-group-agrees-to-give-up-libor-setting-duties.
35. www.bba.org.uk/about-us.
36. That paper set out the case for reform of LIBOR and proposed a range of options for reform of the benchmark. In addition, the paper considered potential alternatives to LIBOR and examined the implications of the Review's thinking on other global benchmarks. www.gov.uk/government/uploads/system/uploads/attachment_data/file/191762/wheatley_review_libor_finalreport_280912.pdf.
37. Ibid., p. 15.
38. www.euractiv.com/euro-finance/libor-scandal-provokes-regulator-news-514639.
39. www.nyx.com/libor.
40. www.forbes.com/sites/maggiemcgrath/2013/10/31/fannie-mae-suing-nine-banks-over-libor-manipulation/.

41. www.lexology.com/library/detail.aspx?g=74ebbe28-2f13-47f5-820b-a1993614916d.
42. www.ft.com/intl/cms/s/0/fb18fc5c-601b-11e3-b360-00144feabdc0.html#axzz2oap3DEJa.
43. Daniel Schäfer, Alice Ross, and Delphine Strauss, "Foreign Exchange: The Big Fix," *Financial Times,* November 12, 2013. www.ft.com/intl/cms/s/2/7a9b85b4-4af8-11e3-8c4c-00144feabdc0.html#axzz2ocUViOOa.
44. www.bloomberg.com/news/2013-10-30/citigroup-jpmorgan-said-to-put-senior-currency-dealers-on-leave.html.
45. Katie Martin and Chiara Albanese, "Banker, Regulators Weigh Forex Fixes," *Wall Street Journal,* November 29, 2013. http://online.wsj.com/news/articles/SB10001424052702304017204579228022791310030.
46. www.reuters.com/article/2013/12/05/eu-forex-probe-idUSL5N0JK-2WQ20131205.
47. http://www.google.com/hostednews/afp/article/ALeqM5g-08Hkm ZNXwq2PpUEETHi0e4dSNg?docId=9e30f5a2-2349-4338-b8e--78e3864607c3&hl=en.

CHAPTER 3

The Lessons of the Recent Financial Crises: The Explosion of Balance Sheets

"Advanced economies have steadily increased leverage for decades. That era is now decisively over. The direction may be clear, but the magnitude and abruptness of the process are not. It could be long and orderly or it could be sharp and chaotic."

—Bank of Canada and Bank of England Governor Mark Carney

The transformation of the landscape of the U.S. capital markets led to structural evolutions that added substantial nonbanking assets to the balance sheet of commercial banks and long-term assets in the balance sheets of investment banks: the removal of the Glass-Steagall Act[1] showed its limitations and was followed by corrective measures of the Dodd-Frank Act of 2002.

Since the beginning of this century the total assets of United States banks increased from $6.2 to $13.4 trillion. At the same time, the gross domestic product (GDP) grew from $10 to $15.7 trillion. They now represent 85 percent of the country's GDP (see Table 3.1).

Even in the United States, about half the balance sheet is composed of loans. A deleverage such as the one that is contemplated in the leverage ratio of Basel III should not mean that banks need to cut their lending activities. It is an argument that is often used, but not substantiated by the figures.

TABLE 3.1 Federal Deposit Insurance Corporation Assets

Year	No. of Inst.	Cash and Due From	Investment Securities	Total Loans and Leases	Allowance for Losses Loans and Leases	Net Loans and Leases
2012	6,096	1,333,763,534	2,750,149,789	7,047,941,339	152,157,881	6,895,783,458
2011	6,291	1,195,924,598	2,541,235,366	6,719,065,712	178,635,735	6,540,429,978
2010	6,530	922,704,016	2,351,738,355	6,594,996,347	217,973,473	6,377,022,874
2009	6,840	976,572,935	2,199,577,511	6,495,186,596	213,817,010	6,281,369,586
2008	7,087	1,041,802,864	1,746,327,228	6,838,447,027	156,659,219	6,681,787,808
2007	7,284	482,162,433	1,590,801,925	6,626,408,618	89,179,154	6,537,229,464
2006	7,401	432,960,082	1,666,204,374	5,981,812,474	69,059,839	5,912,752,635
2005	7,526	400,266,590	1,572,201,667	5,382,110,196	68,730,817	5,313,379,379
2004	7,631	387,555,301	1,551,101,104	4,906,361,549	73,496,034	4,832,865,517
2003	7,770	387,437,399	1,456,248,388	4,428,946,848	77,124,191	4,351,822,658
2002	7,888	383,845,820	1,334,727,452	4,156,249,955	76,982,950	4,079,267,003
2001	8,080	390,340,367	1,172,539,507	3,884,328,453	72,273,347	3,812,055,108
2000	8,315	369,930,621	1,078,984,624	3,815,497,766	64,120,431	3,751,377,337

Source: http://www2.fdic.gov/hsob/HSOBRpt.asp.

The obvious cut should be in investment securities whose share has moved from 15 to 20 percent over the past 10 years. The same applies to "other earning assets." It is so obvious that one wonders how they can still continue to state what is obviously not correct and manage to influence the Federal Reserve Bank to smooth their positions. A trillion dollars more in cash also requires an explanation—unless it is the direct result of quantitative easing.

STRUCTURAL OVERBANKING OF EUROPE[2]

The vast majority of financing in Europe goes through the balance sheet of banks (see Table 3.2). It is far away from the U.S. reality. The reasons for this overbanking are a combination of history, complacency, political lobbying, and power.

Sooner or later, whether it will be under pressure of the new capital adequacy, liquidity and leverage ratios, or otherwise, this situation will need to change. However, Table 3.2, published by the European Central Bank, presents some interesting characteristics.

Other Earning Assets	Bank Premises and Equipment	Other Real Estate	Intangible Assets	All Other Assets	Total Assets
1,227,730,246	112,656,827	34,887,119	351,249,514	684,895,878	13,391,116,364
1,171,968,519	112,006,014	41,017,289	348,296,671	698,058,071	12,648,936,506
1,177,979,870	110,663,798	46,653,051	373,186,055	705,541,375	12,065,489,394
1,108,124,671	110,514,321	35,858,537	386,800,490	723,909,857	11,822,727,909
1,627,921,002	109,680,964	22,915,563	392,528,324	685,932,947	12,308,896,700
1,513,678,238	105,021,581	9,791,860	423,218,397	514,139,524	11,176,043,422
1,149,123,213	96,829,468	5,467,171	358,512,075	470,109,360	10,091,958,378
942,514,776	91,725,352	4,026,107	302,891,742	414,333,686	9,041,339,299
889,528,599	86,799,336	3,852,709	275,726,003	388,186,243	8,415,614,796
780,437,642	83,391,964	4,530,717	158,174,341	379,501,717	7,601,544,836
709,197,457	79,234,720	4,430,808	124,850,466	361,358,124	7,076,911,860
620,534,054	76,643,935	3,829,583	120,143,368	356,207,938	6,552,293,846
584,102,387	75,793,540	3,209,509	103,803,239	278,358,478	6,245,559,732

European banks hold on average 80 percent of their equity in European government securities and approximately 40 percent in the form of loans. This makes them extremely vulnerable to sovereign debt crises, as we have seen since 2009.

Around 2 trillion euros of sovereign debt (23 percent of the total) are in the balance sheets of European banks. That represents on average 73 percent of their equity. Italian banks are the euro champion, with 110 percent of sovereign debt/equity. Since Italy has a 130 percent debt/GDP ratio, and growing, this interdependence between the Italian banks and the Italian government debt is potentially the most explosive imbalance for the world banking system.

The European banks' loan portfolio is on average funded by deposits and is equivalent of half of their balance sheets. This is a very sound structure that allows a decrease of the balance sheet without affecting their lending activity. The largest global banks, however, have one third of their balance sheet in the form of loans. Like U.S. banks, their lending activities do not exceed 55 percent of the balance sheets.

The Liikanen Report gives an impressive visual of the European balance sheet evolution (see Figures 3.1 and 3.2). In Europe, bank assets reach 350 percent of the EU GDP.

TABLE 3.2   Aggregate Balance Sheet of Euro Area Monetary Financial Institutions (MFIs)

2.1 Aggregated balance sheet of euro area MFIs[a]
   (EUR billions; outstanding amounts at end of period)

1. Assets

| | | Loans to Euro Area Residents | | | |
	Total 1	Total 2	General Government 3	Other Euro Area Residents 4	MFIs 5
Eurosystem					
2011	4,700.4	2,780.5	18.0	1.0	2,761.5
2012	5,287.6	3,351.2	16.9	1.0	3,333.3
2013 Q2	4,399.4	2,572.6	15.1	1.2	2,556.3
Q3	4,303.2	2,455.0	15.1	1.2	2,438.7
2013 July	4,364.2	2,508.6	15.0	1.2	2,492.4
Aug.	4,353.7	2,485.8	15.0	1.2	2,469.5
Sep.	4,303.2	2,455.0	15.1	1.2	2,438.7
Oct.*	4,228.5	2,399.5	15.1	1.2	2,383.3
MFIs excluding the Eurosystem					
2011	33,533.5	18,476.5	1,159.6	11,163.1	6,153.8
2012	32,697.6	17,992.9	1,153.4	11,042.6	5,796.9
2013 Q2	32,009.2	17,529.1	1,101.8	10,978.7	5,448.6
Q3	31,385.2	17,303.4	1,090.4	10,781.1	5,431.9
2013 July	31,695.8	17,418.7	1,105.2	10,897.7	5,415.7
Aug.	31,536.9	17,384.6	1,090.2	10,768.4	5,526.0
Sep.	31,385.2	17,303.4	1,090.4	10,781.1	5,431.9
Oct.*	31,354.5	17,192.5	1,103.0	10,737.5	5,352.0

2. Liabilities

| | | | Deposits of Euro Area Residents | | | |
	Total 1	Currency in Circulation 2	Total 3	Central Government 4	Other General Government/Other Euro Area Residents 5	MFIs 6
Eurosystem						
2011	4,700.4	913.6	2,609.0	63.8	12.1	2,533.1
2012	5,287.6	938.2	3,062.2	81.4	64.5	2,916.4
2013 Q2	4,399.4	936.8	2,350.7	107.9	45.7	2,197.1
Q3	4,303.2	944.6	2,225.0	82.0	49.2	2,093.8
2013 July	4,364.2	944.3	2,281.6	114.7	50.6	2,116.3
Aug.	4,353.7	945.3	2,250.3	81.3	46.3	2,122.7
Sep.	4,303.2	944.6	2,225.0	82.0	49.2	2,093.8
Oct.*	4,228.5	950.4	2,153.1	79.7	69.2	2,004.2
MFIs excluding the Eurosystem						
2011	33,533.5	-	17,312.0	195.5	10,752.1	6,364.4
2012	32,697.6	-	17,201.8	170.8	10,869.2	6,161.9
2013 Q2	32,009.2	-	17,074.6	236.7	11,085.1	5,752.8
Q3	31,385.2	-	16,854.3	190.9	10,929.7	5,733.8
2013 July	31,695.8	-	16,947.4	203.8	11,006.4	5,737.3
Aug.	31,536.9	-	16,949.0	181.5	10,950.5	5,817.0
Sep.	31,385.2	-	16,854.3	190.9	10,929.7	5,733.8
Oct.*	31,354.5	-	16,766.5	165.5	10,918.8	5,682.2

| Holdings of Securities Other Than Shares Issued by Euro Area Residents | | | | Money Market Fund Shares/Units[b] | Holdings of Shares/Other Equity Issued by Euro Area Residents | External Assets | Fixed Assets | Remaining Assets[c] |
| Total | General Government | Other Euro Area Residents | MFIs | | | | | |
6	7	8	9	10	11	12	13	14
717.2	557.0	10.1	150.1	-	20.3	779.2	8.1	395.0
723.1	568.4	10.5	144.2	-	23.4	799.9	8.3	381.8
741.7	588.9	25.3	127.4	-	23.6	665.0	8.3	388.4
727.9	576.7	26.5	124.7	-	24.6	690.7	8.3	396.8
737.8	586.7	25.9	125.2	-	23.9	693.9	8.3	391.6
730.1	579.4	25.9	124.8	-	24.0	711.3	8.3	394.2
727.9	576.7	26.5	124.7	-	24.6	690.7	8.3	396.8
724.6	575.7	25.7	123.3	-	25.2	671.7	8.4	399.0
4,765.1	1,395.9	1,517.3	1,852.0	50.2	1,212.0	4,253.5	232.3	4,543.9
4,901.6	1,627.0	1,423.3	1,851.3	66.8	1,227.8	4,044.0	214.6	4,249.9
4,959.6	1,785.2	1,407.3	1,767.1	50.9	1,246.4	4,003.4	209.5	4,010.4
4,841.3	1,744.7	1,392.8	1,703.8	58.9	1,232.9	3,894.1	210.4	3,844.2
4,916.0	1,753.1	1,405.8	1,757.1	52.2	1,249.2	3,942.2	210.1	3,907.5
4,893.2	1,755.3	1,401.8	1,736.1	58.1	1,223.4	3,949.8	210.1	3,817.7
4,841.3	1,744.7	1,392.8	1,703.8	58.9	1,232.9	3,894.1	210.4	3,844.2
4,825.2	1,763.9	1,374.6	1,686.7	55.8	1,234.5	3,950.4	209.0	3,887.1

| Money Market Fund Shares/Units[d] | Debt Securities Issued[e] | Capital and Reserves | External Liabilities | Remaining Liabilities*) |
7	8	9	10	11
-	0.0	481.3	284.3	412.2
-	0.0	536.1	298.7	452.4
-	0.0	421.4	241.3	449.3
-	0.0	444.8	225.4	463.5
-	0.0	449.5	232.9	455.8
-	0.0	469.1	229.4	459.5
-	0.0	444.8	225.4	463.5
-	0.0	444.4	213.5	467.1
570.6	5,008.2	2,229.1	3,805.2	4,608.3
534.7	4,848.9	2,343.9	3,491.0	4,277.2
486.9	4,590.6	2,391.8	3,407.5	4,057.8
476.8	4,470.5	2,392.7	3,271.7	3,919.2
487.0	4,538.1	2,405.1	3,363.3	3,954.9
502.5	4,506.4	2,388.8	3,339.6	3,850.6
476.8	4,470.5	2,392.7	3,271.7	3,919.2
474.6	4,447.5	2,398.9	3,296.8	3,970.3

Source: ECB.

a) Data refer to the changing composition of the euro area. For further information, see the General Notes.

b) Amounts issued by euro area residents. Amounts issued by non–euro area residents are included in external assets.

c) In December 2010 a change was made to the recording practice for derivatives in one Member State, leading to an increase in this position.

d) Amounts held by euro area residents.

e) Amounts issued with a maturity of up to two years and held by non–euro area residents are included in external liabilities.

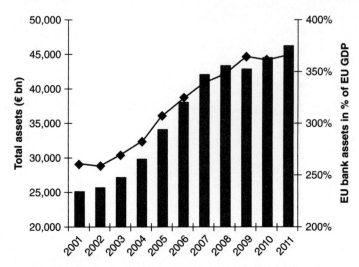

Note: Bar charts show total assets, dotted line shows assets in % of GDP.

FIGURE 3.1   Total Assets of MFIs in EU 2001–2001
Source: ECB data.

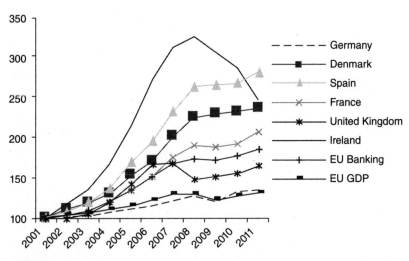

FIGURE 3.2   Total MFI Assets 2001–2011 (Index, 2001 = 100)
Source: ECB data.[3]

TABLE 3.3   Size of EU, U.S., and Japanese Banking Sectors (2010)

	EU	USA	Japan
Total bank sector assets (€ trillion)	42.9	8.6	7.1
Total bank sector assets/GDP	349%	78%	174%
Top 10 bank assets (€ trillion)	15.0	4.8	3.7
Top 10 bank assets/GDP	122%	44%	91%

Note: Top 6 banks for Japan.
Source: European Banking Federation, 2011.[4]

What those data cover is a huge discrepancy among the main parts of the world. This explains the dependency of the European authorities and governments on the banking sector (see Table 3.3).

First steps have been made to reduce the balance sheets, but they are clearly insignificant in the context of this structural overbanking. Clearly, European banks are more focused on complying with Basel III.

> *In compliance with the new bank regulations, known as Basel III, the risk-weighted assets of European banks were cut by 817 billion euros ($1.1 trillion) from December 2011 to June 2013, while core tier 1 capital rose by more than 80 billion euro in the same period, according to the EBA report, which was released Monday. The capital ratio is a measure of how well banks can cushion heavy financial losses, and it rose to 11.7 percent from 10 percent.*[5]

LACK OF TRANSPARENCY OF THE DERIVATIVE MARKETS

Poor accounting and execution standards have been hiding a gross $600 trillion bubble[6] that was neither counted for nor seriously regulated. The Self-Regulation of the International Swap and Derivative Association (ISDA)[7] could not provide the necessary infrastructure and reporting of derivative exposures, and derivative markets were by and large unregulated.

The situation was very well documented, and the reports of the BIS and central banks were vocal about the need to ensure proper back-office structure, accounting of swap contracts, and many other aspects of the derivatives markets.

The question is hotly debated between regulators and industry professionals. The main confusion comes from the fact that while regulators need to have a full transparency to be able to exercise their oversight role, the question of full transparency through public information is questioned.

> *The big derivatives dealers have argued that too much transparency could harm markets by making it more difficult to provide liquidity. But a group of nine global regulators meeting in Toronto this week agreed to continue to push for publicly available volumes in swaps, said Gary Gensler, chairman of the CFTC.*[8]

The Institute of International Finance recently took a cautious view on the subject, but does not favor full transparency.

> *Transparency should not require disclosure of the results of assessments of, or the text of, individual financial institutions' recovery or resolution plans. The criterion should provide that such reports should not be understood to require disclosures of the results of assessments of, or otherwise non-public portions of, individual financial institutions' recovery or resolution plans or other information not required to be made public by the relevant substantive law or regulations.*[9]

EMERGENCE OF THE CREDIT DEFAULT SWAP (CDS) MARKET[10]

> *Credit default swaps are financial instruments investors can use for hedging. In the case of government debt, investors use the swaps to express an opinion about the creditworthiness of a government, and to protect themselves in the event a country defaults or undertakes a debt restructuring.*[11]

They are marketable instruments aiming to insure some credit risks: at any given time, the level of trading of the risks associated with corporate and sovereign bonds. As most bellwethers, CDSs were not only indicating risk deteriorations, but also, due to their relatively small size, amplified it.

Since it was the only readily available barometer of the health of companies, banks, and countries, the media started to report it systematically and gave it an undue prominence that led to aggressive reactions of those institutions that were seeing their credit deteriorating.

The snowball effect of this prominence increased the problem of the creditworthiness of the targeted institutions, and added to its natural course, leading to the perception that this instrument and the speculation associated with it was in fact the cause of the problem.

European authorities have been proactive in trying to regulate the CDS market.

Investment banks' lucrative role as the middlemen of derivatives markets have long been under regulatory attack. But Brussels is not only rewriting rules for future trading and clearing; it could now punish banks for their past dominance.[12]

THE REGULATORY LANDSCAPE IS NOT GLOBAL BUT LARGELY NATIONAL

To be effective, global regulation needs a legal system, court jurisdiction, and statutory rights. They don't exist. Regulators were totally unable to deal with the global consequences of the global crisis.

Not only did they not have the instruments to assess the global position through the fragmentation of regulation, but also the solution had to be dealt with in national courts and jurisdictions.

As a result of this situation, owners of debt instruments or financial assets would end up being treated differently in New York than they were in London. The procedures were also vastly different, and it took five years to resolve the problems of Lehman's collapse, and cost $2.2 billion in legal fees alone.[13]

NOTES

1. U.S. Senate, The Financial Modernization Act, 1999. www.gpo.gov/fdsys/pkg/CRPT-106srpt44/pdf/CRPT-106srpt44.pdf.
2. http://sdw.ecb.europa.eu/reports.do?node=100000137.
3. Ibid., p. 12.
4. Ibid., p. 12.
5. www.ibtimes.com/basel-iii-capital-ratio-requirements-chop-more-1-trillion-european-bank-assets-european-banking.
6. This is the web site part of the Bank for International Settlements, which publishes statistics about the size of the derivative markets: www.bis.org/statistics/derstats.htm.
7. International Swap and Derivatives Association web site: www2.isda.org/.
8. www.ft.com/intl/cms/s/0/7e7f7160-946d-11e1-8e90-00144feab49a.html#axzz2kqXzi5vD.

9. www.financialstabilityboard.org%2Fpublications%2Fc_131121f
.pdf&ei=okfEUsufCoy_sQSQsICQDQ&usg=AFQjCNFSoXIsyakR2X
fgPzV2s62szgII7g&bvm=bv.58187178,d.cWc.

10. Martin Oehmke, Columbia University, and Adam Zawadowski, Boston University, "The Anatomy of the CDS Market," January 11, 2013.
www.gsb.columbia.edu/faculty/moehmke/papers/OehmkeZawadows
kiCDS.pdf.

11. IMF, "Credit Default Swaps on Government Debt Are Effective
Gauge," April 11, 2013. www.imf.org/external/pubs/ft/survey/so/2013/
POL041113B.htm.

12. www.ft.com/cms/s/0/86c7fd06-e255-11e2-a7fa-00144feabdc0
.html#ixzz2jVDotpdo.

13. www.hartfordbusiness.com/article/20130913/NEWS02/309139992.

CHAPTER 4

Global Financial Regulation: The Institutional Complexities

"Every administrative agency that has put out a broad rule has had to cut it back, sometimes cutting it back 50 percent or more. The agencies are not only paralyzed, they are inundated. They are unable to meet the pace set by Congress. Beyond that, they are extremely risk averse right now. They are focusing on the trivia rather than the broader issues."

—Columbia Law School Professor John Coffee

In his message to JPMorgan Chase shareholders, its chairman and CEO, Jamie Dimon, mapped in 2011 the regulatory web his bank is subject to, emphasizing the impossible and ineffective complexity (see Figure 4.1).

A robust financial system needs coordinated and consistent regulation that is strong, simple and transparent. The regulators should have clear authority and responsibility. Just one look at the chart on the next page (Figure 4.1) shows that this is not what we now have. Complexity and confusion should have been alleviated, not compounded.[1]

Did he ever expect that JPMorgan Chase would be buried under massive fines from several of those institutions?

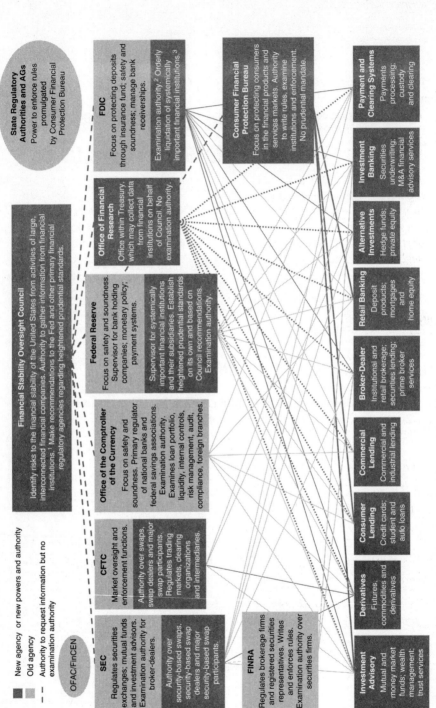

State Regulatory Authorities and AGs
Power to enforce rules promulgated by Consumer Financial Protection Bureau

FDIC
Focus on protecting deposits through insurance fund; safety and soundness; manage bank receiverships.

Examination authority.[2] Orderly liquidation of systemically important financial institutions.[3]

Financial Stability Oversight Council
Identify risks to the financial stability of the United States from activities of large, interconnected financial companies. Authority to gather information from financial institutions.[1] Make recommendations to the Fed and other primary financial regulatory agencies regarding heightened prudential standards.

Consumer Financial Protection Bureau
Focus on protecting consumers in the financial products and services markets. Authority to write rules, examine institutions and enforcement. No prudential mandate.

Office of Financial Research
Office within Treasury, which may collect data from financial institutions on behalf of Council. No examination authority.

Federal Reserve
Focus on safety and soundness. Supervisor for bank holding companies; monetary policy; payment systems.

Supervisor for systemically important financial institutions and their subsidiaries. Establish heightened prudential standards on its own and based on Council recommendations. Examination authority

Office of the Comptroller of the Currency
Focus on safety and soundness. Primary regulator of national banks and federal savings associations. Examination authority. Examines loan portfolio, liquidity, internal controls, risk management, audit, compliance, foreign branches.

CFTC
Market oversight and enforcement functions.

Authority over swaps, swap dealers and major swap participants. Regulates trading markets, clearing organizations and intermediaries.

SEC
Regulates securities exchanges; mutual funds and investment advisors. Examination authority for broker-dealers.

Authority over security-based swaps, security-based swap dealers and major security-based swap participants.

FINRA
Regulates brokerage firms and registered securities representatives. Writes and enforces rules. Examination authority over securities firms.

New agency or new powers and authority

Old agency

Authority to request information but no examination authority

OFAC/FinCEN

Payment and Clearing Systems
Payments processing; custody and clearing

Investment Banking
Securities underwriting; M&A financial advisory services

Alternative Investments
Hedge funds; private equity

Retail Banking
Deposit products; mortgages and home equity

Broker-Dealer
Institutional and retail brokerage; securities lending; prime broker services

Commercial Lending
Commercial and industrial lending

Consumer Lending
Credit cards; student and auto loans

Derivatives
Futures, commodities and derivatives

Investment Advisory
Mutual and money market funds; wealth management; trust services

Note: Green lines from SEC and CFTC represent enhanced authority over existing relationships.

FIGURE 4.1 Regulatory Institutional Complexity—JPMorgan 2011 Annual Report

At a global level, few attempts were made to discuss regulation at a global level prior to the 2008 crisis. The Bank for International Settlements (BIS) publishes a list of regulators on its web site.[2] Not surprisingly, most of them are national central banks.

The institutional complexity is of course a reflection of the subject, but it is not coherent, and sometimes plainly unnecessary. In an article published in 2010 (see Table 4.1), Eric Pan emphasizes:

The importance of (i) coordination and information sharing among regulatory agencies—noting that the achievement of such coordination and information sharing is more important than the structural question of a single regulator versus twin peaks system; (ii) active participation by the national regulator in multilateral and bilateral negotiations with foreign regulators; and (iii) additional resources for enforcement and supervision.[3]

GROUP OF 20 (G20)

The G20 finds its origin in an attempt to involve countries other than the richest countries in the world, named the G7, which became the G8 after Russia was included. It was becoming indecent that crucial economic issues were being discussed without China, India, Brazil, Mexico, or Saudi Arabia. These 20 countries represent 90 percent of the world gross domestic product (GDP).

The G20 was formally established in September 1999 when finance ministers and central bank governors of seven major industrial countries (Canada, France, Germany, Italy, Japan, the United Kingdom and the United States) met in Washington, D.C. in the aftermath of the financial crisis of 1997–1998, which revealed the vulnerability of the international financial system in context of economic globalization and showed that key developing countries were insufficiently involved in discussions and decisions concerning global economic issues.

The G20 brings together finance ministers and central bank governors from 19 countries: Argentina, Australia, Brazil, Canada, China, France, Germany, India, Indonesia, Italy, Japan, the Republic of Korea, Mexico, Russia, Saudi Arabia, South Africa, Turkey, the United Kingdom, the United States of America plus the European Union, which is represented by the President of the European Council and by Head of the European Central Bank.[4]

TABLE 4.1 Summarized Description of the Global Regulatory Framework

	International Organizations	State-to-State Contact Groups	Transgovernmental Networks	Bilateral and Regional Networks	Private Standard-Setting and Opinion-Making Bodies
Examples	IMF World Bank WTO OECD BIS	G-7 G-8 G-10 G-20	BCBS IOSCO IAIS FSB	FMRD RRD HLMFI ECRDC ERDFS EUI	IASB S&P
Characteristics	▪ Treaty-based ▪ Large secretariat ▪ Policy administrating ▪ Limited policy making	▪ Protocols ▪ No secretariats ▪ Policy-making	▪ MOU/informal ▪ Small secretariats ▪ Information sharing ▪ Policy coordination ▪ Policy administration	▪ MOU/informal ▪ No secretariats ▪ Information sharing ▪ Policy coordination	▪ Private sector experts
Regulatory tasks	▪ Sovereign loans ▪ Economic development ▪ Technical assistance ▪ Standards enforcement	▪ Crisis response ▪ Regulatory initiatives ▪ Networks creation	▪ Rules and standards on prudential aspects of banking ▪ Securities ▪ Insurance	▪ Approximation of rules and standards ▪ Mutual recognition ▪ Market access provision	▪ Technical standards
Examples of achievements	▪ FSAP	▪ Creation of BCBS ▪ FSE	▪ Development of sectoral prudential standards	▪ Opening of Russian market ▪ IFRS roadmap	▪ IFRS ▪ New supervisory tools

Source: Based on Pan (2010), p. 248.

What this description does not include is how it became the body it is today. Shocked by the consequences of the 2008 financial crisis, President Sarkozy left the *Sommet de la Francophonie* in Québec to meet President George W. Bush at Camp David and convince him to organize a meeting of the G20 at the level of heads of state and government. This initiative took place after Barack Obama—who declined to attend the summit in Washington, D.C.—was elected.

This led to the transformation of a group that was originally working at finance ministers' level on economic imbalances and financial stability into the forum where the heads of state and government decided to promote the development of a global regulatory framework and a repositioning of the G20 into a major political initiative surrounded by publicity as well as incendiary declarations before, during, and after the summits.

The wide objectives of the G20 have recently been defined as follows. They are so general that its role in regulation is still modest.

- Policy coordination between its members in order to achieve global economic stability and sustainable growth.
- Promoting financial regulations that reduce risks and prevent future financial crises.
- Modernizing international financial architecture.[5]

It subsequently became a huge undertaking with biannual summits, generally among more or less violent antiglobalization demonstrations.[6] The summit itself became an instrument by its members to ensure that it would support some of their domestic or regional political agendas. The press releases following the summits have become the most fascinating catalog of disparate agendas.

Most important, it became the inspiration of regulatory initiatives that were missing and inspired a number of reforms around the world.

FINANCIAL STABILITY BOARD (FSB)

The G7 finance ministers and central bank governors, following recommendations by Hans Tietmeyer, president of the Deutsche Bundesbank, founded the Financial Stability Forum (FSF) in 1999.[7]

In the absence of an agency working for the G20, the FSF became the FSB,[8] which became the secretariat of the G20 for regulatory matters and issued global policy papers that were directed to national regulators in order to include the policies and principles of the G20 in their regulatory framework and revision. It was created at the London meeting of the G20 in April 2009.

As part of its mandate, the FSB will:

- *Assess vulnerabilities affecting the global financial system and identify and review on a timely and ongoing basis the regulatory, supervisory and related actions needed to address them, and their outcomes;*
- *Promote coordination and information exchange among authorities responsible for financial stability;*
- *Monitor and advise on market developments and their implications for regulatory policy;*
- *Advise on and monitor best practice in meeting regulatory standards;*
- *Undertake joint strategic reviews of the policy development work of the international standard setting bodies to ensure their work is timely, coordinated, focused on priorities and addressing gaps;*
- *Set guidelines for and support the establishment of supervisory colleges;*
- *Support contingency planning for cross-border crisis management, particularly with respect to systemically important firms;*
- *Collaborate with the International Monetary Fund (IMF) to conduct Early Warning Exercises; and*
- *Undertake any other tasks agreed by its Members in the course of its activities and within the framework of this Charter.*

The FSB will promote and help coordinate the alignment of the activities of the standard-setting bodies (SSBs) to address any overlaps or gaps and clarify demarcations in light of changes in national and regional regulatory structures relating to prudential and systemic risk, market integrity and investor and consumer protection, and infrastructure, as well as accounting and auditing.

The G20 decided that the FSF would be transformed into a board, despite the fact that it failed in its mission. Under the auspices of the BIS, it had been given the task, following a previous crisis, to be the focal point of data gathering and analysis of the factors that could destabilize the international financial system. It did not even issue warnings prior to the 2007 subprime crisis and was not worried that it might put the world into its worst banking crisis since the Great Depression.[9]

BANK FOR INTERNATIONAL SETTLEMENTS (BIS) AND THE BASEL COMMITTEE (BCBS)

The BIS[10] is the closest thing there is to a global regulator. It is the forum of world central banks. Ever since global banking regulation became a serious concern for central banks, it was under the auspices of the BIS, located in Basel, that the Basel Committee on Banking Supervision (BCBS)[11] issued rules for banking, particularly capital adequacy rules.

The BCBS issued three series of banking regulatory principles. As its name indicates, it is located in Basel, where the BIS is also located. The BIS is relatively unknown to the public, and yet the meetings of the governors of the world central banks creates not only a unique forum to analyze and discuss the problems affecting monetary and fiscal policy, but those who participated in those meetings form the most tightly bound and powerful group of influential world financial leaders.

> *The BIS was established in the context of the Young Plan (1930), which dealt with the issue of the reparation payments imposed on Germany by the Treaty of Versailles following the First World War. The new bank was to take over the functions previously performed by the Agent General for Reparations in Berlin: collection, administration and distribution of the annuities payable as reparations. The Bank's name is derived from this original role. The BIS was also created to act as a trustee for the Dawes and Young Loans (international loans issued to finance reparations) and to promote central bank cooperation in general.*[12]

This has become known as The Sermon from Basel[13] as *The Economist* named it, or The Tower of Basel as it is described in the *New York Times*. Today, the BIS has reached a kind of enlightened old age as a venue for the BCBS, which seeks to set voluntary global capital standards and act as a repository of financial expertise.[14]

INTERNATIONAL MONETARY FUND (IMF)

When the United States and the United Kingdom gathered in Bretton Woods, a small town in New Hampshire (United States), the mission of the IMF[15] was defined as the institution that would, in a postwar environment, act to assist and support what was called at the time the underdeveloped countries.[16] Its interventions in a number of crises created by overindebtedness and structural balance-of-payment deficits was essential to avoid a collapse of those economies:

> *The IMF's fundamental mission is to help ensure stability in the international system. It does so in three ways: keeping track of the global economy and the economies of member countries; lending to*

countries with balance of payments difficulties; and giving practical help to members.

The International Monetary Fund (IMF) is an organization of 188 countries, working to foster global monetary cooperation, secure financial stability, facilitate international trade, promote high employment and sustainable economic growth, and reduce poverty around the world.[17]

None of this makes the IMF a financial regulator. However, since Christine Lagarde became the IMF director general, interventions of the IMF on the health and reforms of the banking sector have multiplied. Was it part of an objective of her predecessor, Dominique Strauss-Kahn, to make the IMF the central bank of the world? The link is their mandate in the field of financial stability.

In a recent speech on financial stability, Naoyuki Shinohara, deputy managing director of the IMF, was addressing the issues of the banking sector and especially the European one:

The unfinished bank repair in the euro area is very costly as it hinders credit transmission to the real economy. Healthy banks are needed to support economic recovery, so it is critical for the repair of the banking sector to be completed. In some cases, additional bank capital is needed, along with adequate provisioning to enhance overall buffers. It is important that the process of bank repair include a thorough asset quality review, stress tests, and supported by adequate capital backstops. If needed, state-backed asset management companies or other mechanisms could be established to warehouse and manage the stock of badly impaired assets to provide banks with incentive to value and write-down impaired and nonperforming loans.[18]

While it is monitoring the situation of the banking sector in emerging economies, it does not have jurisdiction to intervene to bail out or restructure the banking system. During the financial crisis, severe criticisms of the IMF were wrongly addressed to an institution that had less to do with the lack of foresight of banking crises than the BIS.

Bretton Woods refers to the international monetary arrangement, agreed upon by the allied nations in 1944 in Bretton Woods, US, that created the IMF and World Bank and that set up a system of fixed exchange rates with the U.S. dollar as the international reserve currency. To provide credibility, the United States agreed to exchange dollars for gold at a fixed price.[19]

It is important that the BIS keeps the leadership it developed over several decades for the regulation of banking capital. We certainly do not need a coleadership in this crucial undertaking.

INTERNATIONAL ORGANIZATION OF SECURITIES COMMISSIONS (IOSCO)

Based in Madrid, IOSCO[20] is the forum where securities regulators discuss and publish common rules on a vast array of issues affecting the integrity of the securities markets.

IOSCO, established in 1983, is the acknowledged international body that brings together the world's securities regulators and is recognized as the global standard setter for the securities sector. IOSCO develops, implements, and promotes adherence to internationally recognized standards for securities regulation, and is working intensively with the G20 and the FSB on the global regulatory reform agenda.

However, compared to the previous institutions, IOSCO does not have any form of statutory rights that could impose rules on the national regulators. Among them, the U.S. Securities and Exchange Commission (SEC),[21] while actively participating in the work of this institution, was not prepared to accept the rules proposed as more than recommendations. One finds here the traditional reluctance of the United States to accept any form of multilateral jurisdiction imposing its rules and procedures on itself. When the final report of IOSCO, "Suitability Requirements with Respect to the Distribution of Complex Financial Products," was published in January 2013, the SEC rejected it.

IOSCO published a Final Report entitled, "Suitability Requirements with Respect to the Distribution of Complex Financial Products." We believe it is important to state for the record that we objected to the publication of the Final Report and, therefore, that the Final Report was not approved by the Commission. In our view, the Final Report does not accurately reflect the relevant law in the U.S. Nor should the U.S. regulatory regime conform to the Final Report, the substance of which we disagree with in key respects. We especially disagree with the Final Report's failure to properly respect the distinction between retail and institutional investors when determining the suitability requirements that should apply.[22]

INTERNATIONAL ACCOUNTING STANDARDS BOARD (IASB)

The IASB,[23] based in London, is a foundation that has developed the International Financial Reporting Standards (IFRSs)[24] including those that apply to financial institutions.

> *The principal objectives of the IFRS Foundation are:*
>
> - *To develop a single set of high quality, understandable, enforceable and globally accepted International Financial Reporting Standards (IFRSs) through its standard-setting body, the International Accounting Standards Board (IASB);*
> - *To promote the use and rigorous application of those standards;*
> - *To take account of the financial reporting needs of emerging economies and small and medium-sized entities (SMEs); and*
> - *To promote and facilitate adoption of IFRSs, being the standards and interpretations issued by the IASB, through the convergence of national accounting standards and IFRSs.*

Among the essential tools that are required to create a globally coherent financial system are convergent international accounting standards.[25] The principles are contained in what is called the Conceptual Framework[26]:

> *Without them, the accounting impact of financial assets and transactions can be accounted for in different ways, thereby creating distortions between countries. It is indeed essential that, whatever rules and regulations are set up, a cortex of solid accounting rules that measure the same realities with the same standards supports their application. However, the current rules are the subject of serious disagreements between Europe and the United States.[27]*

It is one of the signs of the neglect in which this undertaking is left that no public sector funding is available, leaving some freedom of interpretation and influence to national or professional interests.

This undertaking is difficult, and the complexity of the task is one of the most complex ones. But there is a key overarching principle: the commitment of the countries in their adoption of IFRSs should be unambiguous. As the Financial Accounting Standard Foundation chairman put it at a conference, no à la carte menu can be accepted:

> *The basic premise of IFRS is what rational choice theorists call a "dilemma of collective action." If we all work together, taking*

into consideration our local knowledge and expertise, to develop a single set of standards of the highest quality, and if we all commit ourselves to abide by the outcome of the standard-setting process that takes into consideration global input gained along the way, then we are all better off. Yet, if some jurisdictions—particularly the larger ones—go back to the à la carte model then we should not be surprised that others will follow.[28]

INTERNATIONAL ASSOCIATION OF INSURANCE SUPERVISORS (IAIS)

The insurance industry has a global regulatory forum, the IAIS,[29] where their principles and policies are discussed. Established in 1994, the IAIS represents insurance regulators and transparency of more than 200 jurisdictions in nearly 140 countries, constituting 97 percent of the world's insurance premiums. It also has more than 130 observers. Its objectives are to:

- Promote effective and globally consistent supervision of the insurance industry in order to develop and maintain fair, safe and stable insurance markets for the benefit and protection of policyholders; and to
- Contribute to global financial stability

Here again, the objective of financial stability plays a crucial role. Its Global Insurance Market Report published for the first time in November 2012, is a comprehensive analysis of the issues facing the insurance industry and its regulators.[30]

The rules of Solvency II, known as Omnibus II, were approved at the political level on November 14, 2013. It was a compromise that reduced the influence of the European Insurance Authority. Insurance Europe, the European insurance industry lobby, declared its satisfaction on the agreement:

However, the deal drew criticism from some quarters for caving in to pressure from national governments on behalf of their domestic lobbies. Proposals for more sweeping and harmonized powers for the European Insurance and Occupational Pensions Authority were largely diluted.[31]

The U.S. Treasury recently called for more supervision of insurance companies. The reason for this call is largely that insurance companies are regulated by states that collect taxes from insurance companies.

The United States Treasury called on Thursday for a greater federal role in the regulation of insurance, particularly in areas like mortgage insurance, the collection and use of personal data to set prices, and the use of secretive entities known as captives to keep risks off the books of insurers.[32]

Global insurance regulation is definitely not a simple matter. While insurance companies are calling for consistent regulation to avoid regulatory arbitrage, they have to take into consideration a number of dimensions of global regulation.

A structured dialogue between the United States and Europe concerned key issues:

This dialogue formally resulted in a paper comparing the two insurance regulatory regimes—including aspects that are expected to be part of Solvency II in the European Union with the U.S. regime.

A group steering committee agreed upon seven topics considered of fundamental importance to a sound regulatory regime and to the protection of policyholders and financial stability.

- *Professional secrecy and confidentiality*
- *Group supervision*
- *Solvency and capital requirements*
- *Reinsurance and collateral requirements*
- *Supervisory reporting, data collection and analysis*
- *Supervisory peer reviews*
- *Independent third party review and supervisory on-site inspection*[33]

The FSB mandated the IAIS to develop straightforward, backstop capital requirements (BCRs) for global systemically important insurers (G-SIIs) to apply to all group activities, including noninsurance subsidiaries:

In the absence of a more comprehensive, global insurance capital standard (ICS), the BCR framework will be the foundation for any higher loss absorbency (HLA) requirements (applied by Jan 2019) as part of the G-SII policy framework.

The FSB and IAIS have indicated that the primary reason for a BCR is to ensure comprehensive coverage of all activities, including non-insurance activities, and a reasonably even base and comparability for the calculation of HLA targeted to nontraditional and non-insurance (NTNI) activities across jurisdictions and G-SIIs.[34]

The preoccupation is clearly to ensure that insurers and especially the G-SII companies have adequate capitalization to avoid them becoming a systemic risk. That makes the insurance groups subject to their own web of regulators.

On December 19, 2013, the IAIS came with its second consultation on the following questions:

The second consultation will specifically invite comments on a range of questions regarding the BCR and its relationship with other existing and proposed regulatory measures affecting G-SIIs and Internationally Active Insurance Groups (IAIGs), such as:

1. *Is the purpose of the BCR clear enough?*
2. *At what level should the BCR be calibrated compared to existing national benchmarks?*
3. *Is the BCR expected to be a temporary measure, until the risk-based group-wide global insurance capital standard (ICS) is in place, or will it continue to apply?*
4. *Should a backstop capital measure be introduced to complement the proposed ICS, in addition to or instead of the BCR? If so what should the purpose of such a backstop capital measure be, compared to the BCR?*
5. *Will the proposed approach to valuation of assets and liabilities provide sufficient global comparability?*
6. *Can a reasonable balance of risk sensitivity and simplicity be achieved using a factor based approach?*
7. *How should the BCR be integrated into national or regional frameworks which are in the process of being implemented or modified?*
8. *How should supervisors enforce the BCR in a consistent manner across jurisdictions.* [35]

The AIG debacle, worse than any individual banking bailout, has clearly sent a serious message on the risks associated with financial activities of insurers. The process is only starting but has to be taken extremely seriously. The executives who brought the company down are still pursuing New York ethics complaints.

Former American International Group executives are pursuing an ethics complaint against the New York prosecutors still bringing the charges that cost them their jobs at the insurance giant in 2005.

> *The complaint at the Joint Commission on Public Ethics by Maurice "Hank" Greenberg and Howard I. Smith alleges Assistant Attorney General David Ellenhorn lied in court stating the 88-year-old Greenberg intends to take public the private Starr Companies, where he's now CEO.*[36]

In the meantime, the implementation of Solvency II has been delayed to January 1, 2016, while the European Insurance and Occupational Pensions Authority (EIOPA), the European regulator, intends to implement some of its pieces in 2014 and 2015.

NOTES

1. http://files.shareholder.com/downloads/ONE/2651019379x0x556144/cafb598e-ee88-43ee-a7d370673d5791a1/JPMC_2011_annual_report_letter.pdf#page=19&zoom=auto,0,770.
2. http://www.bis.org/regauth.htm.
3. http://www.uiowa.edu/~tlcp/TLCP%20Articles/19-3/pan.finalfinal.jyz.121610.pdf.
4. G20 members represent almost:
    1. 90 percent of global GDP.
    2. 80 percent of international global trade.
    3. Two thirds of the world's population.
    4. 84 percent of all fossil fuel emissions produced by G20 countries. http://www.g20.org/docs/about/about_G20.html.
5. Ibid.
6. www.italymagazine.com/italy/sardinia/anti-globalisation-activists-stage-naval-siege-g8.
7. G7 ministers and governors had commissioned Dr. Tietmeyer to recommend new structures for enhancing cooperation among the various national and international supervisory bodies and international financial institutions so as to promote stability in the international financial system. www.financialstabilityboard.org/about/history.htm.
8. www.financialstabilityboard.org/activities/index.htm.
9. Jason Liberi, "The Financial Stability Forum: A Step in the Right Direction . . . Not Far Enough," *University of Pennsylvania Journal of International Economics.* www.law.upenn.edu/journals/jil/articles/volume24/issue2/Liberi24U.Pa.J.Int%27lEcon.L.549%282003%29.pdf.
10. www.bis.org/about/history.htm.
11. The Basel Committee on Banking Supervision provides a forum for regular cooperation on banking supervisory matters. Its objective is to

enhance understanding of key supervisory issues and improve the quality of banking supervision worldwide. www.bis.org/bcbs/.

12. www.bis.org/about/history.htm.
13. www.economist.com/blogs/schumpeter/2013/06/money-talks-june-24th-2013.
14. Today, the BIS has reached a kind of enlightened old age as a venue for the Basel Committee on Banking Supervision, which seeks to set voluntary global capital standards, and as a repository of financial expertise. www.nytimes.com/2013/07/21/books/review/tower-of-basel-by-adam-lebor.html.
15. www.imf.org/external/about/overview.htm.
16. IMF Staff Paper, "On Global Trade Liberalization and the Developing Countries," November 2001. www.imf.org/external/np/exr/ib/2001/110801.htm.
17. www.imf.org/external/about/ourwork.htm.
18. Naoyuki Shinohara, *The Path toward Greater Financial Stability: Where Are We and What Needs to Be Done?* 8th Conference on Risk, Banking and Financial Stability. Bali, Indonesia, September 25, 2013. www.imf.org/external/np/speeches/2013/092513.htm.
19. Landmark agreement signed at an international conference in 1944 at Bretton Woods, New Hampshire, aimed at ensuring a stable monetary system after World War II, mainly through the use of fixed exchange rates. The agreement also established the World Bank and the International Monetary Fund. http://lexicon.ft.com/term?term=bretton-woods.
20. IOSCO's membership regulates more than 95 percent of the world's securities markets. Its members include over 120 securities regulators and 80 other securities markets participants (i.e., stock exchanges, financial regional and international organizations, etc.). IOSCO is the only international financial regulatory organization, which includes all the major emerging markets jurisdictions within its membership. www.iosco.org/.
21. The mission of the SEC is to protect investors, maintain fair, orderly, and efficient markets, and facilitate capital formation. www.sec.gov/about/whatwedo.shtml.
22. "Suitability Requirements with Respect to the Distribution of Complex Financial Products." www.sec.gov/News/PublicStmt/Detail/PublicStmt/1365171492100#.UoVWsOK6nj5.
23. www.ifrs.org/The-organisation/Pages/IFRS-Foundation-and-the-IASB.aspx.
24. www.ifrs.org/IFRSs/Pages/IFRS.aspx.
25. Brian Booth, "The Conceptual Framework as a Coherent System for the Development of Accounting Standards." *Abacus* 39, October 2003, pp. 310–324. Available at SSRN: http://ssrn.com/abstract=480891.

26. The IASB published for public comment a Discussion Paper exploring possible changes to the IASB's Conceptual Framework for Financial Reporting. The Discussion Paper is the first step toward issuing a revised Conceptual Framework (July 18, 2013). www.ifrs.org/Alerts/Project Update/Pages/IASB-publishes-a-Discussion-Paper-on-the-Conceptual-Framework.aspx.

27. Mario Draghi and Robert Pozen, "US-EU Regulatory Convergence: The Case of Capital Markets." Harvard University, John Olin Center for Law, Economics and Business, October 2003. www.law.harvard .edu/programs/olin_center/papers/pdf/444.pd.

28. www.ifrs.org/Alerts/Conference/Documents/2013/Michel-Prada-FASF-November-2013.pdf.

29. IAIS web site: www.iaisweb.org/.

30. The Global Insurance Market Report. www.iaisweb.org/Global-Insurance-Market-Report-GIMAR-962.

31. http://online.wsj.com/news/articles/SB10001424052702303289904579197382105891634.

32. http://dealbook.nytimes.com/2013/12/12/treasury-urges-more-federal-oversight-of-insurance/?_r=0.

33. KPMG, "Evolving Global Insurance Regulation. www.kpmg.com/Global/en/IssuesAndInsights/ArticlesPublications/evolving-insurance-regulation/Pages/international-developments.aspx.

34. IIF. "Global Regulatory Update," November 2013. www.iif.com/regulatory/.

35. www.iaisweb.org/index.cfm?pageID=1141.

36. http://abcnews.go.com/US/wireStory/aig-executives-pursue-ny-ethics-complaint-21290823.

CHAPTER 5

Capital Adequacy, Liquidity, and Leverage Ratios: Sailing toward the Basel III Rules

"Specific policies to counteract the structural vulnerabilities created by short-term wholesale funding are a priority, not just for the stability of our large prudentially regulated institutions, but for the financial system as a whole."

—Federal Reserve Governor Daniel K. Tarullo

As markets became more global, the temptation was huge for some countries to use weak domestic regulation as a way to compete in the global financial arena. Competitive regulation had to be addressed at a global level and key stability ratios could not be left to national regulation.

But it is also fair to say that there remains no clear consensus on the balance to be struck between international (whether global or European) and national regulation. Faced with domestic political critics, governments and regulators have worked on their own bespoke responses, which may well complicate the task of achieving stronger international coordination.[1]

Besides the competitive aspect, there is a more substantial risk. If some countries develop weak stability ratios, they become more vulnerable to a banking crisis. The interconnectedness of the financial system creates an

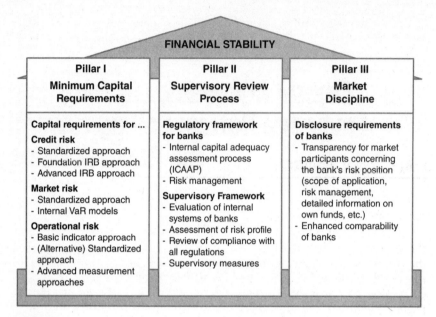

FIGURE 5.1   The Three Pillars of Financial Stability
Source: http://basel-certification.com/wp-content/uploads/2009/10/basel-pillars.jpg.

immediate contagion. It is therefore essential for the development of a more stable financial environment that the banking community adopts the same rules and criteria for adequacy of their balance sheets (see Figure 5.1).[2]

> *"Basel III" is a comprehensive set of reform measures, developed by the Basel Committee on Banking Supervision, to strengthen the regulation, supervision and risk management of the banking sector. These measures aim to:*
>
> - *Improve the banking sector's ability to absorb shocks arising from financial and economic stress, whatever the source*
> - *Improve risk management and governance*
> - *Strengthen banks' transparency and disclosures.*

Traditionally, *capital adequacy* was the main ratio. It measures the relationship between the bank's equity and the risks its balance sheet carries. Equity was, and still is, the core asset of banks: their ability to lend and to grow is closely connected to the level of own funds that they have on their balance sheet. The recent financial crisis did, however, provide evidence that a liquidity crisis could emerge well before a credit crisis and that a *liquidity ratio* needed to be developed. It was not enough for a bank to have adequate equity for its assets and liabilities; it needed to manage its liquidity risk so that a crisis of confidence would not immediately destabilize it.

More recently, for reasons that remain controversial, the BIS added a third ratio: a *global leverage ratio*. How much equity does a bank have in regard to the total size of its balance sheet?

The calendar for Basel III (see Table 5.1) is still in flux, but the final date is 2019. A series of milestones have been imposed for this implementation.

PART I: CAPITAL ADEQUACY

The attempts to regulate capital adequacy are at their third phase, hence its name Basel III (see Table 5.2).

The interconnection of finance makes even strong banks vulnerable to the contagion of banks with inadequate capitalization. Immediately after the Lehman crisis, negotiations started for a new round of capital adequacy rules in Basel. It had become obvious that the Basel II rules were outdated since several bank failures happened in institutions that were applying the Basel II ratios.

The application of Basel III in various legislations is a challenge. It is unclear whether the Federal Reserve of the United States[3] and the European Commission[4] will transform them into legislation as they are being published. The capital adequacy ratios measure equity against a risk defined as the risk-weighted assets (RWAs).

A bank's total risk-weighted assets would be the sum of its credit risk-weighted assets and risk-weighted assets for operational risk, minus the sum of its excess eligible credit reserves (ECL) (that is, its eligible credit reserves in excess of its total (ECL) not included in tier 2 capital and allocated transfer risk reserves.[5]

The capital adequacy ratios[6] are substantially increased and will create additional needs to recapitalize several banking institutions. One of the most interesting rules relates to the haircuts that the banks have to take on assets (see Table 5.3).

One of the most interesting elements is that sovereign bonds are no longer zero-weighted. In other terms, even for the best credits, banks will have to allocate 2 percent of the value of their investment in the AAA-AA sovereign bonds if their maturity exceeds one year. Even for short maturities, a haircut of 0.5 percent will be applied. This is the end of what banks and sovereigns could consider a free lunch. It will affect those countries with excessive indebtedness.

TABLE 5.1 Basel III Phase-in Arrangements

	Phases	2013	2014	2015	2016	2017	2018	2019
Capital	Leverage Ratio		Parallel run 1 Jan 2013–1 Jan 2017 Disclosure starts 1 Jan 2015				Migration to Pillar 1	
	Minimum Common Equity Capital Ratio	3.5%	4.0%	4.5%				4.5%
	Capital Conservation Buffer				0.625%	1.25%	1.875%	2.5%
	Minimum common equity plus capital conservation buffer	3.5%	4.0%	4.5%	5.125%	5.75%	6.375%	7.0%
	Phase-in of deductions from CET1*		20%	40%	60%	80%	100%	100%
	Minimum Tier 1 Capital	4.5%	5.5%	6.0%				6.0%
	Minimum Total Capital		8.0%					8.0%
	Minimum Total Capital plus conservation buffer		8.0%		8.625%	9.25%	9.875%	10.5%
	Capital instruments that no longer qualify as noncore Tier 1 capital or Tier 2 capital		Phased out over 10-year horizon beginning 2013					
Liquidity	Liquidity coverage ratio—minimum requirement			60%	70%	80%	90%	100%
	Net stable funding ratio						Introduce minimum standard	

*Including amounts exceeding the limit for deferred tax assets (DTAs), mortgage servicing rights (MSRs) and financials.

-- transition periods

Source: www.bis.org/bcbs/basel3/basel3_phase_in_arrangements.pdf.

TABLE 5.2 Regulatory Objective—(2) Increased Quantity of Capital

Basel III contains various measures aimed at increasing the level of capital held by institutions, as well as providing countercyclical mechanisms.

Description of the Key Changes	Implications
Minimum common equity Tier 1: ▪ Increased from 2.0 percent to 4.5 percent ▪ Plus capital conservation buffer of 2.5 percent ▪ Bringing total common equity requirements to 7.0 percent ▪ To be phased in from 2013 to 2019 **Minimum total capital:** ▪ Increased from 8.0 percent to 10.5 percent (including conservation buffer) ▪ To be phased in from 2013 to 2019 Countercyclical capital buffer is being developed, which is expected to be implemented by increases to the capital conservation buffer during periods of excessive cedit growth.	▪ Banks will face a significant additional capital requirement, and the bulk of this shortfall will need to be raised as common equity or otherwise by retaining dividends. ▪ In principle, banks will be able to draw on the capital conservation buffer during periods of stress, but it seems unlikely that they would choose to do so, given the associated constraints on their earnings distributions. ▪ Consequently, banks are likely to target a higher common equity ratio and the market expectation for common equity Tier 1 appears to be moving to approximately 9 percent. ▪ There is likely to be further add-ons for Pillar 2 risks, systemically important firms, and the countercyclical capital buffer, so banks may target a total capital ratio of 13–15 percent.

Source: 2011 KPMG LLC. www.kpmg.com/Global/en/IssuesAndInsights/ArticlesPublications/Documents/basell-III-issues-implications.pdf

The Regulatory Failure of Basel II

Initially called the McDonough ratio, from the name of the president of the Federal Reserve of New York, Bill McDonough, the Basel II ratios lost their names when the Federal Reserve decided not to impose their application to U.S. banks, bending under a heavy lobbying of the American banking system that eventually led to the financial crisis.

TABLE 5.3 Proposed Numerical Haircut Floors for Securities-against-Cash Transactions

	Haircut Level	
Residual Maturity of Collateral	Corporate and Other Issuers	Securitized Products
≤1 year debt securities, and FRNs	0.5%	1%
>1 year, ≤5 years debt securities	1%	2%
>5 years debt securities	2%	4%
Main index equities	4%	
Other assets within the scope of the framework	7.5%	

Source: www.secfinmonitor.com/sfm/wp-content/uploads/2013/09/haircuts.jpg.

Some of the recent banking collapses evidenced the inadequacy of capital resources of the banking system. Even though the previous Basel II standards did not provide enough protection, it became apparent in some instances where banks were in trouble and had applied the Basel II standards. The decision was taken for those reasons to move directly to stronger standards.

Basel I: A Quarter Century of Common Rules

Known as the Cooke ratios, from the name of the vice governor of the Bank of England who ran the commission, these initial ratios were specifically centered on the nature of the assets. While sovereign risk was deemed not to require any capital allocation, investments in equity had to be matched one-for-one by equity.

The experience of these relatively simple ratios led, however, to unintended consequences: banks started to look for assets on the basis of the equity allocation needed, trying to minimize the use of equity, rather than enhancing the quality of the assets.

A recent analysis by *Forbes* casts a positive light on the progress made by U.S. banks that are not having capital adequacy ratios in excess of their Basel III requirements.[7]

The European Capital Requirements Directive IV

While Michel Barnier, the European Commissioner in charge of the internal market, stated that the European Commission has wanted a proposal that fully respected the spirit, the letter, the level of ambition and Balance of Basel III,[8] there is a debate about the commitment of Europe to Basel III.[9]

The final texts of the Capital Requirements Directive IV and Regulation (CRD IV/CRR) were published in the *Official Journal of the European*

Union on June 17, 2013, and took effect across Europe from January 1, 2014. Supervisory authorities in European Member States have been consulted on the national measures required to implement CRD IV/CRR.[10]

On December 19, 2013, the Prudential Regulation Authority (PRA) published its rules and supervisory statements, which complement the EU legislative package known as CRD IV, covering prudential rules for banks, building societies, and investment firms. The EU text was formally published in the *Official Journal of the European Union* on Thursday, June 27, 2013 (note the regulation has been subject to a subsequent corrigendum). The bulk of the rules contained in the legislation will apply from January 1, 2014.[11]

EU Commissioner Michael Barnier stated:

> *I welcome the unanimous agreement reached by the Basel Committee on the revised liquidity coverage ratio and the gradual approach for its phasing-in by clearly defined dates. This is significant progress, which addresses issues already raised by the European Commission. We now need to make full use of the observation period, and learn from the reports that the European Banking Authority will prepare on the results of the observation period, before formally implementing in 2015 the liquidity coverage ratio under E.U. law in line with the Basel standards.*[12]

It is unquestionable that by imposing stronger capital requirements than Basel III (8 percent instead of 6 percent), Europe recognizes the insufficient equity buffers needed in times of crisis. Recent changes have been adopted to the CRD IV regulation with the view to enhance financial stability, safeguard the interests of creditors and taxpayers, enhance the level playing field globally while ensuring international competitiveness of the EU banking sector and promoting the integrity of the Internal Market.[13]

However, it is certain that the Capital Requirements Directive includes practical measures that provide throughout the European Union, a *Single Rule Book for Financial Regulation.*[14]

PART II: LIQUIDITY

> *Liquidity refers to the readiness of assets to be converted to cash. By comparing a company's liquid assets with its short-term obligations, we can obtain a general idea of the firm's ability to pay its short-term debts as they come due. Usually, current assets are thought of as the most liquid of a company's assets. Obviously, though, some are more liquid than others, so it's important also to evaluate the specific makeup of current assets.*[15]

The world of finance has evolved dramatically in the allocation of capital and therefore the funding of the financial needs for investors, governments, and corporations alike (see Figure 5.2). The share of deposits in the funding of assets has sharply decreased to represent only a quarter of those assets in the United States. This means that other forms of funding have taken the place of traditional liabilities. The control of those liabilities is therefore escaping the leadership of banks alone.

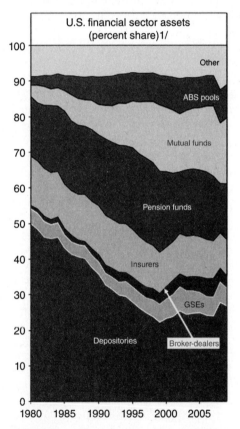

FIGURE 5.2   Capital Adequacy: Key Changes and Implications
Source: Ashok Vir Bhatia, "New Landscape, New Challenges: Structural Change and Regulation in the U.S. Financial Sector." IMF working paper, 2007.

Basel III, having learned the lessons of the liquidity crisis that preceded the credit crisis in 2008, included stringent standards of liquidity, in great detail.[16] While there is no doubt that the liquidity risk is important, it presents a substantial challenge for regulators. If they are too lenient, the ratios will not improve the way banks typically manage that risk. Considering past experiences, it would be a leap of faith that would not be considered as reasonable.

However, the value added of banks is in their ability—their art—to disintermediate. This function is not just to assume the credit risk with deposits. They add value by extending long-term loans or assets to the economy. A liquidity ratio that would be too stringent would in turn create a structural shortage of long-term financing, particularly essential to the manufacturing industry. Striking the right balance between those two objectives is a real challenge.

The Basel III Liquidity Coverage Ratio is designed to ensure "that a bank has an adequate stock of unencumbered high-quality liquid assets that can be converted into cash easily and immediately in private markets to meet its liquidity needs for a 30 calendar day liquidity stress scenario," according to the Basel Committee's statement in January:

> *Under the Basel Committee's rules, a large bank's LCR will be required to be at least 60 percent when the rule is phased in beginning in January 2015, with the requirement rising to 100 percent, once the rules are fully implemented in January 2019. The big banks will also eventually be required to maintain a net stable funding ratio (NSFR) of 100 percent. The NSFR is meant to measure a bank's available "stable" funding, to meet its liquidity requirements over a period of 12 months.*[17]

The liquidity ratio imposes a cushion of long-term debt to cover some of the long-term assets the banks have in their portfolio. One of the stable sources of financing for banks is their deposit basis. After long and protracted decisions, the ratios were amended to respond to the preoccupation of banks that the current proposal was making long-term financing prohibitive, while it is needed for the economy to function.

However, the Federal Reserve does not seem satisfied with the current version of the liquidity ratios. Federal Reserve Chairman Ben Bernanke in Washington said in October 2013 that:

> *Liquidity is essential to a bank's viability and central to the smooth functioning of the financial system. The proposed rule would, for the first time in the United States, put in place a quantitative*

liquidity requirement that would foster a more resilient and safer financial system in conjunction with other reforms.[18]

PART III: LEVERAGE

The Basel III reforms introduced a simple, transparent, non-risk based leverage ratio to act as a credible supplementary measure to the risk-based capital requirements. The leverage ratio is intended to:

- *Restrict the build-up of leverage in the banking sector to avoid destabilising deleveraging processes that can damage the broader financial system and the economy; and*
- *Reinforce the risk-based requirements with a simple, non-risk-based "backstop" measure.*

The Basel Committee is of the view that:

- *A simple leverage ratio framework is critical and complementary to the risk-based capital frame work; and*
- *A credible leverage ratio is one that ensures broad and adequate capture of both the on- and off-balance sheet leverage of banks.*[19]

Not satisfied with the combined effect of the two previous ratios, Basel III introduced a leverage ratio that would limit the size of the balance sheet, irrespective of the quality of the assets.

Intuitively, this ratio seems obvious. Banks respecting the liquidity and capital adequacy ratios might still be made vulnerable to imbalances through the sheer size of their balance sheet. It is particularly true for some countries where the holdings of sovereign debt might not require capital adequacy and liquidity limitations, but could represent a huge percentage of their balance sheet. The case of Italian banks is particularly mentioned. Japanese banks are also vulnerable to such excesses.

The Federal Reserve has decided to delay imposing limits on leverage at eight of the biggest U.S. financial institutions until a global agreement is completed, according to two people briefed on the discussions:

Fed officials want to wait for a finished rule from the Basel Committee on Banking Supervision before completing their own requirement for how much capital U.S. banks must hold as a percentage of all assets on their books, said the people, speaking on condition of anonymity because the process isn't public. The international ac-cord is shaping up as weaker in some respects than the U.S. plan.[20]

It is only in 2014 that the leverage ratio will be defined by the Basel Committee on Banking Supervision (BCBS). It is likely to be 3 percent. This means that a bank will not be allowed to hold assets representing more than 33 times its equity. One would have thought that this would be painless. However, the resistance to this last ratio indicates that, for some banks at least, it might imply further balance sheet deleverage.

The reason for this ratio stems from the fact that then liquidity and the capital ratios might be so complex that banks will respect the ratio while manipulating the risks. At least this one is more difficult to manipulate.

Some in the United Kingdom are arguing to move beyond the 3 per cent leverage ratio proposed by the global Basel III rules. This is unwise. A rate of 4 per cent could create problems for both banks and customers. The leverage ratio could cease to act as an addi-tional "backstop" that enhances financial stability. The higher rate could create perverse incentives, whereby banks prioritise riskier lending over mortgages and other safer forms. Not only could the cost of mortgages increase for customers, it is the exact behaviour policymakers are trying to avoid.

But Osborne and Carney appear committed to doing every-thing they can to promote regulatory convergence. We should only accept a higher leverage ratio on an accelerated timetable if there is clear evidence that it benefits the U.K. economy.[21]

In April 2014, the Federal Reserve announced a 5 percent leverage ratio for U.S. banks

The Insurance Sector Capital Adequacy Ratios in Europe: Solvency II

The most elaborate insurance regulation is the European Solvency II regula-tion that aims to:

- *Take account of current developments in insurance, risk manage-ment, finance techniques, international financial reporting and prudential standards, etc.*
- *Streamline the way that insurance groups are supervised and rec-ognize the economic reality of how groups operate.*

- *Strengthen the powers of the group supervisor, ensuring that group-wide risks are not overlooked.*
- *Ensure greater cooperation between supervisors. Groups will be able to use group-wide models and take advantage of group diversification benefits.*[22]

The question one could ask, however, is the reason for which the European Commission thought it important to create a mirror of its CRD IV ratios adapted to the insurance companies.

I must confess some trouble: insurance companies are much better risk managers than banks. They have imposed some solvency ratios for decades, and they proved to be adequate. The only accident of importance in the insurance industry was AIG. However, it did not occur in the context of its insurance business that remained strong and still is. Its chairman and CEO, Hank Greenberg, without fully informing the board, authorized the utilization of its AAA rating and balance sheet to write derivative contracts that were covering a wide range of risks, and in particular credit default swaps on subprime commitments for a wide variety of banks.

Is it because AIG Financial Products was incorporated in London that the European Commission decided that it needed to reregulate the insurance industry? Could a more global initiative have been more effective?

The net result is, according to Larry Fink, chairman and CEO of Blackrock, the largest asset manager in the world,[23] speaking at the IIF spring meeting in 2013, that insurance companies halved their holdings of stocks. Such an unintended consequence deprives Europe of a key source of equity financing.

While at the same time promoting the need for long-term financing to ensure economic growth, the G20 is taking a direction that might jeopardize this essential political growth.

This might lead to a further consolidation of the industry.

David Simmons, managing director of analytics at reinsurance broker Willis Re, said many small insurers across Europe, particularly mutual insurers, will be hit particularly hard by Solvency II. He said the new regulation may penalize them for a lack of diversification, and they have only limited capacity to raise more capital. They also may not have the resources to pay for the more sophisticated risk management and reporting that Solvency II will require.[24]

Sometimes in an indirect way like for the systemically important financial institutions (SIFIs), global regulations will continue to influence the largest and more international insurance companies. Tower Watson has summarized the main areas of recent developments:

For insurance providers, there are major global regulatory proposals arriving at a time when domestic regulation worldwide is changing. In particular:

- *For Internationally Active Insurance Groups (IAIG), the ComFrame project undertaken by the International Association of Insurance Supervisors (IAIS) is aiming to establish a set of quantitative and qualitative supervisory requirements that would operate in addition to local regulatory requirements, and extend regulatory reach to include non-insurance entities.*
- *For the large, globally interconnected and market-important insurers, measures to address systemic risk in the insurance industry are being established under financial stability proposals.*
- *For all insurers, local regulatory regimes around the world are being compared, for example as part of the Solvency II equivalence process or as part of the E.U.-U.S. Dialogue Project. In several of these regimes, including Solvency II, changes are not yet finalised and have been experiencing significant delays.[25]*

In a summary of the challenges facing the industry, BBVA Research summarizes the likely scenarios in a clear way:

There is a great disparity among countries in the initial situation of the I&P sectors, both in terms of solvency levels and the diversification/riskiness of investment portfolios, which will cause different effects from a country base perspective: Notwithstanding this, there is a common challenge about how to reconcile more risk-sensitive regulation with the search for a yield in a world with consistently low interest rates. As a consequence of these new pieces of regulation, it is possible to anticipate a scenario of: higher fees; lower appetite for corporate debt; higher cost of derivatives hedging; reduced securitisation activity, an I&P industry more involved in infrastructure funding, and more real estate financing activity from the insurance sector.

As regards sovereign debt, the present regulatory statu quo favours a higher demand of these securities by I&P, but the debate on whether to maintain its zero risk weight in Basel III and Solvency II may imply some changes in the future. What is clear in the near future is that regulators of banks, pensions and insurance sectors should analyse the interactions of new regulations; the associated trade-offs and risks and their consistency with a view to avoid creating wrong incentives for the long run.[26]

This implies that some of the key sources of long-term capital (bonds and equities) will become reluctant to risk their credit rating by supporting essential sectors and projects of the economy.

NOTES

1. Howard Davies and David Green, *Global Financial Regulation*. Cambridge, UK: Polity Press, 2011, p. xxxv.
2. Within the web site of the BIS, Basel III is a particular division. www.bis .org/bcbs/basel3.htm.
3. It is the Federal Reserve of New York that holds the regulatory responsibility. As part of our core mission, we supervise and regulate financial institutions in the Second District. Our primary objective is to maintain a safe and competitive U.S. and global banking system. www.newyorkfed .org/.
4. On the European Commission web site, here is the place to start to look at the financial regulatory projects: http://ec.europa.eu/internal_market/ finances/index_en.htm.
5. Federal Reserve Bank, "Basel II Capital Accord Notice of Proposed Rulemaking (NPR) Preamble—V. Calculation of Risk-Weighted Assets," September 5, 2006. http://federalreserve.gov/GeneralInfo/Basel2/ NPR_20060905/NPR/section_5.htm.
6. Basel III: A global regulatory framework for more resilient banks and banking systems. www.bis.org/publ/bcbs189.pdf.
7. www.forbes.com/sites/greatspeculations/2014/03/19/u-s-banks-took-big-strides-towards-basel-iii-compliance-in-2013/.
8. Michel Barnier, press conference, CRD IV, Brussels, July 20, 2011 . http://europa.eu/rapid/press-release_SPEECH-11-533_en.htm.
9. This report presents the conclusions of the Basel Committee's Basel III Regulatory Consistency Assessment ("Level 2") of the EU. The assessment in this report has been based mainly on the 5th Council Presidency's compromise proposal agreed on May 15, 2012. Considering the draft nature of the compromise proposal and in accordance with the Committee's agreed procedures for conducting a Level 2 assessment, this assessment is considered preliminary. A follow-up assessment will take place once the EU authorities have published the final rules that implement Basel III. www.bis .org/bcbs/implementation/l2_eu.pdf.
10. www.lexology.com/library/detail.aspx?g=b55f96b7-2642-410d-ac6c-40e8acf12a34.
11. www.bankofengland.co.uk/pra/pages/crdiv/default.aspx.
12. http://europa.eu/rapid/press-release_MEMO-13-3_en.htm.

13. www.lexology.com/library/detail.aspx?g=c0aa8160-a5a4-48ed-b538-ee3650b938a9.
14. "KPMG Guide to the Single Rule Book for EU Banking Regulation." http://www.kpmg.com/IE/en/IssuesAndInsights/ArticlesPublications/Documents/crd-iv-may-2013.pdf.
15. http://connect.mcgraw-hill.com/sites/0077328787/student_view0/ebook/chapter3/chbody1/liquidity_ratios.htm.
16. www.bis.org/publ/bcbs238.pdf.
17. www.thestreet.com/story/12081632/1/fed-proposes-tougher-basel-iii-liquidity-rules.html.
18. Ibid.
19. www.bis.org/bcbs/basel3.htm.
20. www.moneynews.com/Economy/fedeal-reserve-bank-basel-plan-rules/2013/12/18/id/542498.
21. www.cityam.com/article/1385599169/bank-leverage-ratio-sensible-we-should-be-wary-balkanisation.
22. European Commission, "Future Rules for the Insurance Sector." http://eur-lex.europa.eu/LexUriServ/LexUriServ.do?uri=OJ:L:2009:335:0001:0155:FR:PDF.
23. www.blackrock.com/.
24. http://online.wsj.com/news/articles/SB10001424052702303289904579197382105891634.
25. www.towerswatson.com/en/Insights/IC-Types/Ad-hoc-Point-of-View/Insights/2013/Insights-Global-insurance-regulation.
26. www.bbvaresearch.com%2FKETD%2Fketd%2FDescargas%3Fpais%3DGLOB%26canal%3DRSS%26tipocontenido%3DDOTR%26idioma%3DING%26pdf%3D%2Ffbin%2Fmult%2FWP_1321_tcm348-394284.pdf%26tematica%3D%26tipopublicacion%3D&ei=CKO3UtSxPMmAkQf5q4CIBA&usg=AFQjCNFb2SmOukMXarljhqcPGC1mtNLo9A&sig2=l9z7PgmnuwZuuT5GE9bUXg&bvm=bv.58187178,d.eW0.

CHAPTER 6

Assessing Likely Impacts of Regulation on the Real Economy

We have a financial industry that is still not really providing convincing answers to the questions about the meaningfulness of many modern financial products and trading in securities. The questions are getting louder and require new responses.

—Former Deutsche Bank CEO and IIF President, Josef Ackerman

What will be the consequences of those new rules and ratios for the "real" economy? It certainly does not seem that Wall Street will be more helpful to Main Street. Its stability would, however, have serious benefits to the real economy. There is, therefore, no doubt that, despite some unfavorable consequences, the most important expectation that the real economy has is that authorities find a way to ensure that the "Greed and Glory of Wall Street" is contained to avoid further eruptions of banking-initiated crises.

It is also critical for the corporate world that manipulations of interest rates such as the London interbank offered rate (LIBOR) or foreign exchange fixings be chased and sanctioned. This immediately impacts their ability to compete and to be profitable in their own way. Too much of the world's profits have been captured by the financial services industry.

According to Mian's analysis, U.S. financial services companies in the S&P 500 index are expected to report that they earned aggregate profits of $49 billion in the second quarter. That's almost 20 percent *of the $247 billion in quarterly earnings expected from the S&P 500 companies as a whole.*[1]

Several studies[2] have attempted to quantify the risk of shortage of key financings as a result of the new regulatory environment under which financial institutions will operate.

By regulating finance in vertical silos, regulators fail to integrate the risks associated with the restrictions put on the financing of the real economy. Finance is an enabler, a transformer, and a provider of the financial resources needed to support growth.

These are the main impacts that, conceptually, will affect social and economic developments:

- *Increasing the cost of financing.* The increase of capital adequacy and liquidity ratios will increase the cost of funding of the banks. Lenders will have to integrate an increased cost of equity that will inevitably require the banks to increase the spreads they are asking.

  Assuming the lenders will be able to pass on this increased cost, one cannot expect borrowers to enjoy the same financing terms. That is not, in itself, an objection: before the 2007 crisis erupted, too much money was chasing too few opportunities, and it resulted in financings at spreads that were below reasonable terms.

  Pushing bank capital beyond the point of real need to cover credit losses and other normal risks will raise the cost of financial intermediation with two adverse consequences.

  1. *It will slow investment activity and economic growth.*
  2. *It will create an incentive for the growth of new shadow banking outside the regulatory net and with less transparent risks.*[3]

- *Shortening maturities.* The liquidity ratios have for effect to require that the traditional role of financial intermediation be redefined. The transformation of maturities, one of the key functions of financial intermediation, is not limited by risk management decisions, but by making long-term maturities excessively expensive, and for medium-sized banks, unattainable.

  Bond financing, the key to long-term funding, is obviously accessible to large and global institutions. They might have to offer a higher interest rate as supply and demand might change, but the market is likely to be accessible except in times of liquidity or credit crunch.

  This is not the case for medium-sized banks. This situation is in contradiction with another objective: too big to fail. The new regulatory framework has been so focused on the systemically important financial institutions (SIFIs) that, as it was after the Sarbanes-Oxley Act of 2002, the number of regulations and restrictions was unbearable for smaller corporations.

It is essential for the vitality of the financial sector that registered banks or insurance companies of smaller size continue to have access to long-term funding so as to enable them to extend long-term credit to their clients.

Another dimension of this issue that we will discuss later in the book is the treatment of bank bonds in the resolution mechanism. If, indeed, as appears to be the case now, regulatory authorities might have the right to decide how senior unsecured bank debt might be the subject of principal reduction (sometimes called haircuts), the appetite for bank bonds runs the risk of shrinking.

■ *Drying up liquidities.* The liquidity ratio might have a second unintended consequence: the sheer drying of liquidities. This is particularly critical in the interbank market. We have seen in the recent crisis that access to short term uncollateralized money may dry up at the first alert.

The treatment of repurchase agreements (repo financing) will also affect how banks can safely lend to one another. If it is not successfully dealt with, the role of central banks will continue to be critical as liquidity providers, and for amounts even larger than what they currently have to carry.

The financial world cannot depend exclusively on central banks for its liquidity. While the role of "lender of last resort" is a critical mission of central banks, it should remain the exception. As Paul De Grauwe puts it:

In October 2008 the ECB discovered that there is more to central banking than price stability. This discovery occurred when it was forced to massively increase liquidity to save the banking system. The ECB did not hesitate to serve as lender of last resort to the banking system, despite fears of moral hazard, inflation, and the fiscal implications of its lending.[4]

The same applied at the Federal Reserve[5] in recent years, and the key representatives of the Fed addressed the issue.

Since the onset of the financial crisis in late 2007, the U.S. Federal Reserve (Fed) has, as of December 29, extended roughly $1.2 trillion in credit to the private sector in an effort to restore

*financial stability. These actions have altered the size and composi-
tion of the Fed's balance sheet in ways not seen since its founding
in 1914. According to Alan Meltzer, author of the definitive history
of the Federal Reserve, "[such an extension of credit] is unique, and
the Fed has never done something like this before. If you go all the
way back to 1921, when farms were failing and Congress was lean-
ing on the Fed to bail them out, the Fed always said 'It's not our
business.' It never regarded itself as an all-purpose agency," writes
Kenneth Kuttner in a paper about the Fed interventions in 2008.*[6]

- *Reducing the availability of equity financing.* Banks and insurance companies have been a source of equity financing. Not only do they carry
substantial positions in equities as part of their trading activities, but
they are the ones who engineer the initial public offerings (IPOs) that
give companies access to equity financing.

    The treatment of equity holdings might reduce that ability since equi-
ties are risk capital and require substantial allocations of equity. Banks
will rather keep that capability to finance their equity investments for
their own accounts rather than for accounts of their clients.

    The Volcker Rule maintains the banks' ability to trade equities and
provide the liquidity that the equity markets need. However, the capital
cost of holding equities has been substantially increased under Basel III.
Two major players dominate the trading volume of equities: program
trading and institutional trading. It is critical that banks have an ability to
support exchanges in maintaining an orderly market in equities. The first
one is acting in the short term, even the high-speed market, while the second one is based on investment decisions. Both require a liquid market.

    It is worth noting that, even in the worst days of the Lehman cri-
sis, the stock exchanges managed to keep the market open and active,
avoiding what could have been a terrifying panic.

- *Developing shadow financial services.* Squeezed by capital adequacy
ratios, the banks will inevitably limit their lending activities to the economy, especially in long-term financing. Insurance companies will also
be restricted in their long-term commitments. Both together will reduce
their balance sheets and a substantial part of the current financial activities will inevitably migrate toward other sources.

    The most obvious one will be shadow banking, hedge funds, and even
consumer finance companies. As a result of the financial crisis, the authorities all over the world decided not to leave those activities unregulated. Hedge funds are now regulated by the Securities and Exchange
Commission (SEC) in the United States and by the European Commission

in Europe. Consumer finance companies will be dealt with by banking regulators, who will ensure that they are adequately capitalized.

However, capital markets are likely to be the main source of financing. It will be true for governments, banks, and corporations. But in the most optimistic scenario, securitization will have to become a substantial source of liquidity and credit. While not an important source of financing, "peer-to-peer" financing is developing quickly in the United States.[7]

Capital markets will become a critical source of securitization of loans and financial assets.[8] But the new rules to be applied to securitization will be stricter. It is the lack of rules and regulations, including for rating agencies, that provoked the subprime crisis in the United States.

The International Organization of Securities Commissions (IOSCO) submitted a paper on this subject in 2012 at the request of the Financial Stability Board (FSB):

> *The FSB SRC's request to IOSCO indicated that securitization was a valuable funding technique and an efficient means of diversifying risk. The request referred to a number of problems with securitization that were revealed by the Global Financial Crisis, including an overreliance on ratings, lack of due diligence by investors and inadequate pricing of risk.*[9]

Recent changes announced in Basel, Switzerland, in 2014 will come as a relief to big investment banks that had been fretting they would be forced to raise billions in extra capital. The modifications ease the requirements for products, such as derivatives and repurchase agreements, which make up large parts of their balance sheets.[10]

NOTES

1. www.usatoday.com/story/tech/columnist/shinal/2013/07/14/finance-and-tech-industry-outlook/2509349/.
2. Assessing this impact on a global basis is almost impossible. Here are some studies published on some partial impacts. The world's largest consulting firm, McKinsey, published a number of studies on the impact of regulation. This one is the impact on the U.S. banking system. www .mckinsey.com%2F~%2Fmedia%2Fmckinsey%2Fdotcom% 2Fclient_service%2FRisk%2FWorking%2520papers%2F25_ Assessing_Addressing_Implications.ashx&ei=SlxtUvrfL4iskAev_ YFg&usg=AFQjCNFnwU1j8f-C1bo1KrQJGsXwv4C_jg&sig2=Kkk_ BTC25gnPx1gb_fVoOQ&bvm=bv.55123115,d.eW0.

3. www.mhfigi.com/wp-content/uploads/2013/09/Five-Years-Later-Paper-by-Jeff-Shafer1.pdf.

4. Paul De Grauwe, "The European Central Bank as a Lender of Last Resort," August 18, 2011, in VOX. www.voxeu.org/article/european-central-bank-lender-last-resort.

5. Mark A. Clarkson and David C. Wheelock, "The Lender of Last Resort: Lessons from the Fed's First 100 Years," Economic Research, Federal Reserve of Saint Louis, Working Paper 2012-056B. http://research .stlouisfed.org/wp/2012/2012-056.pdf.

6. Kenneth Kuttner, "The Federal Reserve as Lender of Last Resort during the Panic of 2008." www.google.com/url?sa=t&rct=j&q=&esrc=s &source=web&cd=3&ved=0CEMQFjAC&url=http%3A%2F%2F www.capmktsreg.org%2Fpdfs%2FThe_Federal_Reserve_as_Lender_ of_Last_Resort_during_the_Panic_of_2008.pdf&ei=4ZhtUpOvKIejkQ ewxoCoAg&usg=AFQjCNGpNjeFDSKM7su0sXCw4PftFdXIEA&sig 2=HMvFkEMUAG0lSOKjCrZ51A&bvm=bv.55123115,d.eW0.

7. Peter Eavis, "A Step Toward 'Peer to Peer' Lending Securitization," *New York Times*, Deal Book, October 1, 2013. http://dealbook.nytimes.com /2013/10/01/a-step-toward-peer-to-peer-lending-securitization/?_r=0.

8. Julian Kolm, "Securitization, Shadow Banking and Bank Regulation." www.econ.nyu.edu/user/galed/fewpapers/FEW%20S13/Kolm.pdf.

9. Board of the International Organization of Securities Commission, "Global Developments in Securitization Regulations," June 2012. www .iosco.org/library/pubdocs/pdf/IOSCOPD382.pdf.

10. www.ft.com/intl/cms/s/0/d920db5e-7bb6-11e3-84af-00144feabdc0 .html#axzz2whhYuXdw.

CHAPTER 7

Regulating the Derivatives Market

"The current state of talks would allow markets to continue trading in total opacity and, given the size of its derivatives markets, effectively undermine the reforms that the global regulatory community agreed through the G20."

—European Commissioner Michel Barnier

In their efforts to create safer, more transparent markets policy-makers on both sides of the Atlantic have crafted extensive and aggressive rules that encroached on each other's turf and created confusion.

The result: it is harder to comply with the new regulations, and markets and liquidity are being fragmented, potentially increasing systemic risk. Discontent reached such a pitch that late in the year trade bodies started litigation against the U.S. regulator.

David Wright, secretary general of the International Organization of Securities Commissions, a standards-setting body whose members regulate 95 percent of the world's securities markets, said: "We have clear overlaps of rules. If we don't have mechanisms to deal with these difficulties, the situation will just get more and more complex."[1]

The derivatives market is one of the most difficult to regulate at national levels. They do not take place in the national sphere. Two eminent lawyers and professors at Columbia Law School, Edward Greene and Ilena Potiha, summarize that difficulty:

> *The cross-border derivatives market is difficult to fathom, important to regulate effectively, and central to the proper functioning of global financial transactions. For these reasons, it is critical to achieve a workable framework to create safe markets and effective regulatory coordination with respect to cross-border transactions.*[2]

Contrary to other financial instruments, derivatives are second-level assets that bet on other underlying asset classes, whether they are interest rates, foreign exchange, equities, and bonds. They also take a diversified form and are completely neutral geographically.

Furthermore, derivatives can be issued anywhere in the world for just about any underlying security or asset class. It is important to realize that 80 percent of the derivatives market is associated with fixed-income products—in other words, bonds, and interest rates.[3] As Vania Stravakeva, assistant professor at the London School of Economics, presents it:

> *Derivatives are much more complicated contracts than regular loans, bond and equity purchases and have very different accounting standards. In order to estimate the exposure of banks to systemic crises caused by derivative positions, regulators will need both bank specific transaction level data and fairly complex value at risk models. While some countries have already enforced derivative regulation in one form or another, they are non-transparent and potentially not optimally designed. The US$2 billion loss of JP Morgan due to CDS trades in 2012 and the bail-out of AIG are prime examples of why greater disclosure of information is crucial and regulators should put more effort in designing optimal derivative regulation.*[4]

As history proved, they can affect all kinds of assets and their notional value reached $1,200 trillion at its peak. Until the 2008 financial crisis, it was pretty much an unregulated market with most of its trades taking place in the over-the-counter (OTC) market rather than regulated exchanges.[5]

Treated by Warren Buffett as "financial instruments of mass destruction,"[6] after which he started using them, derivatives are the subject of intense scrutiny. Credit default swaps (CDSs) have been the focus of every single crisis, from Lehman Brothers to Greece.[7]

ORIGIN OF THE DERIVATIVES MARKET

Derivatives have existed as long as finance has. They have also been known by other names: forward foreign exchange, interest rate swaps, and so on. The need to hedge corporate or portfolio risks on a global scale became essential to them as well as to the development of global capital markets. Derivatives are still used for that purpose by corporate and financial investors.

> *The first exchange for trading derivatives appeared to be the Royal Exchange in London, which permitted forward contracting. The celebrated Dutch Tulip bulb mania, which you can read about in* Extraordinary Popular Delusions *and* The Madness of Crowds *by Charles Mackay, published 1841 but still in print, was characterized by forward contracting on tulip bulbs around 1637. The first "futures" contracts are generally traced to the Yodoya rice market in Osaka, Japan around 1650. These were evidently standardized contracts, which made them much like today's futures, although it is not known if the contracts were marked to market daily and/or had credit guarantees.*[8]

As the market grew, derivatives quickly became a substantial asset class and the traders' favorite hedging instrument and literally exploded. The explosion of the derivatives markets was heavily scrutinized, and the authorities blamed them for creating volatility and increasing the pains and difficulties of issuers. It is true that by making speculative instruments easier almost without restrictions, they grew in a way that became completely disconnected to the world economy.

Derivatives are a genuine financial innovation and they respond to needs of chief financial officers (CFOs) and money managers. The derivatives market was, however, allowed to grow without any serious legal framework, and definitely in the absence of any form of financial regulation. In this sense, the "discovery" by the regulatory authorities of the amplitude of the market and the risks associated with it was disingenuous.

On many occasions, central banks expressed the need to establish this framework without, however, offering any avenue for doing so. It was after the Long-Term Capital Management collapse that the industry tried to set up its own standards.

SIZE OF THE DERIVATIVES MARKETS

The size of the derivatives markets is also the source of considerable discussion. It is important to understand the difference between the net and the notional value and the gross market value of derivatives (see Figure 7.1). The notional amount is the cumulative value of all the underlying securities whose derivative contract applies to. For instance, if I buy an option for 5,000 shares at $30, the notional value of the contract is $150,000. However, the cost of the option I bought might be $1: the gross market value of the derivative is $5,000. That value evolves like other securities.

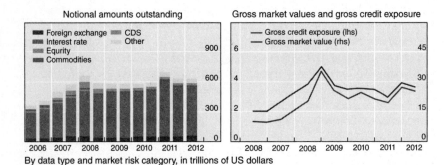

FIGURE 7.1 Global OTC Derivatives
Source: National data, Bank for International Settlements calculations.

U.S. REGULATION: DODD-FRANK ACT

The regulatory structure of derivative markets remains rather confusing. While some of their aspects are part of the securities regulation, some of those derivatives were either traded on different exchange or market places, or regulated by specific regulatory bodies, such as the U.S. Commodities Futures Trading Commission (CFTC). Congress created the CFTC in 1974 as an independent agency with the mandate to regulate commodity futures and option markets in the United States. The agency's mandate has been renewed and expanded several times since then, most recently by the Dodd-Frank Act.[9]

The Dodd-Frank Act[10] divides regulatory authority over swap agreements between the CFTC and Securities and Exchange Commission (SEC) (though the prudential regulators, such as the Federal Reserve Board, also have an important role in setting capital and margin for swap entities that are banks). The SEC has regulatory authority over "security-based swaps," which are defined as swaps based on a single security or loan or a narrow-based group or index of securities (including any interest therein or the value thereof), or events relating to a single issuer or issuers of securities in a narrow-based security index. Security-based swaps are included within the definition of *security* under the Securities Exchange Act of 1934 and the Securities Act of 1933.

> *The fate of one of Gensler's central goals shows why the U.S. attempt to rein in the world's most secretive and profitable financial products falls short of the vision he promoted four years ago. While he won regulators the power to reach deep into a $633 trillion market, Wall Street preserved its dominance in derivatives trading with one of the largest sustained lobbying attacks on a single Washington agency.*
>
> *In the end, the full force of the rules that the CFTC is writing under the authority of the 2010 Dodd-Frank financial regulatory law will apply to only a small share of the global market—possibly less than 20 percent, according to data compiled by Bloomberg.*[11]

EUROPEAN MARKET INFRASTRUCTURE REGULATION (EMIR)

The European Union issued in 2012 a Directive on European Market Infrastructure Regulation (EMIR)[12] that provides for specific rules for the clearance of derivatives through specific clearing mechanisms.

Even today, it remains unclear what the specific objectives of the European Commission are. EMIR is a reflection of this ambiguity. Europe has decided to focus on the whole spectrum of derivative products, and therefore embrace a vast array of institutions and counterparties.

The main obligations under EMIR are:

- *Central Clearing for certain classes of OTC derivatives;*
- *Application of risk mitigation techniques for non-centrally cleared OTC derivatives;*
- *Reporting to trade repositories;*
- *Application of organisational, conduct of business and prudential requirements for CCPs;*
- *Application of requirements for Trade repositories, including the duty to make certain data available to the public and relevant authorities*[13]

The European Securities and Market Authority (ESMA) is the authority empowered to set up the rules and regulations deriving from the EMIR directive. From February 12, 2014, EMIR requires all EU counterparties to a derivative contract to report their trades to a trade repository, irrespective of whether these are traded on or off exchange. Reporting derivative contracts enables regulators to identify and analyze potential risks associated with derivative markets.

The situation remains, however, deeply confusing. EMIR does not include a definition of derivatives and refers to another directive, aiming at another context, MIFID2. The uncertainties of those definitions will obviously make the implementation of the directive difficult and probably not homogeneous throughout the European Union. The City of London Law Society has published a memorandum on the subject.

> We accept that the definition of "derivative" in EMIR must be widely-drawn in order to capture a wide range of exchange-traded and OTC derivatives traded between financial institutions and non-financial institutions, both for speculative and hedging purposes. However, we believe that it is necessary to draw a distinction between OTC derivatives traded between corporate entities and financial counterparties for such purposes, in respect of which there is a discernible "market," and those private arrangements entered into by companies with their employees and shareholders or with other non-financial companies, as part of ordinary corporate transactional business and for very different purposes.[14]

TRANSATLANTIC DIVERGENCES

A deal was struck between Europe and the United States in July 2013. However, in October the United States moved on derivatives regulations in a way that ignores the agreement of July:

> "The Path Forward document has failed at the first hurdle," said Anthony Belchambers, chief executive at the Futures and Options Association in London ..."Barnier was right to ask for more time," said Belchambers. "The reality is the United States is ahead of Europe. That means either the European Union has to catch up— which is unlikely, given the complexity and sovereign powers of its member states—or the United States has to slow down. Unless there's a rationalisation, you get extra-territorial problems. I can

only hope that IOSCO will get a grip on this, because these inter-
national disputes really do have to be sorted out."[15]

The extraterritorial reach of the United States is increasingly resented
in Europe and fuels the feud between them. In the case of derivatives, the
complexity and differences are huge.[16]

SHORT SELLING IS A FORM OF DERIVATIVE

Short selling is not fundamentally different from other derivatives: it simply
does not use an instrument, but they have a similar effect as options or
futures. They have been blamed for the demise of several financial institutions, and new regulations have been looked at, including the banning of
shorting financial institutions stocks.

A recent decision by the European Court of Justice,[17] seized by the
United Kingdom, questions the validity of the European Commission's
rights to ban short selling at all.

The Commission in September 2013 issued new rules for short selling.[18]
It is part of a broader approach that amalgamates short selling and credit
default swaps.

To end the current fragmented situation in which some Member
States have taken divergent measures and to restrict the possibil-
ity that divergent measures are taken by competent authorities it is
important to address the potential risks arising from short selling
and credit default swaps in a harmonised manner. The requirements
to be imposed should address the identified risks without unduly
detracting from the benefits that short selling provides to the quality
and efficiency of markets. While in certain situations it could have
adverse effects, under normal market conditions, short selling plays
an important role in ensuring the proper functioning of financial
markets, in particular in the context of market liquidity and effi-
cient price formation.[19]

The Unites States resorts to Rule 105 to chastise institutions that do not
respect basic rules in short selling:

The federal anti-manipulation rule prohibits investors from short-
ing a public company's shares by restricting the activity in one of
two scenarios, whichever comes first: beginning five business days
before the pricing of the offered securities and ending with the

pricing, or the period beginning with the initial filing of the regis-tration statement for the offering and ending with the pricing, ac-cording to Richards Kibbe & Orbe LLP, a law firm in New York.[20]

The intense lobbying of banks on both sides of the Atlantic leaves little room for hopes that the transparency of the derivatives markets will seri-ously improve. The scope, strength, and depth of this regulation are unlikely to create a level playing field. "Accidents" will continue to occur, and the sta-bility of the financial services industry will be only marginally strengthened.

JPMORGAN CHASE LONDON TRADING LOSSES

In 2012, the U.S. Senate drew important conclusions on the JPMorgan Chase trading losses. The Levin-McCain report makes the following recom-mendations that may curb derivative risks and abuses:

1. *Require derivatives performance data.*
2. *Require contemporaneous hedge documentation.*
3. *Strengthen credit derivative valuations.*
4. *Investigate risk limit breaches.*
5. *Investigate models that substantially lower risk.*
6. *Federal financial regulators should immediately issue a final rule implementing the Merkley-Levin provisions of the Dodd-Frank Wall Street Reform and Consumer Protection Act, also known as the Volcker Rule, to stop high risk proprietary trading ac-tivities and the build-up of high risk assets at federally insured banks and their affiliates.*
7. *Enhance derivative capital charges.*[21]

The diagnostic on what happened at the Corporate Investment Office of JPMorgan Chase was particularly severe. The report of the U.S. Senate includes e-mails that reflect how disrespectful the chief information officer (CIO) was of the basics of best practices is appalling. It did so by "extending" the scope of a loophole of the Volcker Rule that allowed hedging strategies. The reading of the report is distressing. JPMorgan Chase:

1. **Increased Risk Without Notice to Regulators.** *In the first quar-ter of 2012, without alerting its regulators, JPMorgan Chase's Chief Investment Office used bank deposits, including some that were federally insured, to construct a $157 billion portfolio of synthetic credit derivatives. . . .*
2. **Mischaracterized High Risk Trading as Hedging.** *JPMorgan Chase claimed at times that its Synthetic Credit Portfolio*

functioned as a hedge against bank credit risks, but failed to identify the assets or portfolios being hedged. . . .

3. **Hid Massive Losses.** *JPMorgan Chase, through its Chief Investment Office, hid over $660 million in losses in the Synthetic Credit Portfolio for several months in 2012, by allowing the CIO to overstate the value of its credit derivatives. . . .*

4. **Disregarded Risk.** *In the first three months of 2012, when the CIO breached all five of the major risk limits on the Synthetic Credit Portfolio, rather than divest itself of risky positions, JPMorgan Chase disregarded the warning signals and downplayed the Synthetic Credit Portfolio's risks . . .*

5. **Dodged OCC Oversight.** *JPMorgan Chase dodged OCC oversight of its Synthetic Credit Portfolio by not alerting the OCC to the nature and extent of the portfolio. . . .*

6. **Failed Regulatory Oversight.** *The OCC failed to investigate CIO trading activity that triggered multiple, sustained risk limit breaches. . . .*

7. **Mischaracterized the Portfolio.** *After the whale trades became public, JPMorgan Chase misinformed investors, regulators, policymakers and the public about its Synthetic Credit Portfolio. . . .*[22]

It happened four years after the Lehman collapse.

This was the conclusion of the JPMorgan task force that inquired about the reasons for these losses:

The Task Force does not believe that the CIO losses stemmed from any one specific act or omission. Rather, as described in this Report, the Task Force has concluded that the losses were the result of a number of acts and omissions, some large and some seemingly small, some involving personnel and some involving structure, and a change in any one of which might have led to a different result. This experience, as we hope is clear from this Report, has caused substantial and healthy introspection at the Firm and recognition of the need for continued improvement in multiple areas. Ultimately, the Task Force believes that this incident teaches a number of important lessons that the Firm is taking very seriously.[23]

NOTES

1. Anish Puaar, "U.S. and Europe Lock Horns on Derivatives," *Financial News*, December 17, 2013. www.efinancialnews.com/story/2013-12-17/

us-and-europe-lock-horns-on-derivatives-regulation?ea9c8a2de0ee111 045601ab04d673622.

2. Edward E. Greene and Ilena Potiha, "Issues in the Extraterritorial Application of Dodd Frank's Derivatives and Clearing Rules, the Impact of Global Markets and the Inevitability of Cross-Border and U.S. Domestic Coordination," *Capital Markets Law Journal*, 2013.

3. Deutsche Börse, "The Global Derivatives Blue Print," p. 8. http://deutsche-boerse.com/dbg/dispatch/en/binary/gdb_content_pool/imported_files/public_files/10_downloads/11_about_us/Public_Affairs/The_Global_Derivatives_Market_0909.pdf.

4. www.forbes.com/sites/lbsbusinessstrategyreview/2013/09/24/derivative-regulation-why-does-it-matter/.

5. The Chicago Mercantile Exchange and Eurexchange are the two largest derivative exchanges.

6. The rapidly growing trade in derivatives poses a "mega-catastrophic risk" for the economy and most shares are still "too expensive," legendary investor Warren Buffett has warned. http://news.bbc.co.uk/2/hi/2817995.stm.

7. IMF, "A New Look at the Role of Sovereign Credit Default Swaps," Global Financial Stability Report, April 2013. www.imf.org/external/pubs/ft/gfsr/2013/01/pdf/c2.pdf.

8. Don Chance is a professor of finance at Louisiana State University. See "A Brief History of Derivatives, December 20, 2011. http://husky1 .stmarys.ca/~gye/derivativeshistory.pdf.

9. www.cftc.gov/index.htm.

10. This is a summary provided by the SEC of the mains aspects of the Dodd-Frank Act provisions on derivatives. www.sec.gov/spotlight/dodd frank/derivatives.shtml.

11. www.bloomberg.com/news/2013-09-04/how-the-bank-lobby-loosened-u-s-reins-on-derivatives.html.

12. The Regulation (EU) No. 648/2012 of the European Parliament and of the Council of July 4, 2012, on OTC derivatives, central counterparties (CCPs), and trade repositories (TRs) (EMIR) entered into force on August 16, 2012. The Commission Delegated Regulations (EU) Nos. 148/2013 to 153/2013 of December 19, 2012, supplementing EMIR were published in the *Official Journal* on February 23, 2013, and entered into force on March 15, 2013. The implementing technical standards were published in the official journal dated December 21, 2012. www.esma.europa.eu/page/European-Market-Infrastructure-Regulation-EMIR.

13. www.esma.europa.eu/page/European-Market-Infrastructure-Regulation-EMIR.

14. www.bankingtech.com/174272/us-europe-derivatives-rulemaking-deal-falls-at-first-hurdle/.

15. www.citysolicitors.org.uk.

16. Hogan Hovell, a law firm, published in October 2013 a synopsis of the differences between the U.S. and European derivatives regulations that illustrates the substantial differences existing between the two approaches. http://f.datasrvr.com/fr1/713/74638/Oct_2013_Derivatives_Summary_of_key_EU_and_US_regulatory_developments.pdf.

17. The decision was more on the fact that the legal arguments used to support the decision were not correct. It remains to be seen whether the European Commission will be able to find better legal ground to keep its ability to ban some forms of short selling. www.ft.com/intl/cms/s/0/93ed1ea2-1b86-11e3-b678-00144feab7de.html#axzz2jUskzAqO.

18. Guidelines were published recently by the European Commission. http://ec.europa.eu/internal_market/securities/docs/short_selling/20120705-ia-resume_en.pdf.

19. http://eur-lex.europa.eu/LexUriServ/LexUriServ.do?uri=OJ:L:2012:086:0001:0024:en:PDF.

20. http://blogs.wsj.com/moneybeat/2013/09/18/sec-short-selling-crackdown-what-is-rule-105/.

21. www.hsgac.senate.gov%2Fdownload%2Freport-jpmorgan-chase-whale-trades-a-case-history-of-derivatives-risks-and-abuses-march-15-2013.

22. Ibid.

23. www.google.com/url?sa=t&rct=j&q=&esrc=s&source=web&cd=2&ved=0CDAQFjAB&url=http%3A%2F%2Ffiles.shareholder.com%2Fdownloads%2FONE%2F2272984969x0x628656%2F4cb574a0-0bf--4728-9582-625e4519b5ab%2FTask_Force_Report.pdf&ei=Cy0vU9TpHMeZ0AHp_4CYCA&usg=AFQjCNFE12ntfUa3VzfoIMDnDxp6xkQ9_Q&bvm=bv.63556303,d.dmQ.

CHAPTER 8

The Structure of Banking: How Many Degrees of Separation?

"I am speaking of nascent efforts to regulate the multi-trillion dollar asset management industry. This war promises to be even bigger than the one megabanks have waged against the Volcker rule's proposed ban on speculative trading."

—Former FDIC Chair Sheila Bair

"Too big to fail"[1] has become a key element of focus on banking regulation. Is size really the issue? How is size being defined? The debate is heating up after the U.S. Congress came up with a bipartisan plan to deal with this issue. The United States has organized a possible separation of banking from trading in case of excess, followed by European initiatives in April 2014.

These structural reforms are diversely regulated: will they avoid what are fundamentally two different businesses inside a universal banking model? Is there a need to go back to the Glass-Steagall Act in the United States?

SYSTEMICALLY IMPORTANT FINANCIAL INSTITUTIONS (SIFIs)

The definition of systemically important financial institutions[2] and the imposition of additional capital requirements is an important step toward a better oversight of systemic risks by central banks and ministers of finance.

The Financial Stability Board (FSB) published a list of the 28 financial institutions considered to be systemically important.[3] See Table 8.1.

TABLE 8.1 Global Systemically Important Banks as of November 2012 Allocated to Buckets Corresponding to Required Level of Additional Loss Absorbency

Bucket	G-SIBs in Alphabetical Order within Each Bucket
5 (3.5%)	(empty)
4 (2.5%)	Citigroup Deutsch Bank HSBC JPMorgan Chase
3 (2.0%0	Barclays BNP Paribus
2 (1.5%)	Bank of America Bank of New York Mellon Credit Suisse Goldman Sachs Mitsubishi UFJ FG Morgan Stanley Royal Bank of Scotland UBS
1 (1.0%)	Bank of China BBVA Groupe BPCE Groupe Crédit Agricole ING Bank Mizuho FG Nordea Santander Société Générale Standard Chartered State Street Sumitomo Mitsui FG Unicredit Group Wells Fargo

However, this notion is particularly ambivalent. On the one side, by designating those banks as SIFIs, the authorities indicate—*a contrario*—that the financial institutions that are on that list are not systemically important and, in the event of a failure, will be allowed to go bankrupt without benefiting from the resolution system applied to those 28 institutions. The FSB indeed issued a report on the resolution of the SIFIs.[4]

The positive affirmation—*a fortiori*—is that the 28 SIFIs are effectively covered by an implicit government guarantee over and above the ways and means of their national government. The price they pay for it is the additional equity that is required for them. However, with that price comes a series of advantages: their rating will have to take into consideration that situation. Should not some of them be rated AAA/Aaa as a result of this implicit guarantee by the wealthiest nations. The certainty that the bank will not be allowed to fail and will be rescued by its government could be considered to be a competitive advantage.[5]

It is necessary to understand what would happen to those institutions if a crisis occurred: Will there be a special resolution system for them that would apply to each of them independently from their national one? Shouldn't they be forced to choose the single-entry option for resolution?[6]

UNIVERSAL BANKING MODEL

Europe is hesitant to break the universal banking model, and its proposal for separation (the Liikanen Report)[7] raises a series of questions of principle. Furthermore, there is a sharp difference between the European Union and the United Kingdom on this matter.

However, we must also take into consideration the evolution of the U.S. banking system: following the banking crisis, three of the largest independent investment banks were purchased by commercial banks. In a sense, with the exception of Goldman Sachs and Morgan Stanley, the U.S. banking market is led by three major universal banks: Citi, Bank of America (which acquired Merrill Lynch), and JPMorgan Chase (which acquired Bear Stearns). With the acquisition after bankruptcy of the U.S. operations of Lehman Brothers by Barclays Capital, three of the fixed "bulge bracket firms" are now part of a larger universal and global banking group.

I am not convinced that the rules on separation are indeed providing what they pretend to provide: a separation between the risks of deposit and lending banking and capital market activities.

SEPARATION MODELS

Several countries have implemented interesting concepts on separation of activities.

HSBC is the most recent bank to sound out investors about a flotation of its United Kingdom arm, in a move that would realize value from its high street banking business and address regulatory pressures.

UNITED KINGDOM

The Vickers Commission proposed a fundamental change in the way that banks in the United Kingdom are organized. The main change is that a "ring fence" would separate retail "utility" banking work from a range of investment banking and corporate finance activities. It also proposes that banks retain higher capital and loss-absorbing reserves than is currently proposed under the Basel rules. The government has accepted the Commission's main proposals.[8]

> The most controversial recommendation of the Vickers Commission is that U.K. banks' retail operations should be "ring-fenced." Banks will be required to establish a separate legal entity within their corporate group structure to provide retail and commercial banking services in the United Kingdom. The purposes of this subsidiarisation are, first, to insulate retail banking operations from riskier financial activities and risks inherent in the global financial system and, secondly, in the event of failure, to ensure the continuous provision of retail banking services by ring-fenced banks, with reduced bail-out costs for taxpayers.[9]

UNITED STATES

The Dodd-Frank Act[10] provides for some forms of separation of some activities, as well as some limitations to investments considered to have higher risks. The Volcker Rule prohibits an insured depository institution and its affiliates from:

- Engaging in "proprietary trading."
- Acquiring or retaining any equity, partnership, or other ownership interest in a hedge fund or private equity fund.
- Sponsoring a hedge fund or a private equity fund.

Nonbank financial companies designated by the Financial Stability Council of the U.S. Treasury for supervision by the board of governors would not be subject to this prohibition. The act provides, however, that they could be subject to additional capital requirements for, and additional quantitative limits with respect to some activities.

EUROPEAN UNION

Continental Europe built its banking system around powerful national universal banks. For a long time, they were mostly engaged in classical commercial banking activities. As capital markets started developing in Europe, most of those leading banks started developing these activities in their home country. Soon after, they joined the only global European financial center: the City of London.[11]

The European Commission, after the financial crisis, decided to look more closely at its banking system. The Vickers Report had already created a wave of discussions on the separation between banking and trading. At the initiative of Commissioner Michel Barnier, a group of experts was constituted to analyze this question.

The Liikanen Report[12] provided a serious analysis of the various forms of separation between banking and trading that could take place. It takes into consideration the Vickers Report and is advocating a true separation, but some of its aspects are questionable:

> *The central objectives of the separation are to make banking groups, especially their socially most vital parts (mainly deposit-taking and providing financial services to the non-financial sectors in the economy), safer and less connected to high-risk trading activities and to limit the implicit or explicit take of taxpayers in the trading parts of banking groups. The Group's recommendations regarding separation concern businesses which are considered to represent the riskiest parts of trading activities and where risk positions can change most rapidly.*[13]

However, its conclusions stopped where the difficulty of separation starts: the banking group is headed by a holding company that oversees the banking and trading operations. What is the brand going to be? How will the activities be funded? How can proprietary trading be dealt with? What will be the relationship between the trading and the banking groups?

It is through the resolution directive that some of those problems were dealt with, but sometimes the Liikanen Report ended up being at odds with other Commission proposals. There is, as we write this book, no satisfactory definition of a common European banking structure, and the attention is more and more drawn toward the Vickers Report.

In February 2014, the European Commission went further and proposed a separation structure inspired by the Liikanen Report.

The new rules would also give supervisors the power to require those banks to separate certain potentially risky trading activities from their deposit-taking business if the pursuit of such activities compromises financial stability. [14]

SW+ITZERLAND

A parliamentary initiative in Switzerland aims to impose a version of the Glass-Steagall Act that led banks to revisit their structure. The two largest Swiss banks, UBS and Credit Suisse, recently announced their intention to spin off their Swiss banking and wealth management in order to protect their core businesses from the risks associated with their substantial investment banking operations.

> *The argument for doing the split is that it is the only sure way to protect wealth management from potential losses in the investment bank. The snag is that separation would remove the synergies between wealth management and investment banking—the first is a big customer of the second, for example. Above all, it would carry big one-off costs. As a standalone entity, the investment bank would almost certainly require an additional capital injection to be able to finance itself. It's not clear where that capital would come from. Meanwhile, UBS is lumbered with 382 billion Swiss francs of noncore assets that look like a huge obstacle to corporate change.*[15]

VOLCKER RULE AND PROPRIETARY TRADING[16]

> *The final rule has been designed to ensure that banking entities do not engage in prohibited activities or investments and to ensure that banking entities engage in permitted trading and investment activities in a manner designed to identify, monitor and limit the risks posed by these activities and investments. For instance, the final rule requires that any banking entity that is engaged in activity subject to section 13 develop and administer a compliance program*

that is appropriate to the size, scope and risk of its activities and investments.

The rule requires the largest firms engaged in these activities to develop and implement enhanced compliance programs and regularly report data on trading activities to the Agencies.[17]

One of the diagnostics of the reasons for the U.S. banking crisis is the use by banks of their equity for trading purpose. It was a diversion from the *raison d'etre* of equity: it was supposed to be the buffer to absorb possible shocks from the economy or the markets, as well as the credit risks of the bank. It soon became a profit center, and one of the most risky. In a way, the capital account had become a hedge fund that was maximizing its return.

It was ignoring the warning signal of the crisis and when the massive loss of asset values followed the Lehman bankruptcy and the subprime crisis exploded, the banks were hit twice: not only the default on their retail credits—mostly mortgages and credit cards—which in other times would have been covered by equity, were facing heavy losses on the proprietary trading positions. The insurance provided by the equity had, itself, lost its value.

That diagnostic was central to the report Paul Volcker, former president of the Federal Reserve, produced for the President of the United States, Barack Obama. It was recommending limiting proprietary trading to less speculative asset classes. What would be called the Volcker Rule applied to proprietary trading and fund activities by U.S. banking organizations regardless of where the trading or activities are conducted. However, for non-U.S. banking organizations, the Volcker Rule would apply only to proprietary trading and fund activities in the United States, or such activities outside the United States if they involve the offering of securities to any U.S. resident.

While the Volcker Rule has been moderated since its inception, these limitations would have a significant impact on the ability of U.S. banking organizations to provide investment management products and services that are competitive with nonbanking firms generally and with non-U.S. banking organizations in overseas markets. It would also effectively prohibit short-term trading strategies by any U.S. banking organization, regardless of the location of its trading business, if those strategies involve instruments other than those specifically permitted for trading.[18]

It was supposed to end years of speculative proprietary trading that affected several banks. An exception obtained by the banks allowed JP Morgan, through its London office, to stretch the definition and speculate in its Corporate Investment Office.[19]

In Europe, the banking lobby managed to keep this issue off the table of the Commission. When it was eventually examined, the Commission did nothing substantial. The suggestion of the Liikanen Report was ambiguous:

> *The Group proposes that proprietary trading and all assets or derivative positions incurred in the process of market-making, other than the activities exempted below, must be assigned to a separate legal entity, which can be an investment firm or a bank (henceforth the "trading entity") within the banking group.*
>
> *The Group suggests that the separation would only be mandatory if the activities to be separated amount to a significant share of a bank's business, or if the volume of these activities can be considered significant from the viewpoint of financial stability.*[20]

However, the Volcker Rule does have important global implications. The disregard of the United States for the territoriality of its legislation and interventions does apply here:

> *The Volcker rule applies to any banking institution, wherever situated, that has a U.S. branch, agency or bank subsidiary, as well as to the institution's other subsidiaries and affiliates around the globe. Whether an entity is a "subsidiary" or "affiliate" of another entity for purposes of the Volcker Rule depends on whether it controls or is under common control with the other entity, but, significantly, control can be found to exist based on an equity ownership interest of only 25 percent or more.*[21]

Since most SIFIs do fall under that definition, one can reasonably assure that when it will be applicable, the Volcker Rule will become a global standard.

Banks have decided to pursue legal action against the Volcker Rule in the United States, right after the final rules were agreed by seven government agencies. They probably do not realize how trust and confidence in their integrity relies on their recognition that equity is sacred and that proprietary trading threatens their stability.

> *Though the current dispute centers on an obscure and complex investment product, the association's lawsuit could become an early test of how much the industry can successfully push back against the Volcker Rule. The rule was devised to stop regulated banks from speculatively trading with their depositors' money and other funds in an effort to avoid some of the problems that led to the bank bailouts in the wake of the 2008 financial crisis.*[22]

In February 2014, the European Commission sent to the Parliament a proposal banning proprietary trading for large banks, to be applied in January 2017.[23]

TOO BIG TO FAIL (TBTF): IS SIZE THE PROBLEM?

Ever since the expression "too big to fail" was coined, it has become the subject of a number of variations that are not innocent:

- *Too big to fail* addresses the impact of a failure of large financial institutions that cannot be allowed to go bankrupt since their impact would have systemic consequences on the financial system and, as a consequence, the rest of the economy.
- *Too crooked to fail* was used in articles about some of the largest banks.
- *Too big to prosecute or to jail* is a concern for the Department of Justice and prosecutors around the world.

Attorney General Holder told the Senate Judiciary Committee, "I am concerned that the size of some of these institutions becomes so large that it does become difficult for us to prosecute them when we are hit with indications that if we do prosecute—if we do bring a criminal charge—it will have a negative impact on the national economy, perhaps even the world economy. I think that is a function of the fact that some of these institutions have become too large.[24]

- *Too big to regulate* is certainly a crucial one. The Chicago Council on Global Affairs organized a forum on May 9, 2013, on this subject:

From Dodd-Frank to Basel III and beyond, financial regulators are struggling to keep pace with the rapid evolution and increasing complexity of global finance. To combat the systemic risks that revealed themselves during the financial crisis, regulators have implemented new rules covering everything from bank capital requirements to derivative and commodity markets. While some argue that regulators have not gone far enough, others argue that new regulations are unfairly prohibitive or even anti-competitive. Against this backdrop, what is working and what needs to change in global financial regulation? How do we mitigate excessive risk taking and prevent another crisis while simultaneously keeping America's financial institutions competitive in the global economy?[25]

While regulators would not easily admit that they are unable to regulate large global financial institutions, their track record is poor: they did not see it coming and, against evidence, constantly believed that the problem will solve itself. One of the reasons lies in the fragmentation of regulation. This is what makes the special regime for SIFIs so important.

The FSB is in charge of the TBTF problem, on behalf of the G20. In its recent report, dated September 3, 2013, it concluded:

There are signs that firms, markets and rating agencies are adjusting to authorities' determination to address TBTF. As such, rating agencies have lowered their assumptions on the likelihood of government support in light of the considerable progress that has been made in devising a credible and feasible resolution plan for certain firms. In the case of other firms, markets have not yet changed their assumptions of reliance on extraordinary public support, in part due to lack of disclosure around the progress in making the firms more resolvable and in developing credible resolution plans, coupled with uncertainties relating to the legislative reforms of resolution regimes. It will understandably take time to fully establish the credibility of the new framework in addressing TBTF.[26]

■ *Too big to manage.* The question nobody wants to face is the question of the management capabilities of these huge and complex large and global institutions. It is, however, the most important subject. Managements failed miserably when they launched themselves into new activities they could not even understand. It raises questions that go way beyond the TBTF issue. Why should a bank be allowed to trade commodities? Why should it own hedge funds?

Ben Heineman, the former general counsel of GE, published an interesting blog post in the *Harvard Business Review*. He happens to know something about the problem: GE Capital had 22 businesses and was only one of GE's businesses. The Ponzi scheme of Joe Jett that broke Kidder Peabody was one of the consequences of this overextended management challenge.

The range of problems in the financial sector is striking: Bad trades with unforeseen and poorly understood billion dollar losses. Poor controls over risk and valuations. Deceptive communication within the company and to the board. Flawed mortgage origination, loan modification and debt collection practices. Manipulation of energy markets. LIBOR rate rigging. Participation in money laundering that helps drug smugglers or terrorists. Questionable hiring of sons and daughters of Chinese officials. Some of these problems occurred before the 2008 crisis and some since then. But they are not the regulatory esoterica that critics of Dodd-Frank worry about—if proven, these are core issues of wrongdoing.[27]

Nothing concrete has been done. Bank balance sheets continue to grow, activities have remained as diversified as they were, and behaviors and mind-set have not changed, as the London interbank offered rate (LIBOR) crisis and the London Whale demonstrated. One of them is bound to be mismanaged, misregulated, or simply too complex or too large. Short of gradually shrinking them and limiting their scope, they will inevitably be the source of another mega-crisis.

PROHIBIT THE TRADING OF COMMODITIES BY BANKS

What is even more worrying is that banks continue to be allowed to trade assets that are not financial by nature, and of which their understanding is far from certain. The scandals that emerged around the trading of commodities as well as the necessity to increase their capital adequacy ratios have led many banks to sell or close that activity. The most recent one, announced in March 2014, is the sale for $5.3 billion of that activity to Mercuria, a Swiss trading company.[28]

There is no justification for the banks' involvement in this market, and their ability to manipulate markets has had substantial consequences to the real economy—the AIG manipulation of electricity in California, the JPMorgan manipulation in its now-defunct commodities trading activities, and more important, manipulation that led to a substantial increase of the price of oil and the price of food.

Commodities exchanges are there for a purpose, and banks can certainly act as broker for their customers. They should not be traders, however, and not own positions for the purpose of trading. It would reduce a substantial risk that has nothing to do with the mission of financial institutions. They should not go beyond assisting customers.

Several firms started disposing of or closing these businesses. The last one, announced on December 20, 2013, is Morgan Stanley:

Morgan Stanley has sold the majority of its global physical oil trading operations to Russian state-run oil major Rosneft, becoming the latest Wall Street firm to dispose of a major part of its commodity business.[29]

The deal represents a bold move into the U.S. market by Russia's top oil producer, which is headed by Igor Sechin, a powerful ally of Russian President Vladimir Putin. The Russian state owns almost 70 percent of Rosneft.[30]

NOTES

1. Andrew Ross Sorkin, *Too Big to Fail: The Inside Story of How Wall Street and Washington Fought to Save the Financial System—and Themselves*. New York: Viking Penguin, 2009. Sorkin, a *New York Times* financial journalist gives a fascinating account of the collapse of the U.S. and global financial markets in 2008. The book was written based on interviews the author conducted with the major players in the financial crisis. These interviews are documented through tapes, notes, presentations, calendars, call logs, and more. The level of detail is nothing short of amazing, and makes the story well documented. The author keeps it interesting. http://bizfinance.about.com/od/bookreviews/fr/Too_Big_to_Fail.htm.

2. Deloitte published a study called "SIFI Designation and Its Potential Impact on Nonbank Financial Companies: A Roadmap for Nonbank Financial Companies through the New World of Systemically Important Financial Institution Designation." www.deloitte.com/assets/Dcom-UnitedStates/Local%20Assets/Documents/us_aers_grr_crs_SIFI%20Designation%20%20_0313.pdf.

3. This is the updated list of the SIFIs by the FSB in November 2012. www.financialstabilityboard.org/publications/r_121031ac.pdf.

4. www.financialstabilityboard.org/publications/r_130716b.pdf.

5. Fitch Rating, "Level and Mix of G-SIFI Debt Buffer Key Rating Variables," September 6, 2013. www.fitchratings.com/gws/en/fitchwire/fitchwirearticle/Level-and-Mix?pr_id=801411.

6. The notion of "single point of entry" will be further defined when we analyze the resolution and recovery regulations. *American Banker* comments on the FDIC approach. www.americanbanker.com/dodd-frank/fdics-single-point-entry-plan-is-option-to-solve-tbtf-1059149-1.html.

7. Commissioner Michel Barnier established a high-level expert group on structural bank reforms in February 2012. Our task has been to assess whether additional reforms directly targeted at the structure of individual banks would further reduce the probability and impact of failure,

ensure the continuation of vital economic functions upon failure, and better protect vulnerable retail clients (Letter of the Chairman). http://ec.europa.eu/internal_market/bank/docs/high-level_expert_group/report_en.pdf.

8. www.parliament.uk/briefing-papers/SN06171.
9. The Vickers Report and the Future of U.K. Banking. Blog post by Barnabas Reynolds, Shearman & Sterling, on March 29, 2012, at the Harvard Law School Forum on Corporate Governance and Financial Regulation.http://blogs.law.harvard.edu/corpgov/2012/03/29/the-vickers-report-and-the-future-of-uk-banking/.
10. www.cftc.gov/ucm/groups/public/@swaps/documents/file/hr4173_enrolledbill.pdf.
11. Few European leaders would agree with the thesis of the *New York Times* that the City of London is the savior of EU finance. www.nytimes.com/2013/05/20/business/global/the-city-of-london-as-savior-of-eu-finance.
12. http://ec.europa.eu/internal_market/bank/docs/high-level_expert_group/report_en.pdf.
13. http://ec.europa.eu/internal_market/bank/docs/high-level_expert_group/report_en.pdf.
14. http://europa.eu/rapid/press-release_IP-14-85_en.htm.
15. http://dealbook.nytimes.com/2013/05/02/why-a-ubs-split-would-not-be-the-best-move/?_r=0.
16. www.federalreserve.gov/newsevents/press/bcreg/20131210a.htm.
17. www.sec.gov/rules/final/2013/bhca-1.pdf.
18. www.skadden.com/newsletters/FSR_The_Volcker_Rule.pdf.
19. www.bloomberg.com/news/2012-11-21/jpmorgan-turned-cio-into-prop-trading-desk-pensions-say.html.
20. http://ec.europa.eu/internal_market/bank/docs/high-level_expert_group/report_en.pdf, p. v.
21. Frederick J. Knecht, Keith A. Noreika, and Carey S. Roberts, "The Volcker Rule: Troublesome Implications for non-US Banks," *Financier Worldwide*, December 2010. www.financierworldwide.com.
22. http://dealbook.nytimes.com/2013/12/24/banks-suit-tests-limits-of-resisting-volcker-rule/.
23. http://europa.eu/rapid/press-release_IP-14-85_en.htm.
24. Ted Kaufman, "Are Banks Too Big to Tolerate?" *Forbes*, July 5, 2013. www.forbes.com/sites/tedkaufman/2013/05/07/are-banks-too-big-to-tolerate/.
25. www.thechicagocouncil.org/Files/Event/FY13/05_May_13/Global_Finance__Too_Big_to_Regulate_.aspx.
26. www.financialstabilityboard.org/publications/r_130902.pdf.

27. Ben Heineman Jr., "Too Big to Manage: JP Morgan and the Mega Banks," *Harvard Business Review*, October 3, 2013. http://blogs.hbr.org/2013/10/too-big-to-manage-jp-morgan-and-the-mega-banks/.
28. http://dealbook.nytimes.com/2014/03/19/jpmorgan-to-sell-commodities-unit-for-3-5-billion/?_php=true&_type=blogs&_r=0.
29. www.reuters.com/article/2013/12/27/us-rosneft-morganstanley-commodities-idUSBRE9BQ05G20131227.
30. www.reuters.com/article/2013/12/21/us-rosneft-morganstanley-commodities-idUSBRE9BJ1FU20131221.

CHAPTER 9

Banking Resolution and Recovery

"I am concerned that decision-making may become overly complex and financing arrangements may not be adequate. We should not create a Single Resolution Mechanism that is single in name only."

—ECB President Mario Draghi

History has seen governments and international institutions stepping in to avoid previous financial crises that would otherwise create systemic damages. Because the recent banking crisis was not due to macroeconomic external problems but to the financial system itself, the authorities looked at ways to prevent a repetition of a situation where they ended up being in charge of crisis resolution and being forced to use taxpayers' money to do so.

The Bank of England[1] defines *resolution* as having five key objectives, which must be considered in choosing which resolution tools to use:

- *Protect and enhance the stability of the financial systems of the United Kingdom;*
- *Protect and enhance public confidence in the stability of the banking systems of the United Kingdom;*
- *Protect depositors;*
- *Protect public funds;*
- *Avoid interfering with property rights in contravention with human rights*

Recent regulatory reforms were inspired, more or less explicitly, by the same philosophy and pursue the same objectives.

MORAL HAZARD

Former BIS Director General Alexandre Lamfalussy stated:

> *The widespread belief that systemically important financial institutions will always be bailed out has two devastating consequences: it encourages reckless risk taking by such institutions and provides them with unfair competitive edge over the rest of the financial industry by ensuring cheaper financial resources for them. To avoid this happening, it has to be made clear that no financial firm, and especially banking firm, should be able to count on being protected from failure.*[2]

One can only agree with such intentions. Over the past 50 years, many governments have had to use taxpayers' money. This in turn has launched an ethical debate about the risks associated with the belief that banks can do whatever they want. In any event, public money will always be there to rescue them.

The concept of moral hazard was born in the insurance sector. It refers to the chance that the insured will be more careless and take greater risks because he or she is protected, thus increasing the potential of claims on the provider.[3]

Having looked for many broader definitions, I thought the Cambridge dictionary was the simplest and clearest one: a situation in which people or organizations do not suffer from the results of their bad decisions, so may increase the risks they take.[4] A more straightforward definition might be a situation in which you no longer bear the responsibility for your actions and become more likely to engage in reckless behavior that others will incur the cost of.[5]

Often enough, and rightly so, moral hazard has been a sincere preoccupation of governments. The crisis of 2008 has given that problem a new dimension.[6] Banks were not falling out of on an outside crisis but on their own sword. That became politically, ethically, socially, and economically unacceptable.

However, the focus on avoiding the use of taxpayer money could boomerang:

> *Much of the policy focus since the financial crisis has centered on the wish to put in place regulation so that public money never has*

to be called on again to support the financial system. Some have argued that the capacity of the authorities to respond to a crisis, should it occur, ought to be dismantled, and indeed Dodd-Frank somewhat curtailed the emergency lending authority of the Federal Reserve. This approach is like putting in place strong building codes and then eliminating the fire department. We need both building codes and fire departments to keep people and property as safe as possible from fire. And we need both strong oversight and regulation, and a strong lender of last resort, to keep people and their wealth safe from financial calamity.[7]

CAN THE BAIL-IN CONCEPT AVOID TAXPAYERS' BAILOUT?

One has to recognize that the new concept of banks resolving their own problems (bail-in) is mostly aiming at protecting public funds—taxpayers' money. From a concept of bailout, most countries or groups of countries are moving toward a concept of bail-in.[8]

A bail-in takes place before a bankruptcy and under current proposals, regulators would have the power to impose losses on bondholders while leaving untouched other creditors of similar stature, such as derivatives counterparties. By quickly addressing the problems of sickly institutions, they would also help stabilise the financial system by removing uncertainty.[9]

Rather than being rescued by outside sources of financing, financial institutions are now expected to set up plans that will use internal resources to prevent and, if necessary, provide an effective recovery mechanism, regulated and monitored by regulatory agencies.

Untested so far, the bail-in system is a revolution and will force the management and the boards of directors of financial institutions to better manage their risks and avoid having their shareholders, bondholders, and even depositors come to the rescue. It provides for solutions where the main victims of a crisis will be the shareholders, the bondholders, and even the depositors.

Professor John C. Coffee outlines the possible options:

Because the quickest, simplest way for a financial institution to increase its profitability is to increase its leverage, an enduring tension will exist between regulators and systemically significant financial institutions over the issues of risk and leverage. Many have suggested that the 2008 financial crisis was caused because financial institutions were induced to increase leverage because of flawed systems of executive compensation. Still, there is growing evidence that shareholders acquiesced in these compensation formulas to cause managers to accept higher risk and leverage. Shareholder pressure then is a factor that could induce the failure of a systemically significant financial institution.

What then can be done to prevent future such failures? The Dodd-Frank Act invests heavily in preventive control and regulatory oversight, but this paper argues that the political economy of financial regulation ensures that there will be an eventual relaxation of regulatory oversight ("the regulatory sine curve"). Moreover, the Dodd-Frank Act significantly reduces the ability of financial regulators to effect a bail-out of a distressed financial institution and largely compels them to subject such an institution to a forced receivership and liquidation under the auspices of the FDIC.[10]

LESSONS FROM THE FINANCIAL CRISIS

The experience of previous financial crises has certainly taught us a few hard lessons. Financial crises, even if they have largely been anticipated, have a natural tendency to culminate in a maelstrom that erupts after the tectonic plates collide. At that stage, it is a *sauve-qui-peut* that requires *decisive time management, planning, and communication.*[11]

The bankruptcy of Lehman Brothers has taught those who have the responsibility for the financial stability that it becomes a tremendous challenge when the institution being rescued is global. Conflicts of jurisdictions at a global scale were plenty, and yet, in the case of Lehman Brothers, some substantial parts of its activities were sold to Barclays Capital (UK) for the U.S. broker dealer operations,[12] and by Nomura (Japan) for the international operations.[13]

LIVING WILL, OR HOW BANKS WANT TO BE TREATED IF THEY ARE CLOSE TO COLLAPSING

The experience of the financial crisis showed a level of improvisation that made the rescue of several financial institutions more complex and expensive than it should be. This is the planning part of crisis management. Regulators have been designing diverse forms of what the British call a "living will":

These are detailed plans that would enable banks to stipulate in advance how they would raise funds in a crisis and how their operations could be dismantled after a collapse.[14]

UNITED STATES

This process has now reached the level of implementation. The Federal Reserve Board has received the resolution plans of the 15 banks that have been asked to provide it with such a plan. As is often the case, those plans are published. The last version is dated October 1, 2013:

> *The Dodd-Frank Wall Street Reform and Consumer Protection Act requires that bank holding companies with total consolidated assets of $50 billion or more and nonbank financial companies designated by the Financial Stability Oversight Council for supervision by the Federal Reserve submit resolution plans annually to the Federal Reserve and the Federal Deposit Insurance Corporation (FDIC). Each plan, commonly known as a living will, must describe the company's strategy for rapid and orderly resolution in The Dodd-Frank Wall Street Reform and Consumer Protection Act requires that bank holding companies with total consolidated assets of $50 billion or more and nonbank financial companies designated by the Financial Stability Oversight Council for supervision by the Federal Reserve submit resolution plans annually to the Federal Reserve and the Federal Deposit Insurance Corporation (FDIC). Each plan, commonly known as a living will, must describe the company's strategy for rapid and orderly resolution in the event of material financial distress or failure of the company.*[15]

They all follow the same pattern. The published plans are an interesting reading of the principles rather than the actual action plan: they all resemble each other and have approximately 30 pages.

If we were not convinced that the detailed plan would be discussed behind closed doors, the current documents could cast a doubt on the seriousness of the Federal Reserve's approach to living wills. Do they really believe in it?

Jeffrey Lacker, the president of the Federal Reserve of Richmond, has a candid answer to that question:

> *I don't think we are where we need to be, but we're making good progress. I think people have learned a lot over the last two years in preparing these reports about what a bankruptcy filing for a large bank holding company would look like. The key objective is that in a crisis this is something a policymaker would choose as the course of action to resolve a large financial institution using the U.S. bankruptcy code, which is what it's made for, without extraordinary government*

support. If we can't get to a point where people believe policymakers would make the choice of bankruptcy in a crisis, then we're going to have too big to fail with us, because creditors will believe they will get rescued in a crisis, and we will have solved very little.[16]

THE CITI RECOVERY PLAN

I took the time to read the recovery plan of Citibank[17] one of the most global and complex U.S. bank. A glance at the other plans produces similar plans. While most of the document does not disclose anything that the Federal Reserve does not know, and even the public could have access to, the part is the high-level description of resolution strategy:

- *Save the Bank: the clear message is that it is the banking structure that will first be saved. That requires several actions: first,* **recapitalize the banking organization.** *One strategy for resolution contemplates that before a failure of Citigroup Parent, CBNA would be supported and, if necessary, recapitalized, by Citigroup Parent, which Citi believes has sufficient resources to do so even under a severe stress scenario.*
- *The second strategy is the* **sale of assets:** *wind-down or sell Citi's operations in an orderly manner that affords customers continuity of service while they migrate to other service providers. Under this strategy, Citi's businesses and assets are either sold or wound down in an orderly fashion, leveraging Citi's capital resources to fully protect depositors and its liquidity resources to enable an orderly and deliberate wind-down of its activities.*[18]

While this seems perfectly reasonable, the lessons of the previous financial crisis are contradicting these scenarios somewhat.

- The parent company does not have the money to recapitalize.
- The market was not willing to participate in such a recapitalization.
- Liquid assets generally will have been disposed of or served as additional collateral for existing liabilities.
- The remaining assets and operations would probably take months to dispose of.

The plans as they are published have not been met by a warm welcome from regulators. It is, once more, the same lawyers' blueprint that avoids taking any serious commitment. At best, it is a description of the lay of the land from which detailed plans should be drawn.

They were not prepared by the executives who would respond in the event of another financial crisis. "They are an exercise while things are fine, prepared by lawyers and not representative of what might happen," said Mark Williams, a former Federal Reserve Bank examiner and a professor of finance at Boston University.[19]

ROLE OF THE FEDERAL DEPOSIT INSURANCE CORPORATION IN THE UNITED STATES

Since the savings and loan association crisis,[20] the United States has created a recovery mechanism, a system separating good and bad banks. At the center of the banking resolution problems is the Federal Deposit Insurance Corporation (FDIC), a federal agency in charge of handling the various bank failures.

The FDIC is an independent agency created by the Congress to maintain stability and public confidence in the nation's financial system by:

- *Insuring deposits,*
- *Examining and supervising financial institutions for safety and soundness and consumer protection, and*
- *Managing receiverships.*[21]

Sheila Bair was the chair of the FDIC during the financial crisis:

Not long after she took charge in June 2006, Bair began sounding the alarm about the dangers posed by the explosive growth of subprime mortgages, which she feared would not only ravage neighborhoods when homeowners began to default—as they inevitably did—but also wreak havoc on the banking system. The F.D.I.C. was the only bank regulator in Washington to do so.[22]

This essential role has been confirmed through some essential dispositions of the Dodd-Frank Act.

Title II, the Orderly Liquidation provision of the Dodd-Frank Act, provides a process to quickly and efficiently liquidate a large, complex financial company that is close to failing. Title II provides an alternative to bankruptcy, in which the Federal Deposit Insurance Corporation (FDIC) is appointed as a receiver to carry out the liquidation and wind-up of the company. The FDIC is given certain powers as receiver, and a three to five year time frame in which to finish the liquidation process. Title II is aimed at protecting the financial stability of the American economy, forcing shareholders and creditors to bear the losses of the failed financial company, removing management that was responsible for the financial condition of the company, and ensuring that payout to claimants is at least as much as the claimants would have received under a bankruptcy liquidation.[23]

In an interview with its chairman, Jim Wigand, the FDIC gave some idea of this process:

It envisions the government seizing a failed giant at the holding company level and continuing to operate its subsidiaries. Shareholders would be wiped out, management would be replaced and a plan for resolving the company would be created and executed by a bridge company.

Wigand was unequivocal when asked if a company leaving the Orderly Liquidation Authority process would resemble the one that entered. "The answer to that is a definite no," he says. "This company has to be non-systemic as it exits the overall process."

Assets may be sold, whole lines of business may be spun off, but the company will be smaller and simpler when the FDIC is finished. The process may take longer than the six months that the FDIC anticipates running any bridge company, so Wigand says the FDIC could continue to influence the company's operations through a supervisory agreement.[24]

The FDIC will play a critical role in the resolution of bank crises. It favors a system that provides a single point of entry (SPOE) for the deficient financial institution. On December 18, it developed its rules in more detail. However, the SPOE does include risks and challenges.

In its paper on the subject, Shearman and Sterling, the U.S. global law firm articulates these considerations:

SPOE has emerged as the FDIC's preferred OLA resolution strategy in large part because of the advantages it has over other alternatives (namely, sale and liquidation and wind-down strategies) and the fact that it solves many of the resolution impediments that have been identified since the Dodd-Frank Act's enactment. In this regard, although a resolution strategy for a SIFI that contemplates a sale (rather than capitalization) of material assets to a third party has appealing aspects, it faces the fundamental challenge that there may not be acquirers with the desire and financial strength to make the acquisition even if their regulators were willing to permit such an acquisition to go forward.

A resolution strategy that contemplates a full liquidation and wind-down resolution strategy also has a number of significant risks and challenges, including, among other things, that it can be time-consuming and result in the loss of going concern value for creditors and the loss of critical services provided by the SIFI to the overall economy. In contrast to those approaches, the FDIC believes that an SPOE recapitalization can be accomplished relatively quickly, will allow the continued operation of key businesses, and is not dependent on a willing and able acquirer.

Although the SPOE strategy eliminates many of the concerns of other strategies, an SPOE strategy is not itself without issues and impediments. Among the major impediments is the risk that the effectiveness of the SPOE strategy could be impaired by the potential for ring fencing by non-US authorities that have jurisdiction over a SIFI or its assets. To address that risk, the Notice suggests that a multiple point of entry ("MPOE") resolution strategy could be utilized as an alternative. As described, the MPOE strategy would involve positioning multiple levels of holding companies in various jurisdictions that could then be used as a point of entry in the event of a crisis.[25]

The choice is well described in this article published by the *Financial Times*[26]:

Now, the FSB has decided to intervene again—to clarify exactly what it expects from the banks, in guidance issued quietly last month.

It says big global banks will be forced to choose between two "resolution mechanisms," which will dictate how they restructure themselves and ensure that crucial banking functions—payment systems, trade finance and deposit taking—can continue, no matter what happens to the larger group.

These are known as the "Single Point of Entry" (SPE) method, for banks such as Goldman Sachs and JPMorgan that operate as an integrated group, and the "Multiple Point of Entry" (MPE) method, for banks such as Santander and HSBC, that operate as locally capitalised subsidiaries.[27]

UNITED KINGDOM

It is in the United Kingdom that the concept of "living will" was used. It has been adopted as part of the dictionary in the Special Resolution regime included in the Banking Act of 2009.[28] On August 9, 2011, Brooke Masters, the chief regulation correspondent of the *Financial Times,* summarized the situation in the United Kingdom:

> *All U.K. deposit-takers and large investment firms will have to draw up "living wills" . . . that would allow them to be wound down over a weekend and quickly return assets to clients.*
>
> *Six big U.K. banks are already working on such recovery and resolution plans, part of a broad effort to avoid another banking crisis. But the Financial Services Authority said in a consultation paper on Tuesday the requirement would be extended to more than 250 banks and building societies, as well as investment firms with more than £15bn in assets.*[29]

The six main U.K. banks have indeed been dragging their feet and had to be reminded by the Special Resolution Unit of the Bank of England[30] of their living wills. The Deloitte, United Kingdom, analysis of the U.K. living wills contains a critical message: Recovery plans have to be owned by the management. It is ultimately the management that will need to commit to execute this living will, and it is not the regulators who will do it, unless they come to the ultimate sanction of replacing the management.

- *Recovery plan—A plan to prolong the ability of a firm to continue in operation through a period of crisis or stress (market wide or firm specific). The actions considered in the recovery plan could include business or asset disposals, reductions in the risk profile of the business or restructuring of liabilities. Actions should be material enough to have an impact on the capital or liquidity (or both) position of the firm. The recovery plan is owned by management.*
- *Resolution plan—A plan for the orderly resolution of the firm by the relevant resolution authority in the event a firm fails. The resolution plan will be devised and executed by the relevant authorities with a significant amount of analysis required by firms to facilitate planning by the authorities. Resolution planning will seek to avoid impacts on financial stability and maintain provision of critically important functions to the economy without exposing taxpayers to loss.*[31]

EUROPEAN BANKING RESOLUTION AND RECOVERY DIRECTIVE

Europe issued a Proposal of Banking Resolution and Recovery Directive (BRRD)[32] in the fall of 2012 and a new version of it in March 2013. This document provides for a complex way to handle the various liabilities of banks, bail-in instruments to be automatically converted into equity, and the hierarchy of liabilities that will be affected by an internal recovery plan.

The draft Directive would rely on a network of national authorities and resolution funds to resolve banks. While this network would be a major step forward to minimizing different national approaches and fragmentation of the Single Market, it would not be sufficient for Member States who share the common currency or are supervised by the European Central Bank (ECB) in the Banking Union.

Common powers and instruments aim to pre-empt bank crises and to resolve any financial institution in an orderly manner in the event of failure, whilst preserving essential bank operations and minimising taxpayers' exposure to losses.

The directive would establish a range of instruments to tackle potential bank crises at three stages: preparatory and preventative, early intervention, and resolution.

Institutions would be required to draw up recovery plans, and update them annually, setting out the measures they would take to restore their financial position in the event of significant deterioration. Resolution authorities would have to prepare resolution plans for each institution, setting out the actions they might take if an institution were to meet the conditions for resolution.

Authorities would also have the power to appoint special managers to an institution if its financial situation were to deteriorate significantly or if there were serious violations of the law.[33]

Despite these rules, Italy had to bail out its third bank in 2013. Monte dei Paschi di Siena,[34] one of the oldest banks in Europe, could have collapsed under the weight of overleverage, overpayment of the acquisition of Banco Antonveneta,[35] and a series of derivative products provided by Deutsche Bank[36] and Nomura, aiming to hide hundreds of millions of euros of losses. The contracts were kept hidden in the safe of the chairman.

Since then, Unicredit, the largest Italian bank, took the bold move to write off more than 20 billion euros to clean the consequences of bad loans to overpriced acquisitions.[37]

An agreement was reached on the delicate balance between the Member States and the Parliament in March 2014.[38]

REGULATORY TECHNICAL STANDARDS

It is the European Banking Authority that has been put in charge of the rules of the Regulatory Technical Standards (RTSs) for recovery plans. It published a series of guidelines on the scenarios, the assessment, and the contents of the bank recovery plans.

The objective of the recovery plan is to identify the options that might be available to counter a crisis, to assess whether the options are sufficiently robust and whether their nature is sufficiently varied to cope with a wide range of shocks of different natures. The key components of the recovery plan are, therefore, governance, the strategic analysis, the communication plan, and preparatory measures:

- *The governance part should allow for proper development, approval and timely implementation of recovery plans.*
- *Strategic analysis identifies the firm's core businesses as well as critical functions and sets out the key actions to be taken in relation to them and the remaining components of the firm in a stress situation.*
- *For this purpose the recovery plan should include measures to reduce the risk profile of a firm, react to liquidity shocks and reinforce capital as well as strategic options, such as divesture of business lines and restructuring of liabilities.*
- *The communication plan shall aim to ensure effective internal and external communication on issues related to implementing the recovery plan. The recovery plan shall include an analysis of preparatory measures that in a pre-recovery phase could potentially increase the effectiveness of the recovery options identified.*[39]

As the directive on this subject has not yet been finalized, it is hard to predict what those recovery plans will look like. It is, however, interesting that BNP Paribas and Deutsche Bank have already submitted their living wills to the Federal Reserve.[40]

CAN RESOLUTION RULES BE EFFECTIVE?

Crisis resolution is hard to implement unless it has some teeth. It is critical that the legal framework of resolution and recovery mechanisms be actionable without further tergiversations. The decision process during a financial crisis requires a few key individuals who have the authority to make drastic decisions and impose immediate solutions.

In his book on the financial crisis, Hank Paulson, who was secretary of the Treasury during the financial crisis, recounts the numerous conversations that took place over a period of six months prior to the collapse of Lehman Brothers. Even though it did not come as a surprise, the recovery and eventual bankruptcy of Lehman occurred over a weekend. It was dramatic and violent.[41]

The experience of the bankruptcy of Lehman Brothers has taught those who have the responsibility for financial stability that it becomes a tremendous challenge when the institution being rescued is global. Conflicts of jurisdictions at a global scale were plenty, and yet, in the case of Lehman Brothers, some substantial parts of its activities were sold to Barclays Capital (UK)[42] for the U.S. broker-dealer activities and by Nomura (Japan)[43] for the international operations.

AN IMPOSSIBLE EUROPEAN INSTITUTIONAL CHALLENGE

Can Europe design a coherent regulatory system? I asked that question in an article published in the *Columbia Journal of European Law Online*.[44] There is no doubt that the normal challenges of resolution and recovery are compounded in an environment where 27 countries, legal systems, jurisdictions, banking tradition, and cultures are as different as they could be in Frankfurt and Malta or London and Slovakia.

It would therefore be unfair to expect the same level of progress and the same commonality in Europe as it exists in the United States. On top of that, several chapters of European regulation have already been implemented in home countries, whether it is the United Kingdom, Germany, France, or Italy.

Having stated—and emphasized—those difficulties, however, one is entitled to look at the objectives of banking regulation.

The initiative taken by the countries that utilize the euro as their currency, the eurozone, to create a banking union is as remarkable as it is frightening. The audacity of the project cannot be underestimated.

Can the European Banking Union become the reality the Europeans would like it to be? Probably not. But the most interesting and challenging question is, under its historical and cultural diversity, what would it take to achieve the ambitions of the banking union?

The European banking union has three components: first, a single supervisory mechanism (SSM) that confers to the European Central Bank the ultimate regulatory authority on banks in the eurozone.

The European Central Bank (ECB) is preparing to take on new banking supervision tasks as part of a single supervisory mechanism.
The single supervisory mechanism will create a new system of financial supervision comprising the ECB and the national competent authorities of participating E.U. countries. Among these

E.U. countries are those whose currency is the euro and those whose currency is not the euro but who have decided to enter into close cooperation with the single supervisory mechanism.[45]

The second pillar is a European deposit guarantee scheme (DGS). It is the most difficult part of the European banking union and the least likely to see the light of day any time soon. One cannot imagine that banks would become mutually responsible for actions that might affect their deposits and would come to a sort of reciprocal rescue. Can any scheme cover a €6.9 trillion deposit risk? See Table 9.1 and Figure 9.1.

The third pillar that concerns the resolution and recovery of the eurozone banks is included in the draft directive issued by the European Commission:

The proposed directive is aimed at providing national authorities with common powers and instruments to pre-empt bank crises and to resolve any financial institution in an orderly manner in the event of failure, whilst preserving essential bank operations and minimising taxpayers' exposure to losses.

The directive would establish a range of instruments to tackle potential bank crises at three stages: preparatory and preventative, early intervention, and resolution.

Institutions would be required to draw up recovery plans, and update them annually, setting out the measures they would take to restore their financial position in the event of significant deterioration. Resolution authorities would have to prepare resolution plans for each institution, setting out the actions they might take if an institution were to meet the conditions for resolution.

Authorities would also have the power to appoint special managers to an institution if its financial situation were to deteriorate significantly or if there were serious violations of the law.[46]

It is currently being tested in the case of the Royal Bank of Scotland (RBS)[47] in the United Kingdom where the decisions will be taken to split the good and the bad bank.

WHO WILL DECIDE TO PUT COMPANIES UNDER RESOLUTION SURVEILLANCE?

The unanswered question of this system is whether it is compatible with the European Union principle of subsidiarity. Lisa McKenna, a student of my seminar at Columbia Law School, wrote a remarkable paper on the sub-

TABLE 9.1 Breakdown of Deposits in Major European Countries, End 2012

| | Deposits € bn | | | | | % of Total Deposits | | | | | |
| | ELIGIBLE | | | | | ELIGIBLE | | | | | |
	Covered	Not Covered	Total Eligible	NOT ELIGIBLE	TOTAL	Covered	Not Covered	Total Eligible	NOT ELIGIBLE	TOTAL	Not Covered & Not Eligible
Italy	461	215	676	449	1,125	41%	19%	60%	40%	100%	59%
UK	925	485	1,410	338	1,748	53%	28%	81%	19%	100%	47%
Belgium	212	90	302	92	393	54%	23%	77%	23%	100%	46%
Portugal	91	56	147	15	162	56%	35%	91%	9%	100%	44%
Sweden	143	96	239	0	239	60%	40%	100%	0%	100%	40%
Greece	103	30	133	28	161	64%	19%	83%	17%	100%	36%
Netherlands	421	121	542	72	615	68%	20%	88%	12%	100%	32%
Ireland	97	35	132	0	132	74%	26%	100%	0%	100%	26%
Germany	1,799	612	2,411	0	2,411	75%	25%	100%	0%	100%	25%
France	1,191	406	1,597	0	1,597	75%	25%	100%	0%	100%	25%
Spain	747	149	896	65	961	78%	15%	93%	7%	100%	22%
Total	6,189	2,295	8,485	1,059	9,544	65%	24%	89%	11%	100%	35%

Sources: EU, RTD, Bank of England, ECB, and Barclays Research.

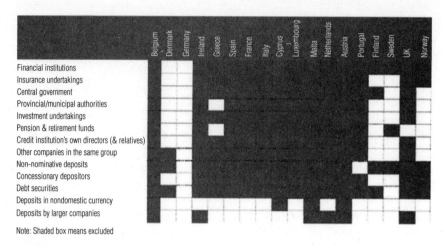

FIGURE 9.1 Deposit Insurance Exclusions

ject. Unfortunately, her conclusion does not support the statements of the European Commission:

> *I argue that the currently proposed SRM (the "proposed SRM") does not fulfill the principle of subsidiarity enshrined in the Treaty of the European Union. The principle of subsidiarity requires that the European Union should only act in an area if the objectives of the proposed actions (1) cannot be achieved by the member states and (2) will be better achieved at the Union level.[48] While current national resolution mechanisms are undoubtedly subpar, the principle of subsidiarity also requires that the objectives of the SRM be better performed at the union level than the national. I assert that the proposed SRM would not do a better job of regulating bank resolution than national governments carrying out a uniform resolution law. In fact, the proposed SRM will do little without concurrent implementation of more far-reaching reforms. I argue that it is only with the creation of a European Federal Deposit Insurance Corporation (European FDIC)—a new, independent mechanism that combines a centralized resolution authority, a common resolution fund and a pan-European deposit guarantee scheme—that a SRM would better manage bank failures and resolutions. While both systems would face numerous legal challenges to their implementation, a European FDIC would satisfy the principle of subsidiarity, and the proposed SRM cannot. As a result, a European FDIC authority is both more legally and practically robust policy option than the proposed SRM.[49]*

The documents issued by the European Commission divulge an intricate web of decision processes as well as institutions that make its project close to impossible to implement (see Figure 9.2).

What the directive calls the decision about nonviability is, of course, the most critical one. The European Commission is trying to take that responsibility and making it political rather than technical.

It would be less problematic if the decision maker were single and fast. Political intricacies create a web of decision makers that ensure its failure.

Resolution is triggered following a process ensuring that a justified and impartial decision is taken in respect of any failing bank:

- *the ECB, as bank supervisor, notifies that a bank is failing to Commission, to the Resolution Board and to the relevant national authorities and ministries the Resolution Board assesses if there is a systemic threat and no private sector solution;*
- *if so, the Resolution Board recommends to the Commission to initiate resolution;*
- *the Commission decides to initiate resolution and indicates to the Resolution Board the framework for applying the resolution tools and for using the Fund to support the resolution action. The*

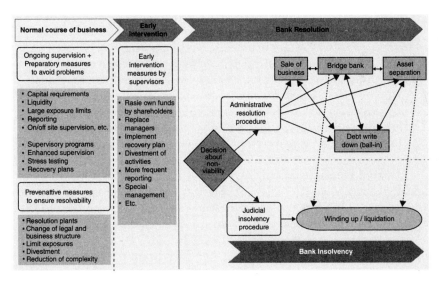

FIGURE 9.2 European Timeline for Bank Resolution
Source: http://eur lex.europa.eu/LexUriServ/LexUriServ.do?uri=COM:2013:0 520:FIN:EN:PDF

Resolution Board adopts, through a decision addressed to the national resolution authorities, a resolution scheme setting out the resolution tools, actions, and funding measures, and instructing the relevant national resolution authorities to execute the resolution measures;

■ *the national resolution authorities execute the resolution measures decided by the Board according to the national law. If the national resolution authorities do not comply with the decisions of the Board, the Board has the power to supersede the national resolution authorities and address certain decisions for the implementation of the resolution measures directly to the banks.*[50]

Any resolution process that includes so many decision makers is probably doomed to fail.

In a remarkable piece on this decision process, the Brussels-based European think tank group Bruegel asked exactly this question. It compares the two last versions of the decision process that demonstrated the overwhelming addition of European Commission competencies.

On December 12, the Economic and Financial Affairs Council (ECOFIN) agreed on the principles of banking resolution:

This law, which applies to all 28 Member States, is an essential piece of the financial regulatory framework that we are building piece by piece for all banks of the European Union in order to draw the lessons from the crisis. Ensuring that failing banks can be wound down in a predictable and efficient way with minimum recourse to public money is fundamental to restoring confidence in Europe's financial sector. The Single Resolution Mechanism, once in place, will be the authority applying these new rules in the context of the Banking Union. With these new rules in place, massive public bail-outs of banks and their consequences for taxpayers will finally be a practice of the past.[51]

It is hard to believe that the Ministers of Finance of the European Union actually believe what they stated. Either it is communication, and it is misleading, or it is incompetence, which would not really be surprising in view of their previous decisions, interventions, and statements.

The last version that emerged in December 2013 is, as Table 9.2 shows, an attempt of the European Commission to establish its leadership on the resolution process. If one can have doubts about the ECOFIN expertise, there is no doubt that the European Commission is a political body with no competence at all in banking resolution. Since they work on the basis of unanimity, once they get into action, they will delay the process, transform it

TABLE 9.2 Comparison of the Initial and Summer 2013 EU Commission Recovery and Resolution Decision Process

	Which level decides which banks to resolve & how?	
	Original Commission Proposal, Summer 2012 (BRRD)	Commission Proposal, Summer 2013 (BRRD + SRM-SBRF)
Who creates a recovery plan to prevent the failure of a troubled bank?	Banks create their own plans, which are approved by the relevant supervisor (either national or SSM).	Banks create their own plans, which are approved by the relevant supervisor (either national or SSM).
Who initiates resolution of a failed bank?	Member States' supervisors based on rules set out in the BRRD.	Resolution Board based on information provided by the ECB and based on rules set out in the BRRD. The Commission approves the Resolution Board's decision.
Who creates the bank resolution plan?	NRA with recommendations from the Systemic Risk Board and European Banking Authority.	The Commission creates the general plan, with the Executive portion of the Resolution Board determining the specific plan. Both are guided by the BRRD toolkit.
Who creates cross-border resolution plans?	Resolution Colleges including the national resolution authorities and the EBA.	The Commission creates the general plan, with the Executive portion of the Resolution Board determining the specific plan. Both are guided by the BRRD toolkit.
Who implements the plan?	NRA	NRA
Who oversees the implementation?	Commission to the extent that the NRA's actions violate the BRRD.	Resolution Board
Sanctions for non-compliance with EU directives/plans?	Commission following the normal procedures as per the TFEU.	The Resolution Board can circumvent the National Resolution Authority and directly implement the part of the plan the NRA is not in compliance with.
How is the plan funded?	National Resolution Funds	Single Bank Resolution Fund

Source: Christopher Gandrud and Mark Hallerberg, "Who Decides? Resolving Failed Banks in a European Framework," *Bruegel,* November 29, 2013. www.bruegel.org/publications/publication-detail/publication/803-who-decides-resolving-failed-banks-in-a-european-framework/.

into a political arena, and their decisions will intervene too late, while their ability to intervene will probably be disastrous.

The way the European Commission handled the European sovereign crisis does not leave any doubt that, in a field where they have some experience, public finance, they will not act effectively. It took two years for the Commission to come up with the disastrous Greek settlement and the even more disastrous Cyprus decisions.

That does not mean that nothing was done.[52]

One of the keys of the new resolution regimes is a decision made by the authorities to put a financial institution under closer supervision to resolve the crisis. While the FDIC does have a long practice of such decisions, there is no common practice at the European level.

Over and above these considerations, we need to be aware that if this should apply to a global financial institution, the decision will be extraordinarily difficult, controversial, and litigated.

Many will pretend that it is that decision that prompted the collapse of the institutions, and that it would have survived had the authorities not announced this extreme measure. That will put enormous pressure on the government(s) involved and their agencies.

The collapse of Lehman Brothers has given us a taste of the differences that existed between the United Kingdom and United States. Needless to say, it might be even more difficult for banks operating in less similar legal and regulatory systems.

NOTES

1. www.bankofengland.co.uk/FINANCIALSTABILITY/Pages/role/risk_reduction/srr/default.aspx.
2. Alexandre Lamfalussy, *In Search of a New World Monetary Order*. Bern, Switzerland: Peter Lang International Academic Publishers, October 2012, p. 171.
3. http://lexicon.ft.com/Term?term=moral-hazard.
4. http://dictionary.cambridge.org/us/dictionary/business-english/moral-hazard.
5. http://voices.yahoo.com/what-moral-hazard-devastate-the-8080702.html.
6. Florian Hett and Alexander Schmidt, "Do Bank Bail-Outs Create Moral Hazard? Evidence from the Recent Financial Crisis," March 1, 2012. www.iwh-halle.de/d/start/news/workshops/20120524/pdf/hett.pd.
7. www.mhfigi.com/wp-content/uploads/2013/09/Five-Years-Later-Paper-by-Jeff-Shafer1.pdf.

8. In a nutshell, a bailout is the injection from outside of additional capital to avoid the financial institution's falling into bankruptcy. Bail-in is a mechanism whereby some liabilities are subject to a "haircut" that decreases their value and, by doing so, recapitalizes the financial institution from within the institution.

9. http://lexicon.ft.com/Term?term=bail_in.

10. John C. Coffee Jr., "Bail-Ins versus Bail-Outs: Using Contingent Capital to Mitigate Systemic Risk." Columbia Law and Economics Working Paper No. 380, October 22, 2010. http://papers.ssrn.com/sol3/papers.cfm?abstract_id=1675015.

11. William R. Rhodes, *Banker to the World: Leadership Lessons from the Front Lines of Global Finance.* New York: McGraw-Hill, 2011.

12. Three days after Barclays, the British bank, failed to reach a deal that would have salvaged Lehman Brothers, it announced Wednesday that it had struck an agreement to buy the broken investment firm's core capital markets businesses for the fire-sale price of $1.75 billion—far less than Lehman had hoped for. www.nytimes.com/2008/09/18/business/worldbusiness/18barclays.html?pagewanted=all&_r=0.

13. This is the presentation Nomura made to its investors on this acquisition. www.nomuraholdings.com/investor/summary/financial/data/2009_2q_leh.pdf.

14. http://lexicon.ft.com/Term?term=living-wills.

15. www.federalreserve.gov/bankinforeg/resolution-plans.htm.

16. www.charlotteobserver.com/2013/11/08/4447563/feds-lacker-on-bank-crisis-bernanke.html#.Un6IruK6nj4.

17. This is the content of the Citibank plan:
Summary: "Citi is stronger than ever" (5 pp)
List of material entities: (1 p)
Description of Core Business lines (4 pp): definition of each business in four lines.
Summary Financial Information: "Citi's funding and liquidity objectives generally are to maintain liquidity to fund its existing asset base as well as grow its core businesses in Citicorp" followed by a summary of financial data. For the rest: got to the last SEC report. (3 pp)
Derivative business: No numbers. Go to SEC filing. (1 p)
Resolution process: in case we thought it would be easy: a complex web of committees, functions, legal entity, and business line management structures work together to support the development and implementation of Citi's resolution planning submission
List of membership of Financial Market Utilities (1 p)
Description of International operations: information including their share of revenues, income and average assets. (4 pp)

Material Supervisory Authorities: the regulatory jungle (1 p)
Principal officers (1 p)
Description of Material information Systems: a great IT mapping (2 pp)

18. www.federalreserve.gov/bankinforeg/resolution-plans/citigroup-1g-20131001.pdf, p. 28.
19. www.nytimes.com/2012/07/04/business/living-wills-of-how-to-un-wind-big-banks-are-released.html.
20. FDIC, "The Savings and Loan Crisis and Its Relation to Banking." Chapter 4 of *An Examination of the Banking Crises of the 1980s and Early 1990s.* www.fdic.gov/bank/historical/history/167_188.pdf.
21. http://www.fdic.gov/.
22. Joe Nocera, "Sheila Bair's Bank Shot." *New York Times*, July 9, 2011. www.nytimes.com/2011/07/10/magazine/sheila-bairs-exit-interview.html?pagewanted=all.
23. Cornell University Law School, Law Information Institute. www.law.cornell.edu/wex/dodd-frank_title_ii.
24. Barbara Rehm, "FDIC Preps Plan to Flesh Out Big Bank Resolution Process,"*American Banker*, June 14, 2013. www.americanbanker.com/issues/178_115/fdic-preps-plan-to-flesh-out-big-bank-resolution-process-1059876-1.html
25. www.shearman.com/en/newsinsights/publications/2013/12/the-volcker-rule–a-comparison.
26. Ibid.
27. www.ft.com/intl/cms/s/0/41be5e44-f2ae-11e2-a203-00144feabdc0.html?siteedition=intl#axzz2b4kw1WGL.
28. www.legislation.gov.uk/ukpga/2009/1/contents.
29. www.deloitte.com/view/en_GB/uk/industries/financial-services/issues-trends/living-wills/index.htm.
30. www.ft.com/intl/cms/s/0/84a3915e-c28e-11e0-9ede-00144feabdc0.html#axzz2kI0vvJvl.
31. www.deloitte.com/view/en_GB/uk/industries/financial-services/issues-trends/living-wills/index.htm.
32. The proposed Directive on Bank Recovery and Resolution (BRRD) would, when adopted, determine the rules for how EU banks in difficulties were restructured, how vital functions for the real economy were maintained, and how losses and costs were allocated to the banks' shareholders and creditors. It would provide more comprehensive and effective arrangements to deal with failing banks at national level, as well as arrangements to tackle cross-border banking failures.
33. www.consilium.europa.eu/uedocs/cms_data/docs/pressdata/en/ecofin/137627.pdf.

34. Valentina Pop, "Monti and Draghi Under Fire in Italian Bank Scandal," *EU Observer*, January 25, 2013. http://euobserver.com/economic/118845.

35. Silvia Ognibene, "Italy Police Search Monte Paschi over Antonveneta Deal," Reuters, May 9, 2012. www.reuters.com/article/2012/05/09/us-montepaschi-taxpolice-searches-idUSBRE8481CI20120509.

36. Elisa Martinuzzi and Nicholas Dunbar, "Deutsche Bank Derivative Helped Monte Paschi Mask Losses," Bloomberg, January 17, 2013. www.bloomberg.com/news/2013-01-17/deutsche-bank-derivative-helped-monte-paschi-mask-losses.html.

37. www.bloomberg.com/news/2014-03-11/unicredit-posts-record-loss-on-bad-loans-goodwill-writedowns.html.

38. www.europeanvoice.com/article/2014/march/deal-reached-on-banking-union/80162.aspx.

39. www.eba.europa.eu/regulation-and-policy/recovery-and-resolution/draft-regulatory-technical-standards-on-the-content-of-recovery-plans/-/regulatory-activity/consultation-paper.

40. www.federalreserve.gov/bankinforeg/resolution-plans.htm.

41. Henry M. Paulson, *On the Brink: Inside the Race to Stop the Collapse of the Global Financial System.*" New York: Hachette Group, 2010.

42. Three days after Barclays, the British bank, failed to reach a deal that would have salvaged Lehman Brothers, it announced that it had struck an agreement to buy the broken investment firm's core U.S. capital markets businesses for the fire-sale price of $1.75 billion—far less than Lehman had hoped for. www.nytimes.com/2008/09/18/business/worldbusiness/18barclays.html?pagewanted=all&_r=0.

43. This is the presentation Nomura made to its investors on this acquisition. www.nomuraholdings.com/investor/summary/financial/data/2009_2q_leh.pdf.

44. Georges Ugeux, "Can Europe Design a Coherent Regulatory System?" *Columbia Journal of European Law Online* 18, 2012. www.cjel.net/wp-content/uploads/2012/09/ugeux_1-18.pdf.

45. www.ecb.europa.eu/ssm/html/index.en.html.

46. www.consilium.europa.eu/uedocs/cms_data/docs/pressdata/en/ecofin/137627.pdf.

47. From Andrew Tyrie MP: Sir, The Parliamentary Commission on Banking Standards welcomes the assurance of the chancellor of the exchequer in his Mansion House speech in June that the government will seek "the right sale" of the Royal Bank of Scotland rather than "a quick sale." We also welcome his support for our report's twin objectives of maximizing RBS's ability to support the U.K. economy and getting value for money

for the taxpayer. www.ft.com/intl/cms/s/0/323d8b46-0bf6-11e3-8f77-00144feabdc0.html.

48. European Union, Treaty of the European Union, Article 5, March, 2010. http://eur-lex.europa.eu/LexUriServ.do?uri=OJ:2010:083:0001:0012:EN:PDF.

49. Lisa Mc Kenna, "Subsidiarity and the Proposed Single Resolution Mechanism: The Case for a European Federal Deposit Insurance Corporation." Columbia Law School, seminar on "European Banking and Finance."

50. http://eur-lex.europa.eu/LexUriServ/LexUriServ.do?uri=COM:2013:0520:FIN:EN:PDF.

51. http://europa.eu/rapid/press-release_MEMO-13-1140_en.htm?locale=en.

52. http://europa.eu/rapid/press-release_MEMO-13-1168_en.htm.

CHAPTER 10

Banking and Shadow Banking

"On its own, a bank capital requirement has the effect of pushing intermediation into the shadow banks, leaving a vulnerability if that sector becomes overleveraged."

—Bank of England Former Deputy Governor Paul Tucker

As new regulations are affecting banks and a variety of regulators affect their ability to operate, banks will need more equity and will not be able to grow as fast as they did. This evolution will fuel the development of alternative sources of financing (see Figure 10.1).

What we learned from the financial crisis is that even shadow banking cannot be left unregulated, and requires some form of oversight and rules. The sense of urgency is increasing as we realize that the needs of the economy are growing again while the capital adequacy and liquidity ratios of Basel III might make financing less readily available from the banking sector.

The question is therefore not to banish or eradicate shadow banking. This is particularly true for Europe, where the bulk of the financial needs of the economy are provided by commercial banks through loans rather than from capital markets through securities financing.

HEDGE FUNDS

The Hedge Fund Association (HFA) is an international not-for-profit industry trade and nonpartisan lobbying organization devoted to advancing transparency, development, and trust in alternative

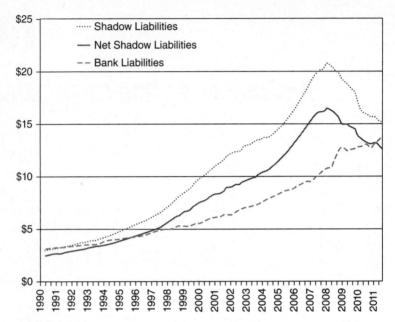

FIGURE 10.1   Shadow Bank Liabilities vs. Traditional Bank Liabilities (in $ trillions)
Source: Flow of Funds Accounts of the United States as of 2011: Q3 (FRB) and FRBNY. www.ny.frb.org/research/staff_reports/sr458.pdf.

investments. Membership in the HFA includes hedge fund firms; global financial institutions with hedge fund offerings, including private banks, asset management firms, and broker-dealers; investors, including funds of hedge funds, family offices, public and private pension funds, endowments and foundations, high-net-worth individuals, and allocators; and service providers, including prime brokers, administrators, custodians, auditors, lawyers, risk managers, technologists, and third-party marketers.[1]

Hedge funds have been the focus of a lot of attention, and were demonized for a number of reasons, one of which was their activism and corporate actions. Their resistance to even a mild form of regulation decided by the Securities and Exchange Commission (SEC) culminated in a Washington court decision that canceled that decision.

The U.S. Court of Appeals for the District of Columbia has invalidated rules requiring certain hedge fund advisers to register with the SEC as investment advisers. The SEC has decided not to appeal the court's ruling, and is instead moving ahead on an aggressive agenda of rulemaking in light of the court's decision. Hedge fund advisers should consider the practical implications of the court's decision.[2]

United States

The resistance of hedge funds to regulation was made impossible by the 2008 financial crisis. The Dodd-Frank Act provides for some limitations to the direct ownership of hedge funds by banks. It does not, however, deal with the financing of hedge funds, generally provided by banks through their prime brokerage operations.

Europe

In Europe, the alternative investment fund managers (AIFM) directive sets up limitations on the activities of the hedge funds and other alternative investment vehicles.

The landmark agreement on the supervision package provided the foundations for a more stable and secure financial system in Europe. We must now build on these foundations by introducing strong and intelligent regulation for all financial markets, products, and actors. Today's agreement on the AIFM directive is an important step in this direction. The directive will increase transparency, reinforce investor protection, and strengthen the internal market in a responsible and nondiscriminatory manner. It will also make full use of the opportunities afforded by the new European supervisory authorities to strengthen supervision and to enhance the macroprudential oversight of this sector." (Statement by Commissioner Barnier.)[3]

This directive was a major source of discontent from the United Kingdom, where most hedge funds were located. Relocation to Switzerland[4] started as a result of this directive.

OTHER TYPES OF SHADOW BANKING

Shadow banking goes well beyond hedge funds, and the development of a new securitization market will be a source of major disagreements between the Anglo-Saxon approach and continental Europe. Securitization will, however, continue to be essential to finance economic growth.

One of the sources of the subprime crisis was the nonregulation of 13,000 sellers of mortgage products that were financed by banks and refinanced by the Fannie Mae[5] and Freddie Mac,[6] two government agencies that needed to be nationalized during the financial crisis.[7]

The U.S. mortgage market is entirely in the hands of those two institutions. The loans granted by banks, even though they are granted directly by the bank to its customer, do not remain on the balance sheets of the banks that do not keep any of the risks associated with those loans. Together, the two government-sponsored enterprises carry $4 trillion of those loans on their balance sheets.

CAPITAL MARKETS AND SECURITIZATION

There is an understanding that bad U.S. subprime lending, not the more simple highly rated pools of mortgages that made up most European securitisations, was at the root of the financial crisis. Global bank regulators and European insurance overseers have just eased demands for the amount of capital to be held against asset-backed bonds. Progress indeed, writes the Financial Times *Lex column of January 2, 2014.*[8]

In this context, the role of capital markets will be crucial, and market participants, whether they are investment banks or trading activities of large global banks, will need to benefit from a global regulatory framework that provides common rules and transparency.

Securitization was considered as the source of the problems of the U.S. financial crisis, and especially the subprime crisis. It became a synonym of financial fraud. However, we should not confuse the instrument and the abuse that was made of it.

Securitization is a process whereby a bank is "packaging" a series of assets (car loans, credit card loans, asset-based financing) into one single security that is rated and provides a yield to the owner of the security. Securitized loans were then placed, through a private placement or public offering, in the capital markets and subscribed by institutional investors and hedge funds. So far, there is nothing reprehensible to this technique that corresponds to another form of collateralized financing.

However, asset-based securities (ABSs) were not issued by a real borrower, let alone by the bank that was selling—and getting rid of—those loans. It was issued by a special-purpose vehicle (SPV) that was borrowing against those securities. Nothing could be done to change the nature of the assets or negotiate changes of terms and conditions on the loans.

The securitization was fraud with several anomalies. First, the banks were not exercising what would be a normal credit underwriting. They were lending against the assets without consideration for the ability of the customer to service the debt. Second, the loans were accompanied by a two-year "tease," in other words, a reduced interest rate, and the inevitable increase of the rates after two years was lost in the marketing brochures in a mischievous, albeit legal, way. Third, the securities were rated by complacent rating agencies that were competing for fees and rated many of those assets with the highest AAA/Aaa rating.

The combination of these three key precautions that were not taken created securities: those were not worth the value that was presented to the subscribers, mostly institutions and hedge funds. As in musical chairs, when the music stopped, one by one, those securities started losing value, and the market collapsed. This subprime crisis was the start of the U.S. financial crisis. It is also those securities that were massively purchased by banks since they had a prime rating and a better return than bonds.

Some abusive practices of the securitization process do not disqualify the process itself. Securitization is starting again and will become essential to the funding of the banks and the financing of the economy.

With the recent Chinese developments, worries about shadow banking in emerging markets are increasing. The Bank of England's Mark Carney sees shadow banking in emerging markets as biggest global risk:

> *Bank of England Governor Mark Carney has warned that the global financial crisis is rotating from West to East, with shadow banking excesses in emerging markets now posing the biggest threat to the international economy.*[9]

It makes the analysis of the impact of the extraterritorial implications of U.S. securitization regulation on Asian markets particularly important.[10]

New initiatives have been taken as authorities are gradually realizing that the economy will not survive without some form of asset securitization. "IOSCO and the Basel Committee are close to agreeing on a working group to look at how the securitization markets are working, and to see whether new thinking is needed," IOSCO Secretary General David Wright told Reuters on the sidelines of a Chatham House financial conference in March 2014.[11]

NOTES

1. http://thehfa.org/aboutus.
2. www.dechert.com/files/Publication/bcf4b9dd-5bf3-40b7-81dc-7c66cab77162/Presentation/PublicationAttachment/f465ff8d-09c2-40e1-8049-7f581550a7ca/FS_Issue6_august.pdf.

3. http://eur-lex.europa.eu/LexUriServ/LexUriServ.do?uri=OJ:L:2011:174 :0001:0073:EN:PDF.

4. The BBC asked in 2010 whether U.K. hedge funds will take a role in Switzerland. http://news.bbc.co.uk/2/hi/business/8518208.stm.

5. "As the leading source of residential mortgage credit in the U.S. secondary market, Fannie Mae is supporting today's economic recovery and laying the foundation for a better housing finance system. We guarantee and purchase loans from mortgage lenders to ensure families can buy homes, refinance, or rent a good home." www.fanniemae.com/portal/about-us/company-overview/about-fm.html.

6. "Freddie Mac was chartered by Congress in 1970 with a public mission to stabilize the nation's residential mortgage markets and expand opportunities for homeownership and affordable rental housing. Our statutory mission is to provide liquidity, stability and affordability to the U.S. housing market. We participate in the secondary mortgage market by purchasing mortgage loans and mortgage-related securities for investment and by issuing guaranteed mortgage-related securities, principally those we call PCs. The secondary mortgage market consists of institutions engaged in buying and selling mortgages in the form of whole loans (i.e., mortgages that have not been securitized) and mortgage-related securities. We do not lend money directly to homeowners." www.freddiemac.com/corporate/company_profile/.

7. "The Bush administration seized control of the nation's two largest mortgage finance companies on Sunday, seeking to shrink drastically their outsize influence on Wall Street and on Capitol Hill while at the same time counting on them to pull the nation out of its worst housing crisis in decades." www.nytimes.com/2008/09/08/business/08fannie.html?pagewanted=all.

8. www.ft.com/intl/cms/s/3/fccde7d6-6982-11e3-89ce-00144feabdc0.html?siteedition=intl#axzz2pFkl2uQc.

9. www.telegraph.co.uk/finance/mark-carney/10516661/Bank-of-Englands-Mark-Carney-sees-shadow-banking-in-emerging-markets-as-biggest-global-risk.html.

10. www.gfma.org%2FInitiatives%2FConsistency-of-Implementation %2FGFMA-Views-on-the-Impact-of-US-Extraterritorial-Legislation-on-the-Asian-Markets%2F&ei=dn_FUsvyO8mtsQTC94HgDQ&usg= AFQjCNEN4Ym9ZiX0uXgIq3TVrsRspFk9OQ&sig2=WchZWtx5Z wRs3Sto3KE5Wg&bvm=bv.58187178,d.cWc.

11. http://www.reuters.com/article/2014/03/17/us-markets-securitisation-idUSBREA2G0TT20140317.

CHAPTER 11

Rating Agencies and Auditors

"The regulatory landscape for rating agencies has been irrevocably changed. Governments have put in place many new rules and regulations to address the issues that led to the crisis. Rating agencies are subject to regulatory controls that did not exist before."

—Standard & Poor's President Doug Peterson

It might be surprising to some that rating agencies and external auditors are put in one category. It is not just because they both miserably failed to identify the weaknesses of financial institutions. Their role in the financial world is arguably even more important than in other industries.

Their function is to provide some form of assurance and valuation of the quality of the financial structure (rating agencies) and the accounts (auditors). They pass a judgment that is supposed to have two characteristics: independence and objectivity. As such, by giving a rating to a bank or approving their accounts, they give guidance to investors and regulators, clients, and depositors. Or at least we thought so until things appeared very different than the reality.

PART I: THE RATING AGENCIES

The rating of banks and financial instruments was influenced by a number of elements. At the bottom of this, three realities emerged from the financial crisis.

1. Their competition was deadly and led to price cuttings, and the quality and the quantity of their work was affected.

2. The fact that they were paid by those they had to judge was creating a strange relationship.
3. Their ownership was in the hands of private companies that were expecting profits ahead of anything else.

The kiss of death was the rating of collateralized securities that were only as good as the underlying assets. However, rating agencies, for the fees they got paid by the bankers, would not look at the quality of the underwriting of the financial institutions. They were giving a rating on the basis of a blend of securities that were modelized.

Ultimately, so many securities were issued that they lent the models to the issuer. Any student who receives the questions and the answers before a test or an examination would do the same. The banks found various ways of gaming the system while the rating agencies turned a blind eye and generously granted an AAA rating to securities whose underlying assets were never really assessed.

Having watched depositions by executives of the rating agencies in front of the U.S. congressional hearings,[1] I was struck by the contrast between the first day, when former executives explained what the daily reality was in churning ratings, and how they were received by their hierarchy, and the second day, where current executives were miserably trying to say that these were only isolated incidents.

Some damning e-mails emerged in a recent lawsuit filed by the liquidators of Bear Stearns in November 2013:

> *In a 141-page complaint, the liquidators cite a trove of emails— some of which had already surfaced in earlier cases—which they say show that the agencies knew their high-quality ratings on the mortgage bonds were a sham.*
>
> *"It could be structured by cows and we would rate it," an S&P employee said to a co-worker in a text message from 2007.*
>
> *"We sold our soul to the devil for revenue," a Moody's employee said in an internal document.*
>
> *In an email, another S&P employee called the firm's ratings practices a "scam."*[2]

Regulating Rating Agencies

The SEC under a special act regulates the U.S. rating agencies.[3] One of the first actions taken deprived rating agencies of their nonaccountability. Unbelievably, they were deemed to be considered as media, and therefore were protected by the freedom of the press. They could not be made accountable, let alone sued.

The Dodd-Frank Act changed that system, and made rating agencies accountable for their judgment and liable to pursuits by parties who could prove the damage they suffered as a result of the ratings.

> *Credit rating agencies should make investors aware of the data on the probability of default of credit ratings and rating outlooks based on historical performance, as published on the central repository created by ESMA.*[4]

Since then, everybody has tried to break the logjam of the payment of the rating agencies. Nobody found a volunteer to pay. I am advocating that the fees to the rating be structured in such a way that, rather than being paid by the issuer who has a vested interest in getting the best possible rating, they become part of the issuance costs. It creates a neutrality of the origin of the fees and decreases the risk of fees paid by interested parties.

Sovereign Ratings

Fourteen countries still enjoy an AAA rating from Standard & Poor's (see Figure 11.1).

The idea to create a public European rating agency for sovereign ratings became very popular in Europe.[5] It was a knee-jerk reaction to the abundance and timelessness of the downgrading of European sovereign bonds. I must confess that I was sometimes mystified by the justifications of some of the changes of rating.

If there is an area where oversight by the Securities and Exchange Commission (SEC) is not appropriate, it is the sovereign ratings: they have neither the competency nor the expertise to rate foreign countries.

I am pleading for a special form of oversight: The International Monetary Fund (IMF) could take on this responsibility, even though it does not like the idea of that new accountability. The IMF would have to approve the methodology. After all, it is itself the nonofficial rating agency of the world's economies. It does have the expertise and experience to exercise that approval.

Periodically, the rating agencies would be audited by the IMF experts, not on the merits of their ratings, but on their compliance with their own models and rules. This would provide some integrity to the rating system without interference in the actual ratings.

However, we should not forget that ratings, as convenient as they are to investors and traders, are not a substitute for their homework, and should no longer allow them to abandon the sound principles of credit analysis. To their credit, rating agencies, despite the unfortunate error during the downgrading of the United States,[6] have gone a long way in explaining their methods, rules, and criteria.

Country	Rating ▼	Outlook	Date
United Kingdom	AAA	Negative	2012-04-13
Australia	AAA	Stable	2012-02-20
Canada	AAA	Stable	2012-02-20
Denmark	AAA	Stable	2012-02-20
Finland	AAA	Stable	2012-02-20
Germany	AAA	Stable	2013-03-27
Hong Kong	AAA	Stable	2011-11-29
Liechtenstein	AAA	Stable	2011-11-29
Luxembourg	AAA	Stable	2013-08-12
Netherlands	AAA	Negative	2012-07-24
Norway	AAA	Stable	2011-11-29
Singapore	AAA	Stable	2011-11-29
Sweden	AAA	Stable	2012-10-24
Switzerland	AAA	Stable	2011-11-29

FIGURE 11.1 Countries with AAA Ratings from S&P
Source: http://en.wikipedia.org/wiki/List_of_countries_by_credit_rating.

PART II: EXTERNAL AUDITORS

Historically, companies have had some form of audit committee reporting on the quality of the financial reports. However, those were often insiders or quasi-insiders, and their credibility was weak, as it still is in Japan, as we saw in the Fujitsu case.[7]

It is from the United States and the United Kingdom that the practice of outside independent auditors was developed. Unfortunately, after the collapse of Arthur Andersen, the number of major global agencies is down to four. Smaller independent auditing firms also had their fair share of scandals. None of the biggest frauds of the past 20 years could have happened without some form or another of complicity or complacency of the external auditors.

This situation creates a huge problem of conflicts of interest, and this oligopoly (I was about to talk about oligarchy) of PricewaterhouseCoopers, Deloitte, Ernst & Young, and KPMG exercises a huge influence.

The Regulation of External Auditors

For a number of years, the industry was fundamentally self-regulated. It never was considered to be liable for its opinion.

It was the closeness of Enron and Arthur Andersen, evidenced by the practice of auditors being recruited by the company, that created a form of complicity between auditors and financial executives. This led to the production of fraud accounts, the death of its chairman and CEO, Kenneth Lay, and the jailing of the previous CEO, Jeffrey Skilling.

One of the solutions to this potential conflict of interest could be the prohibition for auditors to be hired by the companies they audit themselves. From a self-regulatory system, the oversight of the profession and the rule making for their practices were entrusted into a new agency, under the supervision of the SEC: the Public Company Accounting Oversight Board (PCAOB).

> *The PCAOB is a nonprofit corporation established by Congress to oversee the audits of public companies in order to protect investors and the public interest by promoting informative, accurate, and independent audit reports. The PCAOB also oversees the audits of broker and dealers, including compliance reports filed pursuant to federal securities laws, to promote investor protection.*[8]

There is no European oversight, and the national oversight bodies remain in place. The only form of oversight is exercised by the Financial Accounting Standards Board at a global level.

The number of companies whose activities are deployed in Europe would, however, justify such oversight. The lobby of national regulators is too strong to be bent: it will take an accident or a crisis to change the situation. It also explains the defiance of the European authorities, pushed by those national bodies toward some aspects of the Basel III accounting rules, especially when it comes to capital adequacy. They find it hard to resist the pressure that large European companies exercise on them.

The accounting profession has its own integrity problem. There is no hope that trust will be restored in financial institutions unless external auditors can reform themselves to make sure that their approval of audited accounts can be relied upon.

PART III: THE LIMITS OF ACCOUNTABILITY

The impact of a rating or an audit report is important. It also creates a huge problem of responsibility. While we would all like to be able to take some of them to court (especially Grant Thornton in the case of Parmalat and Austria), the reality is that the amounts at stake are so much larger that neither rating agencies nor the audit firms have financial means at the level of the risks such actions would incur.

In most cases, the only answer would be, as it was in the case of Arthur Andersen, to go bankrupt. In that case, individual partners[9] would have been made personally liable and ruined. They decided to let the firm go.

The European Commission took into consideration some important elements that limit the responsibility of auditors:

> *The chosen option of the Commission encourages Member States to introduce a limitation on liability into their national liability regimes. Action, implemented by way of a recommendation, would only fix the objective of having a limitation. The objective could be achieved by introducing high-level principles to ensure that the limitation is fair for auditors, the audited companies and other stakeholders. Member States would have the choice between measures that currently exist such as a cap or proportionate liability, a mixture of both or other methods as they see fit including contractual arrangements. However, limitation of liability would not apply in the case of wilful misconduct on the part of the auditor.[10]*

NOTES

1. "Credit Agencies to Testify Before Congress." www.nytimes.com/2011/07/27/business/economy/credit-rating-agencies-to-testify-before-congress.html.
2. http://dealbook.nytimes.com/2013/11/11/suit-charges-3-credit-rating-agencies-with-fraud-in-bear-stearns-case/.
3. S. 3850 (109th): Credit Rating Agency Reform Act of 2006. www.govtrack.us/congress/bills/109/s3850/text.
4. The Dodd-Frank Act reviews the role and responsibility of rating agencies. www.sec.gov/spotlight/dodd-frank/creditratingagencies.shtml.
5. On several occasions, the European authority looked at the merits of a European rating agency. http://eur-lex.europa.eu/LexUriServ/LexUriServ.do?uri=OJ:L:2013:146:0001:01:EN:HTML.

6. Standard & Poor's did reply to this affirmation by the U.S. Treasury. www.theguardian.com/business/2013/sep/04/standard-poors-us-retaliation-lawsuit.

7. The non-Japanese CEO was ousted by the board of Fujitsu because he had publicly questioned the integrity of the accounts published by the company. "Fujitsu's Corporate Governance 'Is Failing Investors.'" Barclay Simpson, May 2010. www.barclaysimpson.com/news/fujitsu-s-corporate-governance-is-failing-investors--news-19774697.

8. http://pcaobus.org/about/pages/default.aspx.

9. For the case study on Arthur Andersen's collapse published by the Tuck School of Business at Dartmouth, see http://mba.tuck.dartmouth.edu/pdf/2001-1-0026.pdf.

10. http://ec.europa.eu/internal_market/auditing/docs/liability/summary_en.pdf.

CHAPTER 12

Central Banks as Lenders of Last Resort Have a Conflict of Interest with Their Regulatory Role

"I know that it is fashionable to talk about a 'dual mandate,' that policy should be directed to price stability and full employment. Fashionable or not, I find that dual mandate both operationally confusing and ultimately illusionary."

—Paul Volcker, Former Federal Reserve President

Since 2008, central banks have been the main source of liquidity when distrust between banks and financial institutions threatened financial stability and the financing of the economy. On top of that liquidity intervention, they effectively took credit risks that should never have been theirs and massively increased the size of their balance sheets.

This marks a profound evolution of central banking, and has implications on the nature of its role. It will require a complete rethinking of the role of central banks that have been accused of acting more in favor of the banks than the economy as a whole. It seems obvious that the $9 trillion increase of the balance sheet of the main central banks since 2007 cannot be sustained without a reanalysis of their role (see Figure 12.1).

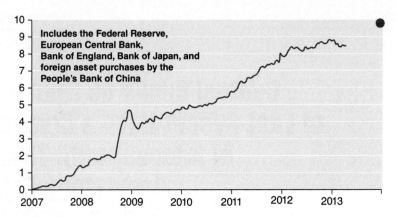

FIGURE 12.1   Earth Nebula, Change in Central Bank Balance Sheets since January 2007 (Trillion $)
Sources: Federal Reserve, Bank of Japan, Bank of England, European Central Bank, People's Bank of China, J. P. Morgan Asset Management estimates.   http://www.mybudget360.com/wp-content/uploads/2013/05/Earth-Nebula_0.jpg.

FINANCIAL STABILITY

One of the key roles played by central banks, generally in coordination with the Treasury of Finance Ministry, is to ensure the stability of the financial system.[1] While this is perfectly legitimate, it does influence their role as regulators: it is more important to them that the financial sector be healthy and stable than to try to supervise them.

This leads to the accusations[2] (common to many regulators) that central banks are too close to the banks and the banking sector. During the financial crisis, several interventions, while sometimes motivated by economic growth and employment, often had the financial system benefiting from these capital injections in the system known as quantitative easing.

> *Federal Reserve officials have been worried that their policy of ultra-low interest rates may be having less of an effect than usual because of a "broken transmission channel." In plain English, this means the money hasn't really been flowing smoothly from liquidity-flooded banks to would-be borrowers.*[3]

UNITED STATES: QUANTITATIVE EASING

Quantitative easing (QE), the modern word for printing money, became a key policy instrument and made the Federal Reserve Bank (FRB) more than just a liquidity provider, but also the depository of all the anomalies affecting the banking system.

- The access to the FRB had to be widened beyond commercial bank, provoking the need for investment banks to create bank holding companies. It was a direct result of the Lehman crisis, when Lehman could not access badly needed liquidity and the U.S. government refused to bail out Lehman Brothers.
- The Federal Reserve in the United States provided liquidity through three waves of QE targeted to subprime assets, U.S. Treasuries, and mortgage loans, respectively.

For almost a year and a half the global financial system has been under extraordinary stress—stress that has now decisively spilled over to the global economy more broadly. The proximate cause of the crisis was the turn of the housing cycle in the United States and the associated rise in delinquencies on subprime mortgages, which imposed substantial losses on many financial institutions and shook investor confidence in credit markets. However, although the subprime debacle triggered the crisis, the developments in the U.S. mortgage market were only one aspect of a much larger and more encompassing credit boom whose impact transcended the mortgage market to affect many other forms of credit. Aspects of this broader credit boom included widespread declines in underwriting standards, breakdowns in lending oversight by investors and rating agencies, increased reliance on complex and opaque credit instruments that proved fragile under stress, and unusually low compensation for risk taking.[4] It is now increasingly clear that the QE was unnecessary and cost taxpayers—who did not even realize that they were taken for a ride—a fortune. In a recent "Confession of a Quantitative Easer" in the *Wall Street Journal*, Andrew Huszar a former senior executive of the Federal Reserve makes Wall Street, not the economy, the main beneficiary of the QE programs of the Fed.

> *Even by the Fed's sunniest calculations, aggressive QE over five years has generated only a few percentage points of U.S. growth. By contrast, experts outside the Fed, such as Mohammed El Erian at the Pimco investment firm, suggest that the Fed may have created and spent over $4 trillion for a total return of as little as 0.25 percent of GDP (i.e., a mere $40 billion bump in U.S. economic output). Both of those estimates indicate that QE isn't really working.*

Unless you're Wall Street. Having racked up hundreds of billions of dollars in opaque Fed subsidies, U.S. banks have seen their collective stock price triple since March 2009. The biggest ones have only become more of a cartel: 0.2 percent of them now control more than 70 percent of the U.S. bank assets.

As for the rest of America, good luck. Because QE was relentlessly pumping money into the financial markets during the past five years, it killed the urgency for Washington to confront a real crisis: that of a structurally unsound U.S. economy. Yes, those financial markets have rallied spectacularly, breathing much-needed life back into 401(k)s, but for how long? Experts like Larry Fink at the BlackRock investment firm are suggesting that conditions are again "bubble-like." Meanwhile, the country remains overly dependent on Wall Street to drive economic growth.[5]

Such assessment increasingly raises the question of the independence of the Federal Reserve, but more important, brings to light the embedded conflict of interest between the role of central banks as guardians of monetary policy and support of the economy and their role in protecting (I was about to say cajoling) the banking system.

Rather worryingly, the new Fed chair, Janet Yellen, who was elected because she believed in QE as a source of jobs, might make this practice a habit. Her nomination hearing faced the opposition of U.S. lawmakers.

Throughout a hearing that lasted more than two hours, Ms. Yellen faced scepticism from Republican lawmakers about the effectiveness, risks, and seemingly open-ended nature of the Fed's easy money policies. One described them as a "morphine drip," another as a "sugar high," and another still as "elitist."[6]

This is why the withdrawal of Larry Summers became good news for Wall Street, which is still milking the cow and benefited from the QE programs.

Lawrence Summers made dismissive remarks about the effectiveness of quantitative easing at a conference in April, raising the possibility of a big shift in U.S. monetary policy if he becomes chairman of the Federal Reserve.

"QE in my view is less efficacious for the real economy than most people suppose," said Mr. Summers according to an official summary of his remarks at a conference organised in Santa Monica by Drobny Global, obtained by the Financial Times.[7]

Despite those fears, the Federal Reserve reduced its quantitative easing that was announced in March to be tapered to $55 billion per month.

EUROPEAN CENTRAL BANK: THE LONG-TERM REFINANCING OPERATIONS (LTROS)

The European Central Bank is now considering what to do with the $ 800 billion that banks are supposed to reimburse at the end of 2014 and early 2015.

The European Central Bank's long-term refinancing operation is a process by which the ECB provides financing to eurozone banks. The stated aim of the LTRO is to maintain a cushion of liquidity for banks holding illiquid assets, and thus prevent interbank lending and other loan origination from seizing up as they did in the credit squeeze of 2008.[8]

While presented as a liquidity injection to ensure the stability of the financial system, the quantitative easing of the ECB was a credit support in disguise. It favored essentially the banks of southern Europe who were the primary beneficiaries. The distribution of this long-term refinancing obligation (LTRO)[9] was indeed mostly favorable to those banks that were getting financial conditions that allowed them to reimburse their more expensive debt and never enhanced their lending activities.

On 21 December 2011 the bank instituted a term of 3 years (36 months); 523 banks that took part in the first auction. Loans totaling €489.2 billion ($640 billion) were announced. The ECB's second 36 month auction, LTRO2, was held 29 February 2012, providing 800 eurozone banks with further €529.5 billion. Net new borrowing under the February auction was around €313 billion— out of a total of €256bn existing ECB lending €215bn was rolled into LTRO2.[10]

LTROs were provided by the ECB in the form of three-year loans at a subsidized 1 percent interest rate for an unlimited amount in two tranches that ended up amounting to €1 trillion. While the objective was to support the liquidity of the banking system, the nature of the operation was unusual:

- The ECB did not limit the amount lent to banks.
- The loans were granted at a rate that was way below market rates.
- The absence of premium based on the risk associated with the nationality of the banks made it a subsidization of the banks from the weakest economies.

- The long-term maturity of three years, for which the ECB has no matching funding.
- The concentration of two one-shot operations threatens some disruptions of markets when two maturities, three months from each other, will require banks to find hundreds of billions of euros.
- In order to achieve that massive transaction, the ECB accepted a weakening of the acceptable collaterals, making its financial position as a creditor particularly uncomfortable.

While there was, at the time of the issuance of LTROs, a liquidity crisis that required the ECB to step in, there is a mystery surrounding their structure. One does not resolve a liquidity crisis by extending three-year loans to the banking sector. It was largely sufficient for the ECB to intermediate short-term liquidity tensions.

By using LTROs as the instrument to resolve the liquidity crisis, the ECB entered in a substantially different field: it was becoming a credit provider, and it was neither differentiating the quality of the borrowers nor the assets that were brought as collaterals.

By doing so, the ECB changed its role: most of the LTROs were subscribed by banks from three countries in difficulty: Spain, Italy, and Portugal. What the ECB did was to palliate to the insufficiency of the European Financial Stability Fund (FSF). It was acting as a substitute to a nonexisting European Treasury, rather than as a central bank.

What is bothering me is the fact that the justifications were, at best, dubious, if not plainly misleading. Now, as expected, banks are trying to lobby the ECB to make sure that when they have to repay those loans, a new LTRO will be put in place.[11]

UNITED KINGDOM

The situation of the United Kingdom was substantially different. To avoid a collapse of the U.K. banking system, HM Treasury had to nationalize three banks: Northern Bank, Lloyds Bank, and Royal Bank of Scotland. By doing so, it would effectively protect the risk that the Bank of England would take by putting together its own version of quantitative easing (that, by respect for Her Majesty, could not be called QE).

The United Kingdom followed the same route but decided in early 2013 not to add further resources through this facility.

In March 2009, the Monetary Policy Committee (MPC) announced that it would reduce Bank Rate to 0.5 percent. The Committee also judged that Bank Rate could not practically be reduced below that level, and in order to give a further monetary stimulus to the economy, it decided to undertake a series of asset purchases.[12]

JAPAN AND ABENOMICS

Bank of Japan Governor Haruhiko Kuroda stated:

The Bank of Japan has engaged in a wide range of monetary easing efforts—
    Including the implementation of the zero interest rate policy, the quantitative easing policy, and comprehensive monetary easing. . . . I have felt strongly that we should make all-out efforts to utilize every possible resource bestowed upon the Bank, rather than to adopt an incremental approach or, put differently, to adopt gradualism.[13]

The Bank of Japan massively purchased Japanese government bonds to counter the appreciation of the yen and restore the Japanese economy. It was a tug of war between the conservative vision of central banking and the action of the Japanese government.

At the core of this political decision was the rush of investors toward yen assets at a time when the U.S. dollar and the euro were weakened by a banking crisis and the QE transactions and the euro was weakened by its sovereign crisis and its LTRO operations.

Japan being an export economy, and having just experience a tsunami and a nuclear catastrophic accident at Fukushima, could not stay idle as the appreciation of the yen was making Japanese exports uncompetitive.

ARE CENTRAL BANK BALANCE SHEETS ETERNALLY EXPANDABLE? HAVE THEY BECOME HEDGE FUNDS?

Without going deeply into the fact that the balance sheet of a central bank is not included in public debt the question will need to be raised (see Figure 12.2). It was addressed by the Chairman of the Federal Reserve in a deposition to the U.S. Congress.[14]

Figure 12.2 shows the importance of the balance sheet of the central banks as a percentage of gross domestic product (GDP). When added to the public debt (what governments refuse to do), it shows the extraordinary dependency of the developed economies on public financing.

I am not convinced by the idea that the balance sheet of a central bank can be expanded almost without limit. I am not the only one to believe that

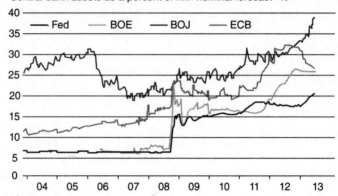

Balance sheets as percent of GDP

FIGURE 12.2   Select Central Bank Balance Sheets as Percentage of GDP

Source: Thomson Reuters Datastream. www.economicsinpictures .com

balance sheet considerations have to be taken seriously. Even the Bank for International Settlements (BIS) believes that it matters.[15] The reason for this opinion lies in a number of basic considerations:

- The equity of central bank balance sheets is generally minimal and was never considered to be the basis of its creditworthiness. This being the case, it assumes that the government will step in should the central bank need equity. There is nothing wrong with this, except that it means that taxpayers' money is on the line and that, maybe, the balance sheet of the central bank might be integrated into public indebtedness.
- The funding of central banks is from two main sources: the bank notes in circulation, which cannot be expanded substantially, and deposits from other central banks and commercial banks. It is quite clear that large expansions of central bank balance sheets have implications both for the real and financial sectors of the economy. They do create risks— and we must watch these closely. In some historical episodes, central banks did expand their balance sheets too much in order to finance profligate government spending. This often had inflationary results. On other occasions, central banks were too slow in reversing expansionary policies when conditions improved.[16]
- In the case of a crisis of confidence in the country, the confidence in its central bank is affected, and the deposits of central banks and commercial banks might be fading quickly.

- The last resort of a central bank is the imposition of higher deposit requirements. However, in most cases, this would effectively create a banking crisis that nobody could control since the central bank would not be able to act as lender of last resort.

IS THIS NOVATION OF CENTRAL BANKS LEGITIMATE OR LEGAL?

The transformation of the role of central banks was a result of the political difficulties to take adequate measures in time and amount that could prevent systemic consequences. This is clearly legitimate, and no questions are asked when the ship is sinking. That does not mean that the risks taken by the central banks were consistent with their original brief, and certainly not with their statutes. Their role is clearly changing and they are increasing their risk profile.

Without entering into the depth of the legal debate, let me just mention that central banks were fundamentally convinced that their impact on employment and growth was critical. Only the hubris of central bankers could convince them of the fact that liquidity injections when interest rates are sometimes below 1 percent could have any effect on the decision of companies to invest and grow.

Mohamed El-Erian, the former CEO of PIMCO, the largest fixed-income asset manager, in a research paper for the Federal Reserve of Saint Louis, advocates for other agencies, in both the public and the private sectors, to urgently work in connection with central bank policies.[17]

NOTES

1. Garry J. Schinasi, "Responsibility of Central Banks for Stability in Financial Markets." IMF Working Paper, June 2003. www.imf.org/external/pubs/ft/wp/2003/wp03121.pdf. This point was recently reemphasized in another paper by Erlend Walter Nier in April 2009. www.imf.org/external/pubs/ft/wp/2009/wp0970.pdf.
2. Alan S. Blinder, "Central Bank Independence and Credibility during and after a Crisis," Jackson Hole Symposium, September 1, 2012. www.kansascityfed.org/publicat/sympos/2012/ab.pdf.
3. Pedro da Costa, "Banks Keeping Most of QE3 Benefits for Themselves." October 17, 2012. http://blogs.reuters.com/macroscope/2012/10/17/banks-keeping-most-of-qe3-benefits-for-themselves/.
4. www.federalreserve.gov/newsevents/speech/bernanke20090113a.htm.

5. www.online.wsj.com/news/articles/SB1000142405270230376380457 9183680751473884

6. www.ft.com/intl/cms/s/0/3e1be888-4d44-11e3-9f40-00144feabdc0 .html#axzz2kqXzi5vD.

7. www.ft.com/intl/cms/s/0/01988daa-f540-11e2-94e9-00144feabdc0 .html#axzz2kqXzi5vD.

8. http://lexicon.ft.com/Term?term=long_term-refinancing-operation-_-LTRO.

9. The euro system's regular open market operations consist of one-week euro liquidity-providing operations (main refinancing operations or MROs) as well as three-month euro liquidity-providing operations (longer-term refinancing operations or LTROs). MROs serve to steer short-term interest rates, to manage the liquidity situation, and to signal the stance of monetary policy in the euro area, while LTROs aim to provide additional, longer-term refinancing to the financial sector. www .ecb.europa.eu/mopo/implement/omo/html/index.en.html.

10. www.euromoney.com/Article/2985829/LTROs.html.

11. "Cheap Loans Are a Hard Habit to Break, ECB's Draghi Learns," *Wall Street Journal,* October 16, 2013. http://online.wsj.com/news/articles/ SB10001424052702304106704579133363168513456.

12. www.bankofengland.co.uk/education/Documents/targettwopointzero/ t2p0_qe_supplement.pdf.

13. Haruiko Kuroda, "Quantitative and Qualitative Monetary Easing." Speech by Bank of Japan Governor, at a meeting held by the Yomiuri International Economic Society in Tokyo in 2013. www.boj.or.jp/en/ announcements/press/koen_2013/data/ko130412a1.pdf.

14. The assets the Fed holds have jumped by over $800 billion, or about 30 percent, to more than $3.6 trillion since it first announced its latest bond-buying program last September. The central bank has been adding $85 billion a month in Treasuries and mortgage-backed securities since early this year. www.reuters.com/article/2013/03/21/us-usa-fed-discount-idUSBRE92K17720130321.

15. Jaime Caruana, "Why Central Bank Balance Sheets Matter," BIS Papers No 66. www.bis.org/publ/bppdf/bispap66b.pdf.

16. Ibid., p. 3.

17. Mohamed El-Erian, *Federal Reserve of Saint Louis Review,* July–August 2012. http://research.stlouisfed.org/publications/review/12/07/243-264El-Erian.pdf.

CHAPTER 13

Financial Institution Governance (or Lack Thereof)

"It seems clear that, if the CEO chooses, he or she can, by example and through oversight, induce corporate colleagues and outside auditors to behave ethically."
—Alan Greenspan, Former Federal Reserve President

Had bank governance been perfect and the supervision by the regulatory authorities been impeccable, the financial crisis would not have happened. The failures of some governance mechanisms must be remedied, and while little has been done to improve governance regulation, some initiatives are gradually changing the way banks operate.

The Financial Stability Board (FSB) is the closest to a global regulator in matters of financial institutions. It issued several directives on some of the aspects of governance. The Organization for Economic Cooperation and Development (OECD) looked at the corporate governance lessons from the financial crisis and organized an in-depth initiative to look at various aspects of bank governance:

A number of weaknesses have been apparent. The risk management systems have failed in many cases due to corporate governance procedures rather than the inadequacy of computer models alone: information about exposures in a number of cases did not reach the board and even senior levels of management, while risk management was often activity rather than enterprise-based. These are board responsibilities. In other cases, boards had approved strategy but then did not establish suitable metrics to monitor its implementation. Company disclosures about foreseeable risk factors and about the systems in place for monitoring and managing risk have also left a lot to be desired even though this is a key element of the Principles. Accounting standards and regulatory requirements have also proved insufficient in some areas leading the relevant standard setters to undertake a review. Last but not least, remuneration systems have in a number of cases not been closely related to the strategy and risk appetite of the company and its longer-term interests.

This article concludes that the financial crisis can be to an important extent attributed to failures and weaknesses in corporate governance arrangements. When they were put to a test, corporate governance routines did not serve their purpose to safeguard against excessive risk taking in a number of financial services companies.[1]

RISK MANAGEMENT

At the center of the questioning of risk management is a question to which partial answers have been given: Did the banks know their risks? Did they deliberately ignore them? Were they simply overoptimistic (a judgment question)?

Several initiatives have been taken to improve the reporting of risks to regulatory authorities, making such reporting more cumbersome. The Institute of International Finance (IIF) published a comprehensive study from the industry on governance for strengthened risk management.[2]

Finance is all about risks and trust. If it does not take risks, it is useless, if it takes too much risk, it loses trust. One would think that the most important function of a financial institution would be considered as a fundamental discipline and that those who are in charge of monitoring risks would be among the most senior officers.

Since the financial crisis, the function of the chief risk officer has been upgraded, and in its October 2012 report, the IIF describes what it should be.

The CRO and the risk function should not be seen as a silo, dealing only with risk and separated from the rest of the business. The CRO should have a strong working relationship with other members of the senior management team, including the Chief Executive Officer (CEO), Chief Financial Officer (CFO), and Chief Information Officer (CIO), as it is this coordination that ensures that risk considerations are taken into account early in the decision-making process.[3]

If the financial crisis might have benefitted financial stability, it is by putting forward the importance of a risk culture that needs transformation. Here again the IIF provides a powerful definition of what the risk culture should be.

> *An organization's risk culture determines the way risks are identified, understood, discussed, and acted upon in the organization. A strong risk culture is an essential building block for effective risk governance and is typically seen as heavily dependent on the "tone at the top" and clear and consistent actions by board members and senior management. Getting risk culture right is fundamental to controlling risk effectively within the organization. It is, above all, about actual behavior—what you do, not just what you say.*[4]

Risks have two major dimensions: ownership and control. There should not be any doubt that the owners of the risk are the business line and its management. The fact that there exists a strong risk management function does not change the accountability of the businesses.

It was one of the key causes of the subprime crisis: once business people could securitize the risks they took, they ignored it and it came back to haunt them through severe liabilities about the quality of their underwriting practices. This explains the amplitude of the fines the banks paid for their marketing practices. JPMorgan paid $7 billion, and Bank of America paid $6 billion.

DYSFUNCTIONAL BOARDS OF DIRECTORS

The biggest weakness of the corporate system is the board of directors. Any director who was sitting around the table of the board of a bank that was hit by the subprime, mortgage, or sovereign crisis should reflect on his or her performance. Yet, most of them are still sitting there, having failed to do their duties to society and to the shareholders they were supposed to defend, and shamelessly parading and cashing substantial fees for this miserable performance.

JPMorgan Chase director and chairman of the board's audit committee, Laban Jackson, did not cause much of a stir in Chicago recently when he stunningly admitted at an institutional investor conference, "We've got these things that we actually are guilty of and we've got to fix them."

Directors are generally very powerful people. Boards are also incredibly badly composed. In a recent case that involved JPMorgan, the chair of the audit committee eventually had to step down. Nothing seems to have been done to improve the quality and expertise of boards of directors. While individual initiatives have been taken in some circumstances, there has been no recognition, no accountability, no sanction or improvement of the boards of financial institutions.

The European Capital Requirements Directive (CRD) IV provides for new criteria, in particular to availability (impossibility to cumulate certain functions).[5]

It is from the Australian Association of Corporate Directors that this list of measures comes:

> *So what should boards be doing? According to Doughty, directors who can agree with most of the following are likely to be sitting on more effective boards:*

> ■ *Board members are clear on what is expected of them.*
> ■ *Board meeting agendas are well planned so that the board is able to get through all necessary board business.*
> ■ *Most board members come to meetings prepared.*
> ■ *Written reports to the board are received well in advance of meetings.*
> ■ *All directors participate in important board discussions.*
> ■ *Different points of view are encouraged and discussed.*
> ■ *All directors support the decisions reached.*
> ■ *The board has a plan for the further development of directors.*
> ■ *Board meetings are always interesting and frequently fun.*[6]

SHOULD THE CHAIRPERSON ALSO BE THE CEO?

The debate of CEO and chairpersons remains widely diverse. While Germany makes it a law, France and the United States keep fighting for this management structure. The last episode was the reaction of a large minority of the shareholders of JPMorgan Chase on the reappointment of its current chairman and CEO.[7]

Under normal circumstances, the system might work, but one would think that the decision might not be left only to the annual general meeting. One of the duties regulators would have is to ensure that, in difficult circumstances, the functions to protect shareholders and the management self-interest must be distinct.

> *It seems that every year calls ring out louder and louder for boards to separate the roles of CEO and chairman. Large companies from Wells Fargo to News Corp. have faced shareholder proposals*

demanding that they replace their CEO with an independent direc-
tor in the role of chairman.

Advocates of splitting the positions argue that an independent
leader will aid the board in more effectively monitoring the CEO's
actions and performance. Critics of the combined CEO/chairman
role include institutional investors, policymakers, and a preponder-
ance of corporate governance experts and advisory firms. Many
executives disagree, however, arguing that such a structure creates
unnecessary confusion and hurts unity of leadership.[8]

Whatever are the official and legal justifications of this trend, we should
not ignore the role played by egos in the boardroom.

REMUNERATION AND RISKS

Regulators around the world have diversely handled the compensation
issues. The G20 recommendations do not seem to have been followed in a
consistent way.

- The United States[9] and Switzerland[10] chose to give a "say on pay" to
  shareholders, recognizing the inability of directors to exercise control.
- Europe decided to limit the bonuses of bankers to 100 percent of their
  salaries, without addressing the issue of global compensation.[11]
- The use of taxation as a way to reduce bonuses or salaries has been
  unevenly used with the United Kingdom[12] take the harshest measures.

PERSONAL OR INSTITUTIONAL ACCOUNTABILITY

Accountability seems to be widely diverse, with some countries using prison
sentences and others not even attempting to look at ways to affect the failures of negotiation.

The fundamental issue is that the financial world has resolved its mistakes, misbehaviors, failures, and ethical aberrations by making the institution liable for them. History tells us that people don't care.

Combinations of measures need to be taken to ensure that those who commit those irregularities that are not crimes or frauds be sanctions by using:

- Personal fines
- Banning from the financial industry
- Recovery of former bonus

There is no hope to change the egomaniac mind-set of finance if the individuals who are handsomely paid are not held personally accountable for their actions. The tendency to fire traders where chief financial officers (CFOs) and managers escape any sanction is part of this lack of personal accountability that is the best way to ensure behavioral changes.

This might be about to change, as the United Kingdom is now embarking on a new approach that aims at the individuals who bear their accountability.

Regulators and politicians in the United Kingdom want bankers to be more accountable for mistakes made by themselves and their teams. But while supervisors are trying to expand the existing sanctions regime, politicians are seeking a more radical overhaul.[13]

This reform comes from the top of the U.K. government and Parliament.

In the United Kingdom, the Committee on Banking Standards proposed a series of sweeping reforms aimed at establishing much great accountability on senior management. Among these would be the "replacement of the statements of principles and the associated codes of practice, which are incomplete and unclear in their application, with a single set of banking standards rules to be drawn up by the regulators. These rules would apply to both senior persons and licensed bank staff and a breach would constitute grounds for enforcement action by the regulators."[14]

NOTES

1. www.oecd.org/daf/ca/corporategovernanceprinciples/42229620.pdf.
2. IIF Report on Governance for Enhanced Risk Management, http://www.iif.com/press/press+364.php.
3. Ibid., p. 3.
4. Ibid., p. 7.
5. Katja Langenbucher, "CRD IV and Corporate Governance of Banks—A New Discipline in the Making," *Zeitschrift fur das Gesamte Handels-und Wirtschaftsrecht* 6, 2012. Available at SSRN: http://papers.ssrn.com/sol3/papers.cfm?abstract_id=2176633&download=yes.
6. www.companydirectors.com.au/Director-Resource-Centre/Publications/The-Boardroom-Report/Back-Volumes/Volume-11-2013/Volume-11-Issue-11/Is-your-board-dysfunctional.

7. In a Harvard Business School blog, Roger Lowenstein described this fight as "the battle Jamie Dimon shouldn't be fighting." http://blogs.hbr.org/2013/05/the-battle-jamie-dimon-shouldn/.
8. Matthew Semandeni and Ryan Krause, "Splitting the CEO and Chairman Roles: It's Complicated." *Bloomberg Business Week*, November 1, 2012. www.businessweek.com/articles/2012-11-01/splitting-the-ceo-and-chairman-roles-it-s-complicated.
9. This Harvard Law School blog by Matteo Tonello, in September 2013, raises the question: "When Do Shareholders Care about CEO Pay?" http://blogs.law.harvard.edu/corpgov/tag/say-on-pay/.
10. The Association of Corporate Counsels describes the new Swiss initiative. www.lexology.com/library/detail.aspx?g=37783d26-2fef-4cfa-99a4-e33ba0ddc333.
11. This *Financial Times* article describes the EU rules on bonuses. www.ft.com/intl/cms/s/0/ca5becf0-91ae-11e2-b4c9-00144feabdc0.html.
12. www.lexology.com/library/detail.aspx?g=a4a54de7-ff1a-4a2c-a-03-62ae937d0d8c.
13. Lucas Becker, "Bank Supervision Gets Personal as United Kingdom Focuses on Accountability," *Risk,* June 27, 2013.www.risk.net/risk-magazine/feature/2276767/bank-supervision-gets-personal-as-uk-focuses-on-accountability.
14. Henri Engler, "Reforming Banking's Risk Culture Requires Breaking 'accountability firewall.'" http://blogs.reuters.com/financial-regulatory-forum/2013/09/11/reforming-bankings-risk-culture-requires-breaking-accountability-firewall/.

CHAPTER 14

Was It a Global Crisis?
The Asian Perspective

"In the face of this global crisis, we have seen Asia emerge; not just with its global economic standing intact, but with its standing strengthened."

—Christine Lagarde, IMF Director General

The first thing that senior executives and government officials I met after the Lehman crisis told me is that, once again, the "West" considers itself like the center of the universe.

They wanted to describe the financial crisis as an "Atlantic crisis." Their statements were actually right. It is what they described as "Western greed" that caused the situation and felt that Asian financial institutions had been largely spared this tsunami.

As a result of this, most Asian leaders watched the drive for financial reforms and global financial regulation more than they led or participated in the effort. It is critical to understand what this means for the financial institutions covering 60 percent of the world population.

When it comes to Basel III, Asian regulators were involved in trying to understand what this would mean for their financial institutions rather than looking at the global perspective. As a result of their structure, they did not try to reach a consensus between Asian banks and insurance companies. We will therefore need to look specifically at the three major financial centers and apologize for not looking closely at others. We will focus on Japan, China, and India.

JAPAN

Japan is the only Asian global financial power. For all the noise around other countries, we should not lose sight that the yen is the third most actively traded currency in the world, that the Japanese government bond market is one of the top five markets, and that the aggregate value of listed companies is second to the United States.

Japanese Financial Institutions Are Global

When the monopoly of the Bank of Tokyo on international transactions stopped, Japanese banks started to operate internationally and quickly established a global position especially in fixed income and equity.

One of the most surprising elements of the subprime and Lehman crises is the absence of Japanese banks in these situations and the absence of significant fines incurred by them. There are several explanations for this situation, but the most credible one is that Japanese banks themselves had just emerged from a crisis that led them to become more conservative and limit their international activities. This explains why Japan has not embarked in an effort to develop a new regulatory framework.

Restructuring the Japanese Financial System

At a recent panel on December 13, 2013, in Tokyo, on vitalizing financial and capital markets members, which included representatives of the Financial Services Agency and the Bank of Japan, some interesting conclusions were drawn:

> *Following the burst of the bubble economy,* **the Japanese financial system** *has restored its soundness after overcoming the financial crisis and the non-performing loan problem,* **and has since remained sound even through the Global Financial Crisis.** *The Japanese financial system must now play an active role in ensuring the economy to take a leap back to the positive equilibrium and in sustaining a vibrant society under such equilibrium. In other words, as part of "the third arrow," a strategic structural reform policy aimed at enhancing growth potential must be pursued in financial and capital markets as well. This effort is exactly what is required to turn the above vicious cycle into a positive cycle and fully accelerate the development.*
>
> *In particular, financial assets held by households, which amount to nearly 1,600 trillion yen ($16 trillion), and public pension funds, are expected to be mobilized as risk money and funding for growing*

businesses, while having the decline in the real value of the those assets minimized in an inflationary environment. Measures should be taken to enhance this shift of financial assets.[1]

Japan is therefore much more focused on the utilization of the huge savings of the Japanese public to support its economic revival. The *shift to financial assets* is a buzzword to cover the use of deposits into securities and other financial assets.

Is the Japanese Banking System Sound?

While Japanese banks have sound assets, they also are massively exposed to Japanese government bonds, and their strength is predicated by the maintenance of the current system that finances the government through domestic financial institutions. Only 4 percent of the Japanese public debt is in foreign hands compared to, say, at least a third for European debts.

It is this interwoven relationship that is the biggest threat to the Japanese banking system, since the indebtedness of Japan amounts to $13 trillion or 245 percent of its gross domestic product (GDP), the largest in the developed world. It is therefore on a strong support of the government that rating agencies are continuing to keep their confidence in the Japanese financial institutions.

While Japanese banks are considered conservative in their domestic activities, they are now encouraged to be involved in supporting the economic policy of the Abe government. It is rated under the Standard & Poor's Banking Industry Country Risk Assessment (BICRA) with a note 2 that is also granted to France, Germany, Australian, Canada, and Hong Kong. It corresponds to an AA– rating. It is based on the following factors:

- Diversified and developed economy with competitive export industries contributing to the trade surplus
- Moderate growth in private-sector debt and sound financial profiles among corporations and individuals
- Core retail deposits constitute a large share of system-wide funding needs

Japanese Public Opinion Has a Different Approach to Moral Hazard

One of the reasons why the SFA has not yet approached the possibility of bail-in of Japanese banking is that it does not feel any specific pressure, neither from the political side nor from public opinion.

The Japanese public is willing to see its government, despite its high indebtedness, bail out banks if necessary. This is in sharp contrast with the approach in Europe and the United States, who seem to be predominantly focused on limiting taxpayers' money.

While Japan is chasing fraud, and recently implemented a new restrictive regulation on short selling and intends to fight insider trading, it is not following the same path as the "Atlantic" governments.

CHINA

The question of the possible regulation of the banking system has to be seen in perspective. The largest Chinese banks are owned in majority and controlled by the Chinese government. Furthermore, since they were listed on the stock market, they have become among the largest banks in the world. It is essential to ensure that the financial stability of China continues and that China does not become a threat to world financial stability.

However, as *The Economist* wrote on August 29, 2013, this rosy picture needs to be further analyzed:

> *At first sight, China seems to have a superb banking system. Its state-controlled banks, among the biggest and most profitable in the world, have negligible levels of non-performing loans and are well capitalised. That appears to suggest that the country's approach should be applauded.*
>
> *Not so. For one thing, though China's banking system is stable, its banks are not as healthy as they seem. The credit binge of recent years has left them with far higher levels of risky loans than they acknowledge. And a profit squeeze is coming. The banks are having to work harder to keep both their biggest depositors, who are tempted by alternative investment products, and their biggest borrowers, who are turning to the bond market instead. As a consequence, the country's Big Four banks—Industrial and Commercial Bank of China, Bank of China, Agricultural Bank of China and China Construction Bank—will no longer make easy money by merely issuing soft loans to state-owned enterprises, or SOEs.[2]*

This problem is never looked at seriously since China has historically supported its banks, injecting $80 billion into state-owned banks and resorting to the good bank/bad bank resolution system. Asset management companies were created and separated from the banks. They were entrusted to professional asset managers, whose role is to manage the toxic loan portfolio. It derived from the fact that banks were automatically funding state-owned enterprises irrespective of their creditworthiness.

However, despite official denial, shadow banking has become a substantial part of the Chinese financial system. It is shadow banking that threatens China and potentially represents a risk to world financial stability. Fortunately, China disposes of massive foreign exchange surplus that is already used to strengthen its financial system.

At the end of December 2013, new rumors of a liquidity crisis, mostly driven by shadow lenders, forced the Chinese government to intervene for the second time in one year. Over three days, RMB300 billion ($50 billion) was injected by the central bank, the People's Bank of China (PBOC). Shadow banking lenders do not have any liquidity resources. Furthermore, the PBOC said that there was RMB1.5 trillion ($2 trillion) of reserves in the banking system. They are therefore sensitive to problems with their borrowers who need more cash.

The risk of crash landing of the Chinese economy in 2014 is not excluded. But the second-largest economy in the world is well managed and its gradual openness under the new Chinese administration provides reassurance.

It is for that reason that the PBOC told lenders to strengthen their liquidity management in January 2014.[3]

INDIA

India's financial system is like a ramshackle engine lovingly maintained by a sect of oil-spattered engineers and wearily tolerated by most people who depend on it. After Indira Gandhi, then prime minister, nationalised most banks in 1969, India slipped towards financial socialism, with a central bank that printed rupees on politicians' command. When India opened up in 1991 a wave of reform took place. The system today is a mishmash. Market forces have a role, but the state looms large.[4]

The Indian government, which interferes often and has not provided adequate equity, holds 60 percent of the banking system. The leading private banks, ICICI and HDFC, took the bold step of listing on the New York Stock Exchange and providing transparency and credible accounts.

The Reserve Bank of India (RBI) has now at its helm Raguram Rajan, a former adviser to the prime minister, but more importantly an International Monetary Fund (IMF) chief economist and a professor at the famous Economics School of Chicago University. He recognized quickly the weaknesses of the

Indian banking system and has asked the government to lift the barriers that prohibit foreign banks' owning more than 25 percent and limit their direct presence to one branch. The new governor of the RBI wants to see the Indian banking system "dramatically" evolve. He said in an interview with the *Financial Times:*

> *I see over the next few years a dramatic remaking of the banking landscape. Both from the. . . new banks which are going to come on board and the foreign banks which are going to be allowed to expand more freely. It will be a multiplier in terms of competition.*[5]

The most recent RBI report on the financial stability of the Indian banking sector, issued in December 2013, is not reassuring:

> *The risks to the banking sector have further increased since the publication of the previous FSR in June this year. All major risk dimensions captured in the Banking Stability Indicator show increase in vulnerabilities in the banking sector.*[6]

The protectionism of the banking system has, however, allowed the largest Indian public bank to stand: the State Bank of India. It dominates the banking system in a way that will need to be ultimately revisited, but it managed to restore its name. The Indian government and the RBI have not yet conducted a deep forensic audit of the loans granted to state-owned enterprises.

However, the Indian banking system does not provide any systemic risk. Their activities are mostly in domestic lending, which represents approximately 70 percent of the Indian GDP. Shadow banking is developing much faster with the creation of a series of nonbank finance companies. Governor Rajan will need time, strength, and persuasion to ensure that, within the next five years, the Indian banking system will match the quality of its corporate world. The 2014 elections will tell us whether he will have the political backing to do so.

ASSESSING THE ASIAN RISK

While the necessity to provide a stronger and more robust regulation in Europe and the United States is essential, it is because the ethics of the "Occidental" financial world have substantial deteriorated.

By and large, banks in Asia are much more traditional, and even though they have gradually become important players in the international capital markets, there is nothing comparable to the Western personal greed and individualism.

■ A solid deposit base fundamentally tempers the risks represented by Asian financial institutions. Asian customers still massively deposit money with their banks.

■ Their reliance on interbank financing and bond financing is also mitigated by the fact that, with the exception of Japan, the rating of their countries negatively affects their own ratings and most of their bonds are at the limit of investment grade.

■ Borrowing is not as widespread in the Asian mentality and the risks of individual and small companies loans are lower. Only large Asian multinationals have been able to substantially leverage their operations.

■ Asian countries do not care about our moral hazard debate: they know, and so does their population, that their governments will have to step in in case of crisis.

The risks in Asia are therefore of a macroeconomic nature. The over-indebtedness of the Japanese government, the development of shadow banking in China beyond the liquidity capabilities of the lenders, and the protectionism and controlling philosophy of the Indian authorities present a systemic risk for the world financial stability.

Standard & Poor's Ratings Services warned in October 2013 of "a threat to the region's financial stability from a credit and debt bubble in China. In a downbeat look at Asia's banking system, the ratings firm said slower economic growth in China could fuel a spike in bad loans even as the shadow banking sector continues to expand."[7]

When Europe and the United States have finalized their mammoth regulatory exercise, it might be advisable to open a more substantive dialogue with Asia.

NOTES

1. www.fsa.go.jp%2Fen%2Frefer%2Fcouncils%2Fvitalizing%2F201312
13%2F01.pdf&ei=iUovU-n1LtPOkQf_1YHABQ&usg=AFQjCNE5f9
2CNTcz6ak9936BbT6WFdjWMQ&bvm=bv.62922401,d.eW0.

2. "Too Big to Hail," *The Economist*, August 29, 2013. www.economist
.com/news/leaders/21584342-chinas-banking-behemoths-are-too-
beholden-state-it-time-set-finance-free-too-big.

3. www.reuters.com/article/2014/01/17/us-china-economy-liquidity-
idUSBREA0G08720140117.

4. "Bridging the Gulf," *The Economist,* November 28, 2013. www
.economist.com/news/finance-and-economics/21590928-financial-system-
intended-promote-equality-and-stability-no-longer.

5. www.ft.com/intl/cms/s/2/7137fc46-502f-11e3-befe-00144feabdc0 .html#axzz2oDwtrtyi.
6. http://economictimes.indiatimes.com/news/economy/indicators/rbi-financial-stability-report-risks-to-banking-sector-have-further-increased/articleshow/28134966.cms.
7. http://blogs.wsj.com/economics/2013/10/03/dont-rule-out-an-asia-banking-crisis-sp-says/.

CHAPTER 15

The Challenges of Global Regulation

"It's a bloody nightmare. The regulators have no respect for one another at all. Each country is looking after itself."
—Senior executive in charge of regulation at one of the world's biggest banks, quoted by the *Financial Times*

The idea of global regulation is probably a utopia or Myth of Sisyphus.[1] However, several key issues need to continue to be analyzed and treated with a deep understanding of the global implications of national regulation.

Everybody is guilty. Germany implemented its hedge fund regulation[2] the day after a European framework had been discussed, ignoring the discussions. France implemented a banking regulation[3] while the European banking union was being launched. The United States implemented a derivative system that contradicted the agreement it had with Europe four months before. When the European Commission proposed its new structure France was the most vocal opponent.

The world we live in will be dominated by global trends. However, its political leadership depends on many elements that are driven by domestic issues. We all regularly wonder how, in the middle of global turmoil, the national instinct takes over. As the BIS puts it:

Challenges in resolving a cross-border bank crisis arise for many reasons, one of which is that crisis resolution frameworks are largely designed to deal with domestic failures and to minimise the losses

165

incurred by domestic stakeholders. As such, the frameworks are not well suited to dealing with serious cross-border problems. Many earlier discussions of these issues have been framed in terms of either a so-called universal resolution approach that recognises the wholeness of a legal entity across borders and leads to its resolution by a single jurisdiction—or a territorial or ring fencing approach—in which each jurisdiction resolves the individual parts of the cross-border financial institution located within its national borders. Neither characterisation corresponds to actual practice, though recent responses, like prior ones, are closer to the territorial approach than the universal one. It is debatable which is optimal in economic or operational terms. However, even in jurisdictions that adhere to a universal insolvency procedure for banks and their branches, such as in the European Union, each national authority is likely to attach most weight to the pursuit of its own national interests in the management of a crisis.[4]

The European plan to create a eurozone recovery system is an interesting combination of a "national" approach (Europe being considered as a nation) and a "cross-border" approach (17 different legal and financial contexts).

The Directive on Bank Recovery and Resolution, when adopted by the European Parliament and the Council, will determine the rules for how E.U. banks in serious financial difficulties are restructured, how vital functions for the real economy are maintained, and how losses and costs are allocated to the banks' shareholders, creditors and uninsured depositors. Bail-in, a key instrument in the resolution directive, would sequentially allocate losses and write down the claims of shareholders, subordinated creditors, and senior creditors. Depositors below €100 000 are in any case excluded from suffering losses, their claims being protected by national Deposit Guarantee Schemes.[5]

This approach makes the whole project questionable: the European Union does have a key principle: subsidiarity. Under this principle, the European Commission should have elaborated more its compliance with subsidiarity and explained why the current elements of its directive could not be effectively exercised through the current national structures. It inevitably will need to rely on them: can anyone imagine that a Finnish European civil servant will be able to step into an Italian bank fighting for its survival?

The Institute of International Finance (IIF) summarizes this issue in its paper on the subject:

> *An effective framework for the resolution of cross- border firms requires both convergence of national regimes and enhanced coop- eration and coordination among resolution authorities, based on legally effective crisis management agreements. Such agreements have the capacity to allow for approaches to resolution that are consistent with the structural and organizational approaches ad- opted by firms, and which avoid increased ring-fencing of countries and fragmentation of the international marketplace. There are sig- nificant benefits to the global and local economies deriving from the diverse range of approaches and structures that global firms deploy. Cross-border resolution arrangements need to preserve these. To be effective such crisis management agreements need to be embedded in national resolution frameworks incorporating a number of provi- sions designed to underpin and support the international market in financial services.*[6]

Regulating global finance is going to be a long quest for financial stabil- ity. The analysis we made does not preclude hope that, over time, regulation might be an enabler of financial stability.

The financial services industry will go through a substantial regulatory reform that is unique in the regulatory history. We will, as it unfolds, be able to assess how much it contributed to a more effective world of finance. Despite the pitfalls, the complexities, and the forces that will aim at weak- ening it or fight against its application, we must constantly improve it (see Figure 15.1).

REGULATION, POLICIES, AND POLITICS

While there are a number of complex challenges in regulating global fi- nance, the real obstacles are of a political nature. To politicians acting on a national and local basis, the global arena is certainly way above their level of competence. In a recent publication, the following examples were quoted:

> *The following quotations suggest that ministers who lack technical competence make bad policy decisions.*
>
> *"I don't know what George Osborne's degree was in. It was certainly not economics." – Alex Salmond, First Minister of Scotland.*

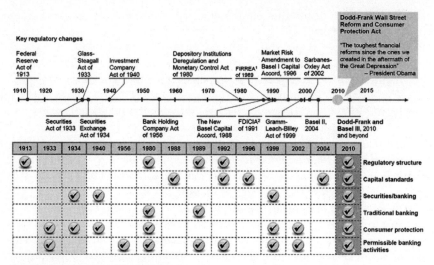

FIGURE 15.1   History of Key Regulatory Changes
Source: Mc Kinsey Working Paper No. 25, 2011. www.mckinsey.com%2F~%2Fmedia
%2Fmckinsey%2Fdotcom%2Fclient_service%2FRisk%2FWorking%2520papers%
2F25_Assessing_Addressing_Implications.ashx&ei=XVWFUoThENjh4AOlx4HAC
w&usg=AFQjCNFnwU1j8f-
C1bo1KrQJGsXwv4C_jg&sig2=BkD0tzzJTWYBHv-
Ca4ffVw&bvm=bv.56343320,d.dmg.

> "[ECB President] Draghi countered the view of [German
> Finance Minister] Schäuble that the Island Republic of Cyprus is not
> 'systemically relevant,' and that a bankruptcy of the country is not a
> danger to the future of the Eurozone. Such a comment is what one
> hears especially from lawyers, argued Draghi. The question whether
> Cyprus is systemically relevant or not is not a question a lawyer can
> answer. It is a topic for economists. Schäuble has a degree in law."[7]

Competence is not the only issue: while governments and parliament
might understand the policy implications of regulation, it does not mean that
they want to use any of their political capital to take the right global decisions
if they hurt their constituencies. Global regulation inevitably is at the cross-
road of conflicting interests, and the incestuous relationship between power
and money, politics and finance will make this undertaking extraordinarily
complex.

REGULATORS AND SOVEREIGN FINANCING

Public regulators are not independent, whatever one pretends. Already in 2002, the International Monetary Fund (IMF) insisted that regulators need independence.[8] Over the past few years the independence of central banks has been redefined. We should not fool ourselves. Regulation is part of sovereignty, and whatever Chinese walls we are trying to build, democracy requires elected officials and representatives to exercise their powers and duties.

Even if regulators dispose of statutory rights to act against wrongdoers, the composition of all regulatory bodies is political. One must recognize that, since the financial crisis, this independence has been decreasing. It is due to the failures of the financial services industry and its regulators, who were too close to keep their independence.

In the case of finance, however, there is a specific field where the incest between finance and politics seems unbreakable. The public sector needs financing and those who provide sovereign financing are precisely the institutions they regulate.

> *The strong link between sovereign and banking stress is frequently emphasised, especially since the start of the European sovereign debt crisis . . . the interdependence between sovereign and banking risk by showing that sovereign and bank credit default swaps (CDS) were positively correlated during 2011 for a number of euro-area countries. It is worth noting that the same graphical result holds not only for periphery countries but also for stronger E.U. economies such as Germany and France. However, the reasons for the interconnectedness between financial and sovereign sector risk are little understood.*[9]

EUROPEAN CENTRAL BANK SUPERVISION: THE E.U. GOVERNANCE CHALLENGES

A recent example illustrates perfectly this dilemma: the European Central Bank (ECB) is taking over the supervision of 124 banks in the eurozone. Prior to undertaking that responsibility, the ECB has decided to submit those banks to a sever audit of their quality, and will in all likely hood, refuse to supervise some of the weakest banks. This audit, however, will bump into the crucial question of the valuation of sovereign bonds in the portfolios of the banks who are probably the largest sovereign bondholders:

> *The ink on the agreements that will hand supervision of the euro area's biggest banks to the European Central Bank (ECB) is barely*

dry. Yet the ECB is already enmeshed in squabbles with national banking supervisors over the extent of its powers and the rigour with which it will undertake its first big task, a warts-and-all review of the balance-sheets of the banks it will take charge of in a year's time.[10]

If they continue, as it was in the case of the long-term refinancing obligation (LTRO), to consider, against all evidence, that all countries are equal and riskless, this audit will produce the same appalling results as the two stress tests produced by the European Banking Authority.[11]

If the auditors recognize what is already obvious—that is, that sovereign bonds are not all equal—who is going to decide the adjusted value risk of each country? Markets and rating agencies provide a very good indication. But should some of those discounts be applied, banks from the weakest European countries might not meet the minimum quality required by the ECB. Would anybody believe that Mario Draghi will haircut Italian sovereign bonds and admit the structural weakness of the banks he was supervising when he was the governor of the Banca d'Italia? What is the current exposure of the ECB to the various countries of the European Union, and what is the geographic distribution of the collateral it took in its lending operations?

The fact is that no answer is given to these questions and Europe expects to be credible without being transparent. A study published on January 3, 2014, casts a serious doubt on European transparency:

Bank supervisors should provide publicly accessible, timely and consistent data on the banks under their jurisdiction. Such transparency increases democratic accountability and leads to greater market efficiency.

There is greater supervisory transparency in the United States compared to the member states of the European Union. The U.S. supervisors publish data quarterly and update fairly detailed information on bank balance sheets within a week. By contrast, based on an attempt to locate similar data in every E.U. country, in only 11 member states is this data at least partially available from supervisors, and in no member state is the level of transparency as high as in the US.

Current and planned European Union requirements on bank transparency are either insufficient or could be easily sidestepped by supervisors. A banking union in Europe needs to include requirements for greater supervisory transparency.[12]

THE RISKS OF REGULATORY FRAGMENTATION

The risks of regulatory fragmentation are particularly critical when it comes to resolution of bank crisis and recovery of these institutions. The IIF has been a strong voice to the IMF and other regulators on the dangers of such fragmentation:

> *The challenge for global leaders is to recapture the political com-*
> *mitment to decisive, coordinated action that made the London*
> *Group of 20 Summit (April 2009) successful in restoring confi-*
> *dence battered by the crisis-and to use that commitment to take*
> *immediate and concerted policy measures within a multilateral*
> *framework. Market participants need to be convinced that the*
> *leaders of these major economies recognize their individual and*
> *collective responsibilities to work towards the goal of balanced*
> *and sustainable global growth.*[13]

The absence of Asia from the fundamental regulatory debate must be a source of concern. While they do take part in the Basel discussions and agree to comply with the capital adequacy ratios, it is less clear whether their national regulators really agree on the liquidity and leverage ratios.

BANK RESOLUTION: THE LEGAL NIGHTMARE

Bank resolution and recovery is probably the single most important issue affecting the future of financial institutions. It is also the most complex legal issue. It crosses legal systems, institutional structures, cultural differences, and generally accepted practices.

Every country operates in a different legal system and has rules that are not necessarily giving their regulators the same regulatory power needed to sanction their banking institutions.

Is it such a good idea to entrust central banks with powers to regulate the banking system? How will they behave in a crisis resolution? Historically, they used their financial resources to bail out the banks. But that would be contrary to the objectives of the bail-in.

> *The reform is the final leg of an ambitious project launched al-*
> *most two years ago to fuse financial oversight in the eurozone and*
> *improve the resilience of the currency bloc against the ravages of*
> *its debt crisis. However, the resolution system has faced criticism,*

including from the European Central Bank, for being too complex and inadequately funded.[14]

BASEL III

Capital adequacy of financial institutions, and especially banking, seems to have a chance to become global. The Basel III regulations are starting to unfold their effects on banking strategies and recapitalization. The European Banking Authority (EBA)[15] has also put forward serious attempts to ensure that European banks are adequately capitalized. The timeline is, however, still far away.[16]

More important, bank lobbying against some aspects of Basel III are at an all-time high. In September 2013, the Federal Reserve issued an interim report on the implementation of Basel III:

> *Rules to implement the Basel III capital reforms in the United States were finalized in July, and will be phased-in beginning in 2014 or 2015, depending on the size of the banking organization. The planning horizon for the next capital planning and stress testing cycle runs from the fourth quarter of 2013 through the fourth quarter of 2015. Thus, the next capital planning and stress testing cycle, which begins October 1, overlaps with the implementation of the Basel III capital reforms.*[17]

Europe would like to make everybody believe that they endorse Basel III, and ensure that the United States does it as well. However, at the same time, they are looking for a compromise.

Three issues have been contentious:

- *Whether member countries should be permitted to enact minimum capital ratios considerably tougher (higher) than those specified under Basel III without approval of the European Union;*
- *Whether the restrictions on what can be counted as high-quality capital under Basel III should be scrupulously adhered to in E.U. legislation; and*
- *Whether the Basel III deadlines for introducing an unweighted leverage requirement for bank capital and two new quantitative liquidity standards (the liquidity coverage ratio and the net stable funding ratio) should be mirrored in E.U. legislation.*[18]

REEMERGENCE OF CAPITAL MARKETS

The objective to reduce the risk of using taxpayers' money to bail out financial institutions is a noble one. However, by ensuring that banks are adequately capitalized, have adequate liquidity, and are not overleveraged, the new wave of regulation is protecting depositors but externalizing a substantial portion of financial assets.

Banks have only started to recapitalize themselves. In the absence of substantial appetite of investors to add equity to banks, asset and business disposals will be the most important way to rebalance the balance sheets.

Nobody is taking seriously the risk of an increase in capital market financing. Are the structures and the rules of securities regulation adequate to avoid crises in capital markets? This will in turn create additional risks since capital markets cannot be domesticated and while banks restructure debts, bonds collapse overnight and immediately affect interest rates and the real economy.

The share of capital markets in global finance will inevitably increase. The Basel III haircut criteria will increase the need to allocate equity to support the sovereign and corporate bond portfolios. Banks will, however, continue to hold bonds.

Will capital markets provide enough capital? The newly designed bail-in instruments will be issued on capital markets. Who will buy those potentially explosive assets? Will capital markets be able to issue enough of those bonds (the *coco bonds*)?

It is paradoxical to see that, while the source of the financial crisis was financial instruments issued on capital markets, securitization and all kinds of securities, the net result of the new regulatory moves will make this source of financing more essential than before.

RESTRUCTURING FINANCE

Banking structure, and in particular "too big to fail" systemically important financial institutions (SIFIs), is evolving in the same direction throughout the world. Even Asian banks are now joining the effort.

- The prohibition of proprietary trading in speculative instruments needs to be generalized. It is the only way the rules of capital adequacy are not going to be undermined by risks affecting the integrity of equity.
- Regulatory coordination is probably the second best to a global regulation: there is no doubt that the global institutions that put around the same table the various types of regulators and the attention to regulation by public opinion make this a core political issue.

It seems impossible that the financial sector will be the same after the heavy and complex regulatory surgery it will be submitted to. Will it be safer? Will it be more efficient? Will it better serve the economy? Those are the real questions to which only partial answers are emerging.

SHOULD FINANCIAL COMMUNICATION BE REGULATED?

The need for additional transparency will make financial communication an essential element of the trust and confidence that regulators will oversee. Without entering into the details of a subject that will require a full book, I would like to make a few observations.

The information published by financial institutions as well as securities issuers has been the source of concern as its complexity increased.

- The first attempt by the Securities and Exchange Commission (SEC) to make it more readable was to require companies to communicate in *plain English* as opposed to legal jargon. It went as far as a *Plain English Handbook: How to Create Clear SEC Disclosure Documents*. In the Preface, Warren Buffett writes:

  For more than forty years, I've studied the documents that public companies file. Too often, I've been unable to decipher just what is being said or, worse yet, had to conclude that nothing was being said. If corporate lawyers and their clients follow the advice in this handbook, my life is going to become much easier.[19]

- A subsequent attempt was made to ensure that the risks associated with a particular security be explicitly explained. It is constantly updated. Following the publication of the Dodd-Frank Act, updated rules were issued:

  These new regulations establish a comprehensive testing methodology that swap and security-based swap counterparties must employ both to determine whether they will be subject to heightened regulation as a major participant and to establish whether they will be shielded from such requirements by a safe harbor. To the extent that an entity satisfies any of the three alternative major participant tests, it will generally become subject to additional statutory and regulatory requirements, encompassing margin, capital, business conduct, recordkeeping, and reporting.[20]

- Last but not least, the disclosure rules were better elaborated. The FD (for financial disclosure) rules issued by the SEC rein in information disclosure and has definitely reduced the information available before.[21]
- Europe has launched a decade-long quest for a European prospectus.[22] It made prospectuses throughout the European Union more consistent.

The investor is as lost as he was before: there are two ways not to be transparent: not publish or publish so much that it becomes impossible to understand. We are at that stage. It is pretty common to have tens of pages of risk considerations, and they have become so similar that they seem to come from the same boilerplate.

These moves have made two sources of information more readily available: financial analysis and the financial media. While new rules have been established to improve the transparency of analyst reports by disclosing areas of possible conflicts of interests between the analysts and the investment banking activities, especially in the case of IPOs, their effectiveness remains uncertain.[23] The reading of the very small footnotes of these disclosures is close to impossible and so uninteresting that these attempts did not help the investors. However, they forced global banks to exercise better governance of their analyst activities.

SHOULD FINANCIAL MEDIA RESPECT A CODE OF CONDUCT?

As a blogger myself, I would never want to curb the freedom of the press. The real financial information, however, happens through the media. In today's world, this includes written press, audiovisual press, Internet publications, social media, and many other channels.

As media need to be dramatic to be sold, we have witnessed during the financial crisis a flurry of dramatizing headlines. The question of the role of the media in spreading rumors, interpretations, and potentially damaging opinions has undoubtedly exacerbated the opinion. The multiplication of financial "media" has a consequence with which we will need to live: finance has gone from the back pages to the front pages. Finance has become sexy and invaded the general press without necessarily adding expertise.

I am not competent to suggest what should be done. However, we are living in a world where this frenzy might have criminal intentions. When an investing institution decides that it has reason to short a particular security, nothing is easier than taking the short position and spreading rumors, whether they are exact or not. By the time the issuer reacts, the securities have tanked and the short seller has been able to cover his or her short position within a few hours, making sometimes hefty profits.

Regulators are very aware of this, but it is often impossible to prove malevolent intention and courts will not support cases that are based only on "strange coincidences" as damning as they might be. However, vigilance is essential. The week before the collapse of Lehman, it was a deluge that precipitated the fall of the stock and the bonds of the company.

Hedge funds were particularly fond of activism in cases of takeovers, mergers, and even capital increases. It is a constant cat-and–mouse game between the issuer and their ability to influence the media in favor of their interests. It is their favorite way to influence markets, and often enough they spread rumors on deals without having even contacted the company. The financial consequences are huge. More important, there is a huge distrust in those operations. The Facebook issue, pricing, disclosure, and management leave a sour taste in most investors' mouths and disbelief in the initial public offering (IPO) process in the United States. The media amplified that propaganda.

However, I would like to pay tribute to the exceptional work that is accomplished in the most manipulative environments by the teams of serious and investigative media. Financial information cannot be taken for granted and honest financial institutions are masters in influencing media. The use of their contribution in this book is a testimony to their added value.

FINANCIAL EDUCATION IS KEY

As the financial crisis put finance forward in the awareness of the general public, financial debates have become part of the political, social, and economic world. Unfortunately, financial education is insufficient, sparse, and generally incoherent. One wonders sometimes how the credulity of the public can be abused so easily.

The promotion of new mortgages in the beginning of this century was completely misleading for people with a basic understanding of borrowing. Banks used treacherous ways to make sure that, while in most cases the information was complete, its packaging was fundamentally misleading. Billions of fines are sanctioning this behavior. The SEC published the list of fines based on various types of misconduct.[24]

This is not over. One would expect banks no longer to resort to malpractices and misinformation. Financial solicitations seem as uncontrolled and dishonest as it was before.

Since it would be naïve to believe that this might change, there is one avenue that needs to be explored. Finance should be part of education. It is absurd that students might leave high school without a basic understanding of the functioning of the financial world, the risks of over-indebtedness, terms of borrowing, and abusive practices of issuers of credit cards.

While it is considered normal to explain the basics of health, history, and geography, finance is not a subject. Governments, corporations, and financial institutions have a vested interest in misleading the financial consumer. Their fight to avoid the creation of the Consumer Financial Protection Bureau was so violent that it could only confirm that they had a firm intention to continue to try, and in many cases, succeed in abusing their clients.

> *We work to give consumers the information they need to understand the terms of their agreements with financial companies. We are working to make regulations and guidance as clear and streamlined as possible so providers of consumer financial products and services can follow the rules on their own.*[25]

Corporate governance has been the topic of many rules and regulations. Boards are still not, by and large, financially literate. Management can easily fool them. However, we need now to seriously work on public governance, imposing basic rules on governments and public officials when they operate in the financial sphere. They lose their sovereignty when they enter that field where they need to be taken to the same standards that they impose on others.

In November 2013, the *Huffington Post* launched a new portal for financial education. Ariana Huffington describes the initiative:

> *Financial Education will be a hub of stories, advice and tools to help you make informed money management decisions, from planning a budget and reducing debt to improving your credit score and refinancing a mortgage.*
>
> *Financial Education is rooted in the belief that by empowering ourselves to take control of our own financial lives, we can reduce the stress that so often accompanies financial decisions and at the same time improve the parts of our lives that are about so much more than money: our health, our families, our careers, our homes. It's a useful paradox: by learning more about how money affects our lives, we can make sure it doesn't take over our lives, and by learning how to look after our financial capital, we can also take better care of our human capital.*[26]

NOTES

1. Albert Camus, *The Myth of Sisyphus*, published by New York University, 1942. www.nyu.edu/classes/keefer/hell/camus.html.
2. This is the publication by BAFIN, the German market regulator. www
.bafin.de/EN/Homepage/homepage_node.html;jsessionid=3C8FF1C830
6A7EE05E34B73911371BB0.1_cid298.
3. www.banque-france.fr/en/banque-de-france/history/the-milestones/
the-banque-de-france-and-the-escb/regulating-and-supervising-the-
banking-system-and-investment-firms/the-banking-and-financial-
regulatory-committee.html.
4. Bank for International Settlements. "Report and Recommendations of the Cross-Border Resolution Group," Basel, Switzerland, December 2010.
5. http://eur-lex.europa.eu/LexUriServ/LexUriServ.do?uri=CELEX:52013
PC0520:EN:NOT. European Commission, COM 2013, 520 FINAL.
6. Institute of International Finance, "Addressing Priority Issues in Cross-Border Resolution," May 2011. www.iif.com%2Fdownload.php%3Fid
%3D615ZrRHRb%2BE%3D&ei=Luq9UoTZF4fgsASWsIKIDg&usg
=AFQjCNGLJvWXz57YNB6bmB02ZgQBPFr9FA&sig2=TNJnSPtYT
LbjV5fYPIHHCA&bvm=bv.58187178,d.cWc.
7. Mark Hallerberg and Joachim Wehner, "The Technical Competence of Economic Policymakers," *VOX*, February 2013.
8. www.imf.org/external/pubs/ft/fandd/2002/12/das.htm.
9. Chiara Angeloni and Guntram B. Wolff, "Are Banks Affected by Their Government Debt Holdings?" Bruegel Working Paper, July 2012. www
.bruegel.org.
10. "Gentlemen, Start Your Audits," *The Economist,* October 3, 2013. www
.economist.com/news/finance-and-economics/21587225-close-scrutiny-
europes-banks-may-turn-up-unexpected-shortfalls-gentlemen-start.
11. www.eba.europa.eu/risk-analysis-and-data/eu-wide-stress-testing.
12. S. Christopher Gandrud and Mark Hallerberg, "Transparency in the European Banking Union," Bruegel Policy Contribution. www.bruegel
.org/publications/publication-detail/publication/807-supervisory-
transparency-in-the-european-banking-union/.
13. www.investmentexecutive.com/-/iif-warns-g20-on-fragmented-regulation.
14. www.ft.com/cms/s/0/b640b02e-b003-11e3-b0d0-00144feab7de
.html#ixzz2wp2jG2k5.
15. For the presentation of the role of the EBA, see www.eba.europa.eu/
regulation-and-policy/market-risk.
16. www.deloitte.com/view/en_nl/nl/industries/financial-services-
industries/basel/timeline/index.htm.

17. www.federalreserve.gov/newsevents/press/bcreg/20130924b.htm.
18. Morris Goldstein, "The EU's Implementation of Basel III: A Deeply Flawed Compromise, *VOX,* May 27, 2012. www.voxeu.org/article/eu-s-implementation-basel-iii-deeply-flawed-compromise.
19. www.sec.gov/pdf/handbook.pdf.
20. www.stblaw.com%2Fcontent%2FPublications%2Fpub1414.pdf&ei=uE0vU4LzBYXRkQe04oHIBQ&usg=AFQjCNFSbYRupRLqzlvodDC1L_Z9HoIGWw&bvm=bv.62922401,d.eW0.
21. www.sec.gov/rules/final/33-7881.htm.
22. http://eur-lex.europa.eu/LexUriServ/LexUriServ.do?uri=OJ:L:2010:327:0001:0012:EN:PDF.
23. Gregg McNeal, "Do Investors Care about SEC Mandated Disclosures of Analysts' Stock Ownership?" *Forbes,* November 30, 2012. www.forbes.com/sites/gregorymcneal/2012/11/30/do-investors-care-about-sec-mandated-disclosures-of-analyst-stock-ownership/.
24. www.sec.gov/spotlight/enf-actions-fc.shtml.
25. www.consumerfinance.gov/the-bureau/.
26. www.huffingtonpost.com/arianna-huffington/huffpost-financial-education_b_4284273.html.

CHAPTER 16

Regulation and Ethics

The worship of the ancient golden calf has returned in a new and ruthless guise in the idolatry of money and the dictatorship of an impersonal economy lacking a truly human purpose.

—Pope Francis

The public is strongly expecting a moralization of finance and the establishment of ethical standards that would ensure proper behavior. Unfortunately, regulation cannot impose ethical behaviors; it can only impose rules to incite such behavior.

The "bankster" name given to the financial profession says it all on the perception of bankers by public opinion. It was the headline of the report by *The Economist* on the London interbank offered rate (LIBOR) crisis in July 2012.

"Since we have not more power of knowing the future than any other men, we have made many mistakes (who has not during the past five years?), but our mistakes have been errors of judgment and not of principle." So reflected J. P. Morgan Junior in 1933, in the middle of a financial crisis. Today's bankers can draw no such comfort from their behaviour. The attempts to rig LIBOR (the London inter-bank offered rate), a benchmark interest rate, not only betray a culture of casual dishonesty; they set the stage for lawsuits and more regulation right the way round the globe. This could well be global finance's "tobacco moment."[1]

It can, however, play a major role in the definition of accountability[2] as well as in the definition and implementation of accountability. The sources of such ethics are coming from moral philosophy and translated into rules of natural law, but not in positive law.

MANAGEMENT INTEGRITY

Despite all efforts to improve regulation, the integrity of the management, the boards of directors, the regulators, and the legislators is a moral issue. Never will regulation be a substitute for ethics.

As the French philosopher Albert Camus put it, "Integrity does not need rules."[3] It is a matter of moral spine. Can regulators do anything to improve management integrity?

Yet, as PricewaterhouseCoopers, the audit firm, puts it: Business integrity is a key to rebuilding reputation.

> *"Customer led, ethically guided" runs a leading bank's slogan. A source of competitive advantage for one bank. But what could it imply about others? That they are less ethical, even unethical? Could this be a clue, a reason for the financial services sector's unpopularity with regulators and the media? What value could firms within the sector derive from demonstrating a genuinely more responsible approach to business conduct?[4]*

ACCOUNTABILITY

Whether some behaviors are against the law or not, do not put an end to the accountability of the financial actors. As we indicated, the only managers or directors who were forced to resign and brought to court were accused of fraud.

There is, however, another court: the court of public opinion. It is a dangerous and unpredictable one. However, generally through the media, the expression of anger against the fact that some behaviors were not sanctioned or that some people who resigned were receiving outrageous severance packages, has forced action by governments, parliaments, or regulators.

We have already expressed the difficulties that exist, especially in the United States, to break the accountability wall and sanction the individuals responsible for misbehavior.

TRANSPARENCY IS KEY

The *Financial Times* lexicon definition of *transparency* is the following:

> *An approach to corporate management that emphasises as much disclosure of information as possible to regulators and stakeholders. The concept can also be applied to governments and international organisations.*[5]

"Don't do anything you do not want to see on the front page of the *New York Times*." This is a negative way to translate the fact that most of the unacceptable ethical behaviors were made possible by not disclosing the information in a transparent and understandable way.

Transparency is a formidable way to induce human beings to behave rightly. It also has its winners and losers.[6]

Congress has played a huge role through its inquiry rules in investigating some scandals in the financial sphere and making public some ethically unacceptable behaviors. Some of us remember the Goldman Sachs[7] deposition where it became abundantly obvious that lawmakers were addressing bankers dealing with clients under a fiduciary duty and were answered by a hedge fund management with no banking experience acting as risk managers accountable to capital markets.

A PRINCIPLED REGULATORY SYSTEM IS NEEDED

Harvard Law School professor Hal S. Scott emphasizes the importance of such an approach to ensure the effectiveness of regulation, on behalf of the Committee on Capital Markets regulation:

> *We believe as much attention should be paid to regulatory effectiveness as to regulatory coverage. Equally vital, we think meaningful reform must be based on fundamental principles rather than political expediency. The most important of these principles— particularly in light of the present crisis—is that regulation must reduce systemic risk. When a systemically important institution is in danger of failure, and its failure could trigger a chain reaction of other failures—the so-called interconnectedness problem—there may be no alternative other than to inject some public money into the institution.*[8]

The legal system of finance is mostly the result of what is called the "Anglo-Saxon common law system," which spells out the details of rules and regulations.

Anglo-Saxon law, the body of legal principles that prevailed in England from the 6th century until the Norman Conquest (1066). In conjunction with Scandinavian law and the so-called barbarian laws (leges barbarorum) of continental Europe, it made up the body of law called Germanic law. Anglo-Saxon law was written in the vernacular and was relatively free of the Roman influence found in continental laws that were written in Latin. Roman influence on Anglo-Saxon law was indirect and exerted primarily through the church. There was a definite Scandinavian influence upon Anglo-Saxon law as a result of the Viking invasions of the 8th and 9th centuries. Only with the Norman Conquest did Roman law, as embodied in Frankish law, make its influence felt on the laws of England.[9]

In other legal systems, and mostly in Europe, the code includes some principle definitions that allow the pursuit of misbehaviors under the principle without the need for a specific rule.

Civil law, also called Romano-Germanic law, the law of continental Europe, based on an admixture of Roman, Germanic, ecclesiastical, feudal, commercial, and customary law. European civil law has been adopted in much of Latin America as well as in parts of Asia and Africa and is to be distinguished from the common law of the Anglo-American countries.[10]

This system includes guidance for behaviors and broad risks in case of infraction of the principles. It would insert more ethics in regulation.

Federal Reserve officials have been worried that their policy of ultra-low interest rates may be having less of an effect than usual because of a "broken transmission channel." In plain English, this means the money hasn't really been flowing smoothly from liquidity-flooded banks to would-be borrowers.

DOING THE RIGHT THING

Our legalistic society has replaced righteousness with compliance. Boards of directors and governments, more often than not, subject their decisions to compliance or legal scrutiny and satisfy themselves with the fact that their lawyers tell them: "It is compliant with the rules and regulations."

This is a poor substitute to what should be the primary preoccupation of a decision maker. Things will change when board members will question management by saying, "Tell us why this is the right thing to do for your company, your clients, and the community at large."

> *By not doing it, the Western financial system has lost the respect of its citizens, the confidence of its clients and the trust of public opinion. Furthermore, the handling of public debt in Europe and the United States is being judged strongly as irresponsible in the rest of the world, especially in Asia. With the deal reached Sunday night, the United States has a good chance of escaping the debt limit showdown with its credit rating intact. The United States government may not be so lucky with its reputation.*
>
> *Even before negotiations went down to the wire, the bitterness, division and dysfunction that resounded around the world in recent weeks as the United States veered toward default did more than just fuel a perception that Washington is approaching Japan-like levels of political gridlock. Among foreign leaders and in global markets, the political histrionics have eroded America's already diminishing aura as the world's economic haven and the sole country with the power to lead the rest of the world out of financial crisis and recession.*[11]

Global financial regulation can be a substantial contributing factor, but it cannot, by itself, create the trust environment that will make financial institutions credible. I leave this subject by sharing the Code of Ethics of JPMorgan Chase:

> *The purpose of this Code of Ethics is to promote honest and ethical conduct and compliance with the law, particularly as related to the maintenance of the firm's financial books and records and the preparation of its financial statements. The obligations of this Code of Ethics supplement, but do not replace, the firm's Code of Conduct. As a finance professional of the firm, you are expected to:*
>
> - *Engage in and promote ethical conduct, including the ethical handling of actual or apparent conflicts of interest between personal and professional relationships, and to disclose to the Office of the Secretary any material transaction or relationship that reasonably could be expected to give rise to such a conflict.*

- *Carry out your responsibilities honestly, in good faith and with integrity, due care and diligence, exercising at all times the best independent judgment.*
- *Assist in the production of full, fair, accurate, timely and understandable disclosure in reports and documents that the firm and its subsidiaries file with, or submit to, the Securities and Exchange Commission and other regulators and in other public communications made by the firm.*
- *Comply with applicable government laws, rules and regulations of federal, state and local governments and other appropriate regulatory agencies.*
- *Promptly report (anonymously, if you wish to do so) to the Audit Committee of the Board of Directors any violation of this Code of Ethics or any other matters that would compromise the integrity of the firm's financial statements. You may contact the Audit Committee by mail, by phone, or by e-mail; contact information is set forth below.*
- *Never to take, directly or indirectly, any action to coerce, manipulate, mislead or fraudulently influence the firm's independent auditors in the performance of their audit or review of the firm's financial statements.*

NOTES

1. www.economist.com/node/21558260.
2. Irvine Lapsey, in *Financial Accountability & Management,* November 2013. http://onlinelibrary.wiley.com/journal/10.1111/%28ISSN%291468-0408.
3. Albert Camus, "The Absurd Man." www.sccs.swarthmore.edu/users/00/pwillen1/lit/absur.htm.
4. www.pwc.com%2Fen_GX%2Fgx%2Fbanking-capital-markets%2Fpdf%2Fjournalaug2005-1.pdf&ei=TWJ2UsSTHce2sAT79oHQBA&usg=AFQjCNHy8J8Jz01hT_VQKuJrzIGAI6zpuA&sig2=jM8XVF1BsPM8vmsQK1Ojug&bvm=bv.55819444,d.cWc.
5. http://lexicon.ft.com/Term?term=transparency.
6. Robert J. Bloomfield and Maureen O'Hara, "Market Transparency: Who Wins and Who Loses?" *Review of Financial Studies* 12(1). Available at SSRN: http://ssrn.com/abstract=122708.
7. *The Guardian,* a U.K. newspaper, published the full senate report on Goldman Sachs. www.theguardian.com/business/2011/apr/14/goldman-sachs-full-senate-report.

8. http://fcic-static.law.stanford.edu/cdn_media/fcic-testimony/2009-1020-Scott-article-3.pdf.

9. www.britannica.com/EBchecked/topic/25121/Anglo-Saxon-law.

10. www.britannica.com/EBchecked/topic/119271/civil-law.

11. The *New York Times* reflects on the world reaction to the last debt-ceiling debate in the United States. www.nytimes.com/2011/08/01/us/politics/01capital.html?pagewanted=all.

Conclusion

What Can We Expect?

Financial stability is a long quest. It requires the financial world to regain trust and confidence from just about any part of society, as well as a process that will eradicate some of the least acceptable behaviors and implement a risk management culture.

Having walked the reader through this complex and arduous journey in global financial regulation, I now need to look at financial stability as it is being prepared by global regulation. There will be no quotes or references, just a plain expression of a personal opinion enlightened by several years of analysis of the consequences of the recent financial crises.

It would be unfair not to recognize the enormous task that has been undertaken and the tens of thousands of regulatory texts that have been written by lawmakers and regulators over the past five years. Dismissing that effort would not make sense, and there is no doubt that the best intentions prevailed through that process.

However, this excruciating analysis should leave us with limited hope. It might be that the size and implications of the next banking crisis of a systemic nature will not threaten global financial stability. I sincerely hope that this will be the case and that progress will have been made in ensuring that financial institutions will not be the source of future instability. I would not be honest if I were not pointing toward a series of issues that need to be further tackled to achieve this ambitious goal:

1. *Financial institutions do not genuinely embrace global financial regulation.* Despite statements to the contrary, their mind-set has not changed. Further scandals such as the "London Whale," the London interbank offered rate (LIBOR), and the foreign exchange manipulations continue to demonstrate collusion and manipulation of capital markets by banks in their own interest. These happened in 2011 and 2012, long after the Lehman crisis. The lesson was not to be learned, and there are no signs that it is changing. It is a cat-and-mouse fight, and it will remain.

2. *The legislative process is corrupt by intense lobbying.* The lobbying of lawmakers by financial institutions has allowed the watering down of what was initially a strong push for global regulation. The champion of this process, the Financial Stability Board, acting on behalf of the Group of 20, has a limited ability to monitor systemic risks and has published loads of papers on administrative matters, without any authority to translate them into some form of statutory directives. Banks continue to spend billions of dollars or euros to avoid sanctions, create loopholes, and make sure lawmakers and regulators will not limit their ability to act in their own interests.

3. *The regulatory process and institutions are too complex to work.* Whether it is the numerous decision levels at the European Union or the 20+ regulators in the United States, the likelihood that we will see a repeat of interagency failures and inability to prevent systemic risks is high. Rather than simplifying and rationalizing, governments have chosen to add new agencies, and the complexity of their rules and regulations will create as many loopholes. There is no political will to make regulation more effective, and the cost of regulation has become an astronomic entry barrier into the sector. Too many vested interests oppose it. Europe created authorities where the 19 eurozone regulators compose the board. The European System of Financial Supervision that followed the de la Rosière Report includes several agencies and national authorities. Nine agencies compose the U.S. Financial Stability Oversight Council.

4. *The banking system did not substantially deleverage.* Contrary to the official statements, the banking system has not really deleveraged or abandoned activities. The "separation" is in the proposals, but they remain marginal. There are differences between the United States and Europe: the equity base of the U.S. banking system has substantially increased, and its capital adequacy is stronger and more robust than the European one.

5. *The overbanking of Europe constitutes in itself a systemic risk.* The universal banking structure in Europe continues to prevail and the ratio of banking assets to gross domestic product (GDP) creates a triple systemic danger. First, it threatens the political democratic system by giving financial institutions a huge power over political decision makers. Second, the assets of banks are still largely exposed to their government's borrowings and bonds, creating an interconnected relationship. Third, it was only in March 2014 that an attempt has been made to limit proprietary trading in Europe, and speculative assets still represent a substantial portion of European banks' balance sheets.

6. *Financial governance has not improved: individuals are not accountable.* By and large, the management and the boards of directors of the

financial institutions are the same as they were prior to the financial crisis. No personal accountability system has been put in place, and fines have taken the place of sanctions against the individuals responsible for failures. Large compensation and low accountability are not compatible. A recent fight by a renowned but embattled bank chairman and CEO to keep both titles exemplified this trend. Boards of directors continue to be free of any accountability.

7. *No effort has been made to disconnect risks and remunerations.* While Europe has put together a limit to the bonus system, it has only led to an increase of base salaries and, rather than reducing the risks associated with some high-powered activities, is effectively making financial institutions more vulnerable to market fluctuations as a result of the increase in fixed costs. The say-on-pay system in the United States was more defendable, but it leaves the shareholders in command and the U.S. corporate system only extends a nonbinding voting right that management can perfectly ignore. In both cases, there is limited correlation with the risks attached to the activities.

8. *Basel III ratios are the only hope to reduce systemic risk.* By combining capital adequacy, liquidity, and leverage ratios, Basel III has the ability to force a major restructuring of the banking system in a way that will limit their growth to their ability to carry the risks associated with them. Furthermore, it will force several banks, especially European, to reduce their balance sheets and recapitalize. So far, Deutsche Bank is the only one that has announced such measures. As time progresses, however, the pressure will increase.

9. *Capital markets and securitization will be essential to economic growth.* The limitations put on banks by the Basel III ratios will inevitably lead to a structural change of the financial systems. Only a fraction of the financial needs will be financed by deposits or bank balance sheets. The current regulatory efforts, by concentrating on the need to reduce taxpayer intervention, are effectively evacuating a substantial part of the financing of the economy into shadow banking and securitization. Those markets are structurally global and will need to be monitored and globally regulated. This task has not even started yet.

10. *Trust has not been restored and the mind-set is the same.* Financial institutions have decided to look at the new regulatory wave from a pure compliance standpoint. Their opposition to necessary reforms such as the Volcker Rule, as well as new scandals and excessive compensation, has done little to enhance the trust of the public and the mind-set of traders. The lessons of the previous crises have not been learned. The same behaviors will inevitably induce the same risks.

11. *Regulation should go beyond compliance and lawyers.* As a law professor, I would be misplaced to question the wisdom and experience of lawyers on matters of regulation. However, as important as the drafting of rules and legal arguments can be, financial regulation remains a challenge. Facing macroeconomic, social, and political turmoil, financial markets are subject to an incredible set of factors. Most of those are not of a legal nature. Regulators and central banks are basically ruled by lawyers and politicians. So far, they have failed to anticipate possible crises. They require integrity.

12. *Regulators have not been given the means to implement their rules.* To fight against attorneys paid over $1,000 an hour, CEOs who get paid eight-figure remuneration, and the best lawyers of companies' legal departments, regulators have been facing budget reductions and their remuneration scale is appallingly low. While public service is a noble task, one cannot expect competent people to accept to be paid low civil servant salaries. Their ability to act has also been reduced by the increased interference of political pressure in the United States and many other countries. While American experts are willing to accept lower compensation for a few years in government, Europe is based on career civil servants.

13. *Central banks have lost independence by becoming lenders.* From a role of liquidity provider to a lending arm of impotent governments, central banks have completely changed the financial landscape. The addition of $9 trillion to the balance sheet of the largest of them has transformed them financially and politically. By losing their independence to become supports of their overindebted governments and banks, they are changing the game, as well as capital markets, in a way that is financially unsound and creates important exit problems. Can they be independent regulators?

14. *Asia must become a partner in global regulation.* Global finance cannot be limited to the Atlantic world. With four billion people, the continent will gradually but surely become a key player in the future of finance. It might be helpful to have a serious dialogue with Asian financial institutions and regulators. While we all pursue an objective of financial stability, it might become obvious that we do not necessarily conceive it the same way. The development of shadow banking structures could become sources of regional, or even global, instability. Asia's tendency to resort to shadow banking is a major systemic threat for financial stability.

Will we be able to achieve global financial stability with those unresolved problems? It will require a combination of courage and competence that has, so far, not been displayed by a nationally obsessed political class.

That certainly does not raise expectations that global regulation will be addressed in a professional way.

We have no choice but to try and persist. To end this book, I remember a quote from the Dutch king Willem Ier of Orange (1533–1583):

It is not necessary to hope in order to undertake,
Nor to succeed in order to persevere.

A Few Books I Read and Found Helpful . . .

THE ACTORS

Henry M. Paulson Jr., *On the Brink: Inside the Race to Stop the Collapse of the Global Banking System*. Business Plus, 2010, 478 pp.

William R. Rhodes, *Banker to the World*. McGraw-Hill, 2011, 249 pp.

William L. Silber, *Volcker: The Triumph of Persistence*. Bloomsbury Press, 2012, 300 pp. + 150 pp. of texts, notes, and documents.

George Soros, *The New paradigm for Financial Markets: The Credit Crisis of 2008 and What It Means*. BBS, 2010, 162 pp.

THE CLASSICS

Ken Auletta, *Greed and Glory on Wall Street: The Fall of the House of Lehman*. Random House, 1986, 282 pp.

Michael Lewis, *Liars' Poker: Two Cities, True Greed*. Hodder & Sloughton, 1989, 224 pp.

THE ACADEMICS

John C. Coffee, *Gatekeepers: The Professions and Corporate Governance*. Oxford University Press, 2006, 390 pp.

Howard Davies and David Green, *Banking on the Future: The Fall and Rise of Central Banking*. Princeton University Press, 2010.

Howard Davies and David Green, *Global Financial Regulation*. Polity, 2008, 200 pp.

Charles Goodhardt, Philipp Hartmann, David T. Llewellyn, Liliana Rojas-Suarez, and StevenWeisbro, *Financial Regulation: Why, How and Where Now?* Routledge (in association with the Bank of England), 2003.

D. Quinn Mills, *Wheel, Deal and Steel: Deceptive Accounting, Deceitful CEOs and Ineffective Reforms*. Harvard Business School, FT Prentice Hall, 2003, 300 pp.

Raghuram J. Rajan and Luigi Zingales, *Saving Capitalism from the Capitalists: Unleashing the Power of Financial Markets to Create Wealth and Spread Opportunity.* Crown Business, 2003, 358 pp.

Michael J. Sandler, *What Money Can't Buy: The Moral Limits of Markets.* FSG, 2012, 244 pp.

Joseph Stiglitz, *Free Fall: America, Free Markets, and the Sinking of the Economy.* Norton, 2010, 442 pp.

Daniel K. Tarullo, *Banking on Basel: The Future of International Financial Regulation: The Essential Guide.* The Peterson Institute for International Economics, 2008.

THE REPORTERS

Maria Bartiromo, *The Weekend that Changed Wall Street: An Eyewitness Account.* Penguin Press, 2010, 232 pp.

William D. Cohen, *House of Cards: A Tale of Hubris and Wretched Excess on Wall Street.* Doubleday, 2009, 68 pp.

Kate Kelly, *Street Fighters: The Last 72 Hours of Bear Stearns, the Toughest Firm on Wall Street.* Portfolio, 2010, 242 pp.

Michael Lewis, *The Big Short: Inside the Doomsday Machine.* W. W. Norton, 2010, 291 pp.

Michael Lewis, *Boomerang: Travels in the New Third World.* Allan Lane, 2011, 213 pp.

Gretchen Morgenson, *Reckless Endangerment: How Outsized Ambition, Greed, and Corruption Led to Economic Armageddon.* Times Books, 2011, 252 pp.

Andrew Ross Sorkin, *Too Big to Fail: The Inside Story of How Wall Street and Washington Fought to Save the Financial System—and Themselves.* Viking, 2009.

James B. Stewart, *Tangled Webs: How False Statements are Undermining America: From Martha Stewart to Bernie Madoff.* Penguin Press, 2011, 474 pp.

THE ULTIMATE MANUAL

Hal S. Scott, *International Finance: Law and Regulation.* Sweet & Maxwell, 2009, 666 pp.

About the Author

GEORGES UGEUX is the founder and owner Galileo Global Advisors LLC, providing CEOs, boards of directors, and governments independent advice on international business development, mergers and acquisitions, and raising capital. Galileo is specialized in cross-border transactions to and from emerging markets, particularly India and China.

Prior to founding Galileo, Georges joined the New York Stock Exchange in September 1996, as group executive vice president, International & Research.

A 68-year old Belgian and U.S. national, Georges began his career in 1970 at Société Générale de Banque (now BNP Paribas Fortis Bank), where he ran the investment banking and trust divisions. He moved to London in 1985, as managing director of Morgan Stanley's Mergers and Acquisitions department. In 1988, he was appointed group finance director at Société Générale de Belgique. In 1992, he became president of Kidder, Peabody Europe. From 1995 until joining the NYSE, Georges served as president of the European Investment Fund and also chaired the Kingdom of Belgium's Privatization Commission. He is on the board of directors of AXA-Tianping Insurance (China).

Georges is adjunct professor at Columbia Law School, where he teaches a seminar on "European Banking and Finance." He is regularly called to speak or comment on international financial matters and recently published a book entitled *The Betrayal of Finance: Twelve Reforms to Restore Confidence,* published in French (Odile Jacob, Paris), English (available at lulu.com and Amazon.com), and Flemish (Lannoo, Belgium).

Index